الى الاخ العزيز الدكتور
صالح شكل مع خالص
المودة والتقدير
عبد الرحمن

Arab & Islamic Silver

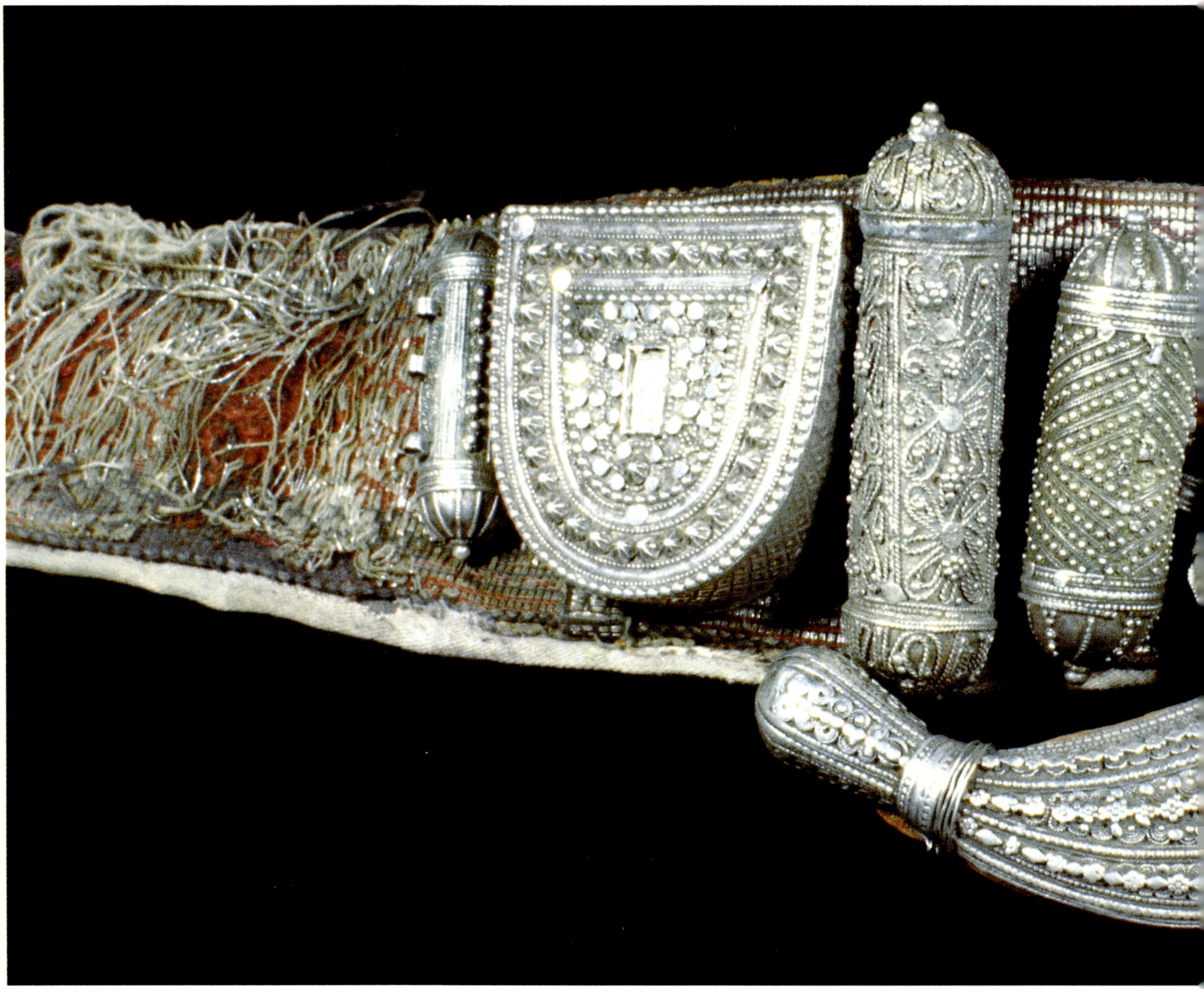

Arab & Islamic Silver

SAAD AL-JADIR

STACEY INTERNATIONAL

Arab and Islamic Silver
First published by Stacey International 1981
128 Kensington Church Street, London W8
London W8 4BH

© 1981 Saad Al-Jadir
© 1981 Maps: Stacey International

Reprinted 1982

ISBN 0 905743 23 7

Design Keith Savage,
           Anthony Nelthorpe MSIAD
Maps: Ian Stephen
Indexers: R. and R. Haig Brown

All rights reserved.
No part of this publication may be reproduced, stored in a retrieval system or transmitted in any form or by any means, electronic, mechanical, photocopying, recording or otherwise, without the prior permission of the copyright holder.

The author wishes to thank Sarah Martin, whose initial work on the English text was most helpful; Sh. Shihab, F. Beer and Marcel Hodges for their photography; staff members of Stacey International and of the Calouste Gulbenkian Foundation.

Set in Times New Roman by
SX Composing Ltd, Rayleigh, Essex.
Printed and bound in Japan by
Dai Nippon Printing Company Ltd, Tokyo.

All the photographs in this book illustrate the author's silver collection and are his property except for those listed below.

Trustees of the British Museum, page 11 (*top and above*), page 12 and page 14 (*below left*); Freer Gallery of Art, Smithsonian Institution, Washington D.C., page 14 (*above*); F. L. Kennett, George Rainbird Ltd/Robert Harding Associates, page 11 (*opposite*); Munzkabinett, Staatliche Museen zu Berlin, page 13; Victoria and Albert Museum, page 15 (*above and above far right*) and page 31 (*opposite below*).

Contents

- 7 Author's Note
- 8 Introduction
- 10 The Early History of Silverwork
- 16 The Functions of Silverwork
- 21 Types of Silverwork
- 30 The Silversmith and his Craft
- 36 The Revival of Folk Art and its Importance

- 38 The Silverwork of North Africa and Spain
- 86 The Silverwork of the Arabian Peninsula
- 126 The Silverwork of the Levant, Mesopotamia, Persia, Turkey and Caucasia
- 170 The Silverwork of Central and South-east Asia

- 212 Conclusion
- 213 Sources of Reference
- 215 Index

Page 1: *This traditional brooch was made in Beni Yeni in the region of Tizi Ouzou. Enamel and use of pendants are typical of the Kabyllian silver works of Algeria.* Pages 2 and 3: *The amulet boxes or* hirz *on this North Yemeni belt are lavishly decorated.* Left: *An incense burner from Iraq consists of two pear-shaped boxes. The larger box on the right has apertures to hold sticks of incense; the other box is for powdered incense. As the heat increases, the birds' silver plumage begins to tremble.*

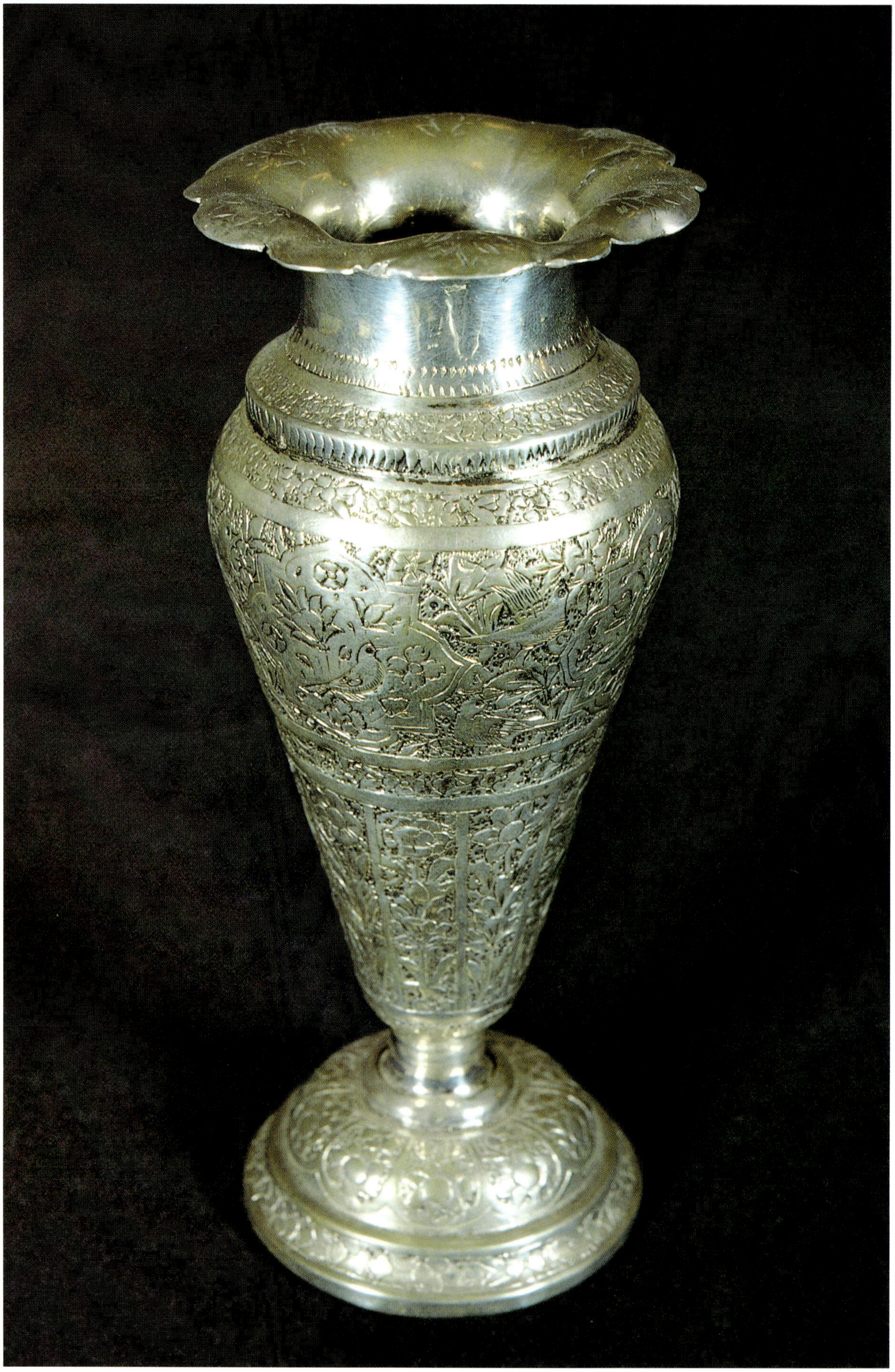

Author's Note

I have led a gypsy life, during which I have published many articles and other works throughout my years as a town planner in North Africa and in Southern Arabia. These complemented my professional life and were mainly concerned with the various societies in which I worked. I wrote on many related subjects: the varieties of existing settlement, their architectural planning, their housing systems, the influence of migration on towns and cities, town planning laws, the role of international consultant companies in regional and town planning and numerous other topics.

My life as a wanderer has brought me into contact with many peoples and cultures. In this book I am moving away from my specialist area into Arab and Islamic silverwork. It was a field unknown to me except in its generality. Little that is dependable has been published elsewhere, and true scholarship in this field is fragmentary. Even now I do not claim to be an expert. But rather than hoard such knowledge as I have until it is complete, I decided to share with the interested reader what I had learned, however imperfectly.

Why? This introduction to Islamic silverwork may help to strengthen the homogeneity of Islam's art, for the collection reveals the common spirituality to which the variety of designs and patterns reach out.

Perhaps it will help, too, to stimulate our modern craftsmen so that they do not just copy older styles but use them as an inspiration for their own, thus carrying on the heritage of Islam. Knowledge of their craft and of its historical place among other crafts is crucial. An artist's appreciation is enhanced by understanding the methods used by fellow artists.

We can approach the study of silversmithing in a scientific way, with geometric drawings and detailed photography. We can search out old references and historical records. We can learn about the technology of the various periods which would have affected the skills of the time. We can inspect the relationship between Arab/Islamic silver and the silver arts of other civilisations which influenced it. Finally, we can consider the tastes and demands of the different periods.

All these approaches have played a part in this book. I would like to have included other sections. For example, a glossary of artistic terms, and of local names for common patterns; a discussion of alloys used with silver; a closer description of techniques and their histories. The task is without end. Here, I claim no more than to have made a start.

Saad Al-Jadir
London

Left: *An engraved Pakistani vase is highly decorated with animals and foliage and the whole piece divided into horizontal and vertical sections.*

Introduction

The investment of time, energy and enthusiasm in a specialist subject can become more than a hobby, and collecting has always been a particularly absorbing pastime. Coins, stamps, rosaries, photographs, birds, flowers, shells, even cigarette cards and matchboxes have all absorbed different people at different times. In an age of unstable currencies there has also been increasing interest in the collection of such things as jewellery, silver, precious stones, works of art, antique furniture, ceramics and crystal, as a store of value.

My own interest started when I became fascinated by the ornaments which people wore, either as jewellery such as earrings and necklaces, or as clothing, such as headdresses, buttons and belts. I began collecting as a student, but really started in earnest during my travels in Libya, Algeria, Tunisia and Morocco, and have now bought from almost all the markets of the Arab and Islamic world. In those early days, when I was working as a town planner in the Sahara, I bought silver jewellery directly from Bedouin women whom I met in desert camps and oases, and I searched through musty shops in remote settlements and towns. Although I have never visited Iran, Afghanistan, Oman or Indonesia, I own many pieces of silverwork from these countries, acquired in Abu Dhabi, London and Frankfurt.

Other major sources of my silver collection have been the antique dealers of European cities, especially in the Portobello Road in London and the Marché aux Puces in Paris. There are several reasons for the multitude of Islamic treasures in their possession. When Europeans came home from the colonies, they brought with them works of art. Many became connoisseurs and built up considerable collections. After their death, uncaring beneficiaries sold these treasures off in the auction houses of Europe. Nowadays many Middle Eastern people emigrate to the West, bringing pieces of silverwork with them from their homelands, sometimes as gifts, more often for sale as their initial means of livelihood. Delegates from the Islamic world exchange fine presents on formal occasions, and if these are unwanted, the recipients sell them; so they too appear on the open market. I have tried to buy back such pieces wherever I can trace them.

In this book I have not attempted to compare Oriental with Western work, for there is remarkably little common ground between the two cultures despite obvious similarities in the usage of ornaments. Islamic silver has its own impressive and distinctive qualities, with cultural roots hundreds and even thousands of years old.

Here I can present the results of eighteen years' experience of energetic collecting, of dealing with silversmiths and traders, collectors and experts, of exploring museums, shops and bazaars and of meeting other lovers of this art form during my travels. I have had to rely almost entirely on these personal researches, as the existing literature is incomplete and inadequate.

As I describe my silver collection, which comprises over five thousand different pieces, I will hope to give the reader some idea of the standards, tastes and habits of Arab and Islamic societies and their environment. Personal adornment is still very important in the Middle East, especially in the rural areas which are cut off from modern civilisation, science and technology. A primitive way of life and economic and social backwardness persist, and these peoples' values, ideals and traditions are little known to the outside world.

Most of the pieces in this book are not of great antiquity: there are some rare pieces more than a hundred years old, some which were made less than a hundred years ago and modern pieces of the very high quality still produced by skilled craftsmen in a few regions. The patterns displayed here provide their own demonstration of the skills and techniques of silversmithing, and show the variety of materials.

Arab and Islamic silversmithing has not received the attention accorded to some other art forms, such as ornamental carving, drawing and architecture, although silver objects and jewellery are regarded as essential in everyday life and have long played an important part in the cultural traditions of Islamic societies.

In recent years Westerners have eagerly bought the distinctive and beautifully-made silver jewellery from the cities of the Arabian Peninsula – Nizwa, Aden, Sana'a and Muscat, and from such cities as Tripoli, Baghdad, Karachi and Delhi. But the legitimate inheritors of this art, the Muslims themselves, have so far shown little interest. One function of this collection is to display, and preserve for their descendants, the accomplishments of thousands of years of the silversmiths' art. In the towns the quality of work has declined, and though the craft still persists in rural areas, the standards of compositions are generally no match for those of the past. This decline increases the value of the treasury assembled here.

Several hundred photographs have been selected from my collection on grounds of variety of function, regional balance and for the quality of the photographs themselves. I could not photograph the entire collection of those older pieces from early Islamic periods which are in bank vaults abroad in several countries, but I am hoping to have the records completed in the future.

After the main essays following this preface, the reader will encounter the collection itself in a distinct order. I have divided the Islamic world into four parts, which bear no relation to political, economic or social divisions but are purely to guide the imagination by linking the silverwork patterns to the areas from which they originated. In each section I have discussed briefly the relationship of Islamic silverwork to other art forms which evolved simultaneously.

For my brother, Khaled Al-Jadir, whose constant support and encouragement have been invaluable throughout my life.

In this Turkish silver-framed calligraphic picture appears a mirror image of the Bismillah al-Rahman al-Rahim – *"In the name of Allah, the compassionate, the merciful".*

The Early History of Silverwork

The art of silversmithing has been sadly neglected by historians. The paucity of surviving examples of early silverwork may be partly responsible for this apparent lack of interest. A few rare pieces exist in museums and in the hands of private collectors, but one must assume that the silver itself has mostly been melted down or has corroded and disintegrated over the centuries. Silver, unlike gold, does corrode with age. It would be optimistic to imagine that there is much Islamic silverwork still buried underground awaiting discovery, but some may well be lying unappreciated in people's homes. History records mass destruction of silverwork at different times. It has always been characteristic of autocratic powers to obliterate as far as possible the traces of alien influence and culture, partly through the need for self-protection while establishing their own rule. We know that in the fourth century, for example, both barbarian hordes and Christians melted down great quantities of silverwork for their different purposes.

Islam covers a wide geographical area and encompasses many ethnic groups which had developed their own cultures, to a greater or lesser extent, before its coming. Evidence of Rock Art found in the Arabian Peninsula, for example, indicates that the earliest tribal groups there had developed an expressive medium. The art of Islam is a fusion of such local cultures and their arts with a prevailing spiritual essence common to all Muslim countries.

It is much more difficult to define particular historic styles of Islamic silversmithing than to distinguish between European works, where artistic schools and their relationships are easily recognisable and closely linked with history. When we speak of Carolingian, Romanesque, Gothic, Renaissance, Baroque, Queen Anne, Rococo, Neo-Classic or Art Nouveau, we recognise their styles and historical implications at once. In Islamic Art too such divisions exist, and there are clear differences to be discerned between the art of the Ummayads, the Abbasids, the Fatimids, the Seljuks, the Safavids, the Mughals, the Ottomans, the Moors, the Andalusians, the Samanids, the Ghaznavids and the Timurids. Islam came into contact with many civilisations as it spread, and drew something from each of their heritages, combining them into a merging of cultures, which is what gives Islamic Art its particular and original flavour. Its boldness and vigour can seem over-elaborate to the undiscerning eye; yet despite its complexity and richness, it has a refinement which reflects spiritual awareness in its architecture, pottery, ceramics, glassware and silverwork.

Metals have been used, wherever they are available, since they were first smelted perhaps six thousand years ago. Copper, bronze, iron and lead were all known from earliest times and used for many purposes, from decorative pieces to weapons and machinery. The Egyptians probably succeeded in purefying silver before 2000 BC and many wars were fought for the vital secrets of mining and refining. Mines which are still being worked in the Arabian Peninsula and Iran have been discovered to date from as early as the first millennium BC.

Rulers in ancient times used gold and silver as a symbol of power. They wore ceremonial jewellery to emphasise the authority of the State over the people. Gold and silver also had religious significance, proclaiming the wearer's special

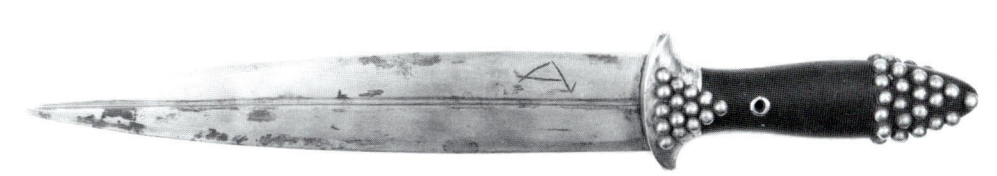

THE EARLY HISTORY OF SILVERWORK

metalwork recording the history of Islamic Art in its various stages of development, silverwork is extremely rare, although silver was widely used to engrave or inlay other metals. Reference to silver is found in paintings, manuscripts and miniatures and in many old folk tales and stories, such as *The Thousand and One Nights*. The Arabs of long ago valued silver highly, comparing it to the moon, as they likened gold to the sun.

Silver is mentioned in the Quran, and the existence of the jewellery of Queen Balkis of Yemen is only one proof that Arabs practised smithing before Islam. Various techniques of metal-working were also known in pre-Islamic days and they are to be seen in rare pieces which have survived, showing that filigree, engraving, openwork and granulation were used, however crudely, in royal jewellery as long ago as 2,500 BC. Another proof that the Arabs were familiar with both sculpture and smithing prior to Islam is the historical record which relates how the Kuraish tribe restored one of their idols, Habal. The Habal sculpture, which was worshipped in the Ka'aba, had a human form and was made of cornelian. When its hand was broken off, craftsmen were brought in to repair it and a new arm was fashioned in gold.

It is not difficult to imagine why the early Arabs had some knowledge of metal working, when we consider such ancient civilisations as those in southern Arabia and in Mesopotamia, where early kingdoms had grown up along the banks of the rivers Tigris and Euphrates. Inter-tribal trading must surely have existed, and settled Arabia had established centres like Makkah and Madinah, where architectural styles had evolved and crafts provided their inhabitants with the necessities for daily life. Makkah was not only an important religious centre, but also a financial and commercial centre, trading with Yemen, Abyssinia, Persia and Byzantium. Taif was a famous agricultural area with a well-known leather industry. Arabia exported spices along its trade routes, and a uniform silver currency was minted in the Peninsula and used from Africa to the Indian Ocean.

The Middle East was constantly visited by people from other civilisations; some passed through to the richer spoils of the East, others established trading centres along the Mediterranean Coast. They brought their armies and their trading

Opposite: *A pectoral in gold cloisonné decorated with semi-precious stones and glass-paste was found in the tomb of Tutenkhamen. In the centre is a winged scarab, a symbol of resurrection. This gold cup* (top) *from the grave of Pu-Abi is now in the British Museum, London.* Above: *The originals of these electrotypes of gold objects found in the royal graves at Ur, c.2600 BC, are in the Baghdad Museum.*

relationship to God and hence his right to rule. This tradition, which is found in different areas of the world – in Mesopotamia, Egypt, Persia and the Inca culture, raised the status of silversmiths by making their craft one of the ruler's means of expressing and demonstrating power.

Collections in the museums of the world reveal the ingenuity of thousands of years ago and man's ancient desire for personal adornment. Some famous examples are the huge quantities of engraved and embossed gold in the tomb of Tutenkhamen, the fabulous treasure of Mycenae and the remarkable jewellery of the Sumerian Queen Pu-abi and her handmaidens found in the tombs of ancient Ur. In South-East Asia, gold-plated statues of the Buddha are renowned. The cultures of Mesopotamia and the Nile civilisations are also represented, as are the workshops of the Roman Empire.

Such notable museums as Baghdad, Cairo, Istanbul, the Louvre, the Hermitage and British Museum display silver jewellery either in cases or on models. Other examples of the worked metal are to be seen on seals, vessels, pottery, porcelain, wallboards and statues. Yet, in relation to the amounts of other ships, but also their laws, their culture and their art. The techniques of silverwork known to the early Arabs had not reached the high standard existing in surrounding areas, for in such places as Greece, Rome, Egypt, Mesopotamia, Persia, India and Urarto, stable empires had permitted the development of richer art forms.

By comparing early Islamic metalwork with Roman silverware dating from the third to the sixth centuries we can plainly see the influence of Rome on Islamic Art. In Roman times most of the available silver was used to make household objects, a tradition which was adopted by Islam, and there are some surviving examples. The Chaourse Treasure found in France, the Water Newton Treasures (which are renowned as the oldest Roman silver from the Christian era yet discovered), the Mildenhall and Corbridge Treasures, and other hoards in Germany, France and Spain have all added to historical knowledge of the development of metalworking. It would seem that silver was highly prized by the Romans, for all silver objects are found buried together, while bronzes, ceramics and glass are found scattered among the ruins of excavations.

We know that the bulk of Roman silverware came from the eastern provinces, from centres such as Antioch in Syria and Alexandria in Egypt. When the western empire declined, Constantinople became the seat of power just prior to the coming of Islam, and other workshops were set up in North Africa and in Constantinople itself, continuing the Roman tradition. Syrian craftsmen were accomplished in metalwork at this time and their high standards of craftsmanship are evident in such examples as the Phela, the Antioch, the Hama and the Riha Treasures. Pieces like those in the Riha Treasure were made for the rulers of Byzantium by Syrian smiths working in Constantinople. They had developed the techniques of filigree, enamelling, gilding and niello. Workshops in Syria itself did not produce such a high standard, since most of their finest craftsmen had been taken to Byzantium; however, much of the gold from Africa destined for Constantinople's workshops never got further than Syria, so that when the Arabs arrived there, they appropriated great stores of precious metals. The Arabs used the gold and the silver for coinage and precious objects, and under their rule Syrian workshops thrived once more.

Of all the outside influences on Islamic metalworking, the Sassanian was perhaps the most dominant. Persia had ancient traditions of metalworking and there are many examples dating from centuries BC which demonstrate advanced techniques, such as engraving, relief and gilding, applied to precious metals. The designs were intricate and marvellously well executed – hunting scenes, floral patterns, fantastic animals, gods and kings – all delicately depicted on silver objects. Many of these techniques had been learned from the Greeks, for when the Kingdom of Macedonia spread to the east, much of Persia was Hellenised and many Greek settlements established.

Although the East adopted Greek art forms, it developed its own spiritual style, firstly under the Parthians and then under the Sassanians. The highest standards of metalworking were reached under the Sassanian kings, whose empire stretched from Syria to western India but whose influence reached further into Asia, even to China. The fineness of Persian work can be seen in the Oxus Treasure found in Turkomania and in the Klimova Treasure found in the Perm region. The Sassanians excelled in every field of metalworking and their craftsmen are still regarded as among the finest in history. Most of their creations are in the Hermitage Museum in Leningrad, although there are some examples in the Bustan Museum in Tehran. Much Sassanian metalwork was traded along the rivers in ancient times and exchanged for furs and slaves. Those pieces still in existence show the skill, imagination and maturity of technique achieved by the Sassanians: ewers, cups and bowls were made in gold, silver, silver gilt and bronze, and their techniques included casting, carving, engraving, repoussé and niello work.

After the fall of Greece, Persia regained her old supremacy and became Rome's main rival. The Empires were so evenly matched that neither could hope to defeat the other. The Middle East acted as a buffer state between these two great powers and was regarded by both as of vital economic importance. Persia took gold and silver and corn from Russia, while Rome drew necessary supplies from Egypt, Nubia and Ethiopia. Syria remained neutral.

The main difference between Roman and Persian Art lies in the Roman depiction of realistic triumphs and of Roman life, whereas Persian Art glorifies

This silver parcel-gilt dish, which has applied relief inscribed in pehlavi and was found in Mazanderen, Persia, forms part of the Oxus Treasure.

the contemporary monarch, who is always larger than any other person or piece in the design. As trade opened up further afield, so Chinese influence affected Persian Art giving it a wider and more diverse flavour. The Persians always had access to large amounts of gold; even Greek historians commented on the ornaments worn by Persian kings and their bodyguards.

Islam rose like a whirlwind from the desert replacing previous Arab cultures. The speed with which it spread and the rapidity of the growth of its influence is only explicable in terms of the appeal of its philosophy. The unique quality of Islam was the successful blending of ethnic and universal elements. This was the core of its magnetism, for while it was born of the desert and the oases and contained elements of such origins, the essence of its concepts was advanced. Islam stressed the brotherhood of man, regardless of race, colour or creed, while it emphasised the supremacy of the Muslim. The early Caliphs did not conquer in order to impose their way of life or their religion on subjugated nations, but were ardently concerned with ruling the world for Allah, as they had been commanded by his Prophet, Mohammed. They did not establish themselves as divine or titular heads of their new religion, preferring to style themselves the servants of Allah.

This was a very different approach in an area of the world which had so often suffered invasions and the imposition of alien religions. Under Islam, a man was free to adopt the new religion and its code of living, but he was not obliged to do so, providing that he recognised the supremacy of the Caliphate. This subtle distinction between the traditional divinity of emperors and the supremacy of the Caliphate may have played a considerable role in the popular acceptance of Islam. Arab conquerors were fierce and successful warriors, but they never gained a comparable reputation for pillage and wanton destruction, for it seems that, despite their nomadic traditions and the hardship of desert life, Arabs had developed considerable appreciation for beautiful things. This emerged initially in their love of language and writing, and their devotion to poetry and the power of the spoken word is still a treasured aspect of the heritage. In addition to these, the Arabs also patronised architecture and the plastic and decorative arts.

They possessed stores of precious metals and raw materials, which led to the development of craftsmanship. There are many references to the use of jewellery by the Arabs at the beginning of the rise of Islam in the work of poets like Omar Ben Kulthum, Hatam Al Tai and Al Nabiga. In manuscripts and miniatures such as Al Mukhassas, Al Tab'akat, Al Teriaq, Makamat Al-Hariri, Al Agani and others, there are mentions of jewels and of smiths. The Arabs prior to Islam wore many kinds of jewellery which had their own functions; some of these pieces were worn by men as well as women. The early Arabs, during the Ummayad period of Islam, had a tendency to rich living and under the Abbasids there was apparently a large market known as the Smiths' Market. There are written descriptions of the preparation of Haroun Al Raschid's jewellery for his wedding to Zoubedah and of jewellery for Mamoon's wedding to Boran. When we look at Islamic Art from its inception, we see that it was influenced by surrounding civilisations but retained a typical Arabian flavour, which reflected the civilisation that had produced Islam itself.

As Islam rose suddenly and strongly in the seventh century, so existing empires like those of Byzantium and Persia declined. The Arabs advanced into areas of economic importance and expanded their influence eastwards to India and Central Asia, incorporating parts of Sassanid territory, and westwards as far as Morocco and Spain, thus diminishing Byzantine influence. As they did so, the Arabs inherited almost all the main sources of Byzantine and Sassanian precious metals, in the Caucasus, Central Asia, Persia, Nubia and Ethiopia. But the Arab craftsmen were not sufficiently skilled to accomplish their masters' desire to rival the old empires, and so their Egyptian and Syrian contemporaries were hired to create new works of art. These men built magnificent edifices and fashioned metal works, adopting the Byzantine tradition of lavishly ornate swords and daggers decorated with silver and gold and Hellenistic and Roman devices. When Persia capitulated to Islam, Sassanian craftsmen enriched Islamic workmanship. The Copts willingly travelled to Damascus bringing skills and designs which dated to Pharaonic times. The Copts, the early Christians of Egypt, had a special talent for working in bronze, and their use of standing lamps and incense burners in their religion may have been introduced into Islam.

The Ummayads were replaced by the Abbasids in the eighth century and the centre of power shifted from Damascus to Baghdad. The Sassanian influence on Islamic Art was now given full rein and many Persian craftsmen migrated from Persia. Very little metalwork survives from the first period of the Ummayad Caliphate, but some of the pieces which do exist are to be seen in the Islamic Museum in Cairo. They include ewers, bowls and jugs, most of which are made in bronze.

The smiths travelled to whichever city was in the ascendant in the Islamic Empire at any one time – Damascus, Baghdad, Isfahan, Constantinople, Cordoba, Cairo or Samarkand. Mosul, too, in Iraq, was one of the most important centres for metalworking, holding much the same position as Augsburg and Nuremburg in European metalwork.

The domination of one ruler over such a vast area transcended existing frontiers and enabled craftsmen to move freely

The obverse and reverse of this coin depict the Caliph Mukhteder of the Abbasid period.

from country to country, where newly-established schools of art drew those who were keen to study new techniques. Sometimes an individual poet or smith became so renowned that a following would gather spontaneously to learn from him; on other occasions a ruler would summon master craftsmen to work on a single project. By these means imaginations were stimulated and different styles and tastes interacted to form the unifying character of Islam – a unity in diversity.

In the early period of Islam the rulers were perhaps too preoccupied with the establishment of their empire as a more powerful force than existing ones, and although fine architecture bears witness to the influence of the Ummayads, the greatest impact was made later by the Abbasid Dynasty under Haroun al-Rashid and subsequently his son, Ma'amoun, who particularly promoted science, mathematics, literature and the arts.

As the Muslim Empire was so vast, art thrived in certain areas under one ruler and declined in others under the same ruler. For example, in Persia, art flourished under the Seljuks and Mughals, but declined under the Mamelukes. The invasions of Ghenghis Khan into Transoxiana and Khurosan in the thirteenth century threatened the livelihood of many craftsmen, who moved to Syria and to other areas where they could practise their skills without danger. A few were taken prisoner by the Mughals, who transported them to India to establish new centres and introduce their designs and techniques. The Ayyubids encouraged craftsmen to leave Mosul for Damascus, Aleppo and Cairo after the

ARAB AND ISLAMIC SILVER

fall of Baghdad and the Abbasid Dynasty in the thirteenth century. Syria superseded Mosul as a centre for metalworking and was itself eclipsed by Cairo under the Mamelukes' rule.

Silver was always most abundant along the main trade routes, and the centres of silverwork have remained substantially unchanged for many centuries. Today the famous bazaars are the Suk al-Hamidiya of Damascus, Khan al-Khalili of Cairo, Suk Ghardaia of Mzab, Suk al-Mushir of Tripoli, Shari' al-Nahr of Baghdad, Suk al-Milh of Sana'a, the Sarafa Bazaar of Karachi and Masjid Jamia of Delhi. These bazaars and others bustle with activity as they have for so long; silver products are bought and sold, bargained for and haggled over. Prices vary in each city and with each dealer.

As we study Middle Eastern metalwork in various international museums, it is possible to draw certain conclusions. Firstly that the surviving jewellery of the Mesopotamians, Egyptians, Phoenicians, Greeks, Etruscans and Romans is more often made of gold than of silver. Secondly, that during these periods metalworkers seem to have been commissioned to produce household and practical objects rather than specialist pieces. Thirdly, that it was in so doing that the craftsmen's originality emerged and decorative designs were created by individuals, who presumably tired of ordinary shapes. Fourthly, that in the hands of master craftsmen, Arabic scripts, geometric patterns, floral designs, human and animal shapes merged in a

A remarkable gold ewer (above) *with winged animal and human head designs dates from the 10th century Buyid period. Below right: Reminiscent of Seljuk tombs, this model's sides are decorated with golden panels of floral design and it is probably Persian. These silver parcel-gilt belt trappings* (below left) *were crafted in the Seljuk Sultanate of Rum which held sway in Anatolia in the 13th century.*

THE EARLY HISTORY OF SILVERWORK

Above: *Some examples of Islamic silverwork found in Russia and documented by Smirnov. This Turkish silver parcel-gilt coffee pot* (far right) *dates from the 18th century.* Right: *This incense burner may have originated either in Egypt or Syria, but it is unique because such a piece is usually only found in copper or brass with Arabic inscriptions in museums.*

wonderful and infinite variety of ways, which became a "language of decoration," reflecting the spirit of Islam. This artistic vocabulary united the diverse cultures and peoples of the Islamic Empire as it became common to the entire range of art. Finally we can see that the designs of the eleventh and thirteenth centuries are the finest in existence.

In examining this metalwork one can see that many of the pieces now known to us were made in baser metals, such as copper, brass and iron. Very few are made of silver. This does not mean that they did not exist in silver, for we have historical records which prove otherwise – for example, in the work of the historians Makrizi and Ibn Khaldoon. In many of the pieces available to us silver is used to inlay other metals. The fact that similar patterns to these were made in silver is supported by Smirnov's book *Vostochnoye Serebro* (Eastern Silver), published in 1909. He demonstrates that many eastern silver pieces found within Russian territory or in the neighbouring areas have Islamic patterns and designs. Some even have Arabic inscriptions.

Today much Islamic silverwork is still fashioned in the designs of these ancient craftsmen, who so many years ago combined their independent heritages, skills and imaginations to produce a new art form that would reflect the magnificent empire of their Islamic masters.

ARAB AND ISLAMIC SILVER

The Functions of Silverwork

Jewellery reflects the aesthetic values of a people. In the Islamic world it is sometimes difficult to distinguish people's dress from their ornaments, because the two blend so well together. In some national costumes this blending is total. Neck, wrist and waist jewellery, once independent additions to the costume, have become an integral part of it. Cloth ornamentation with the same geometric and floral designs are sewn on to the dress itself, making colourful bands round the neck, waist and sleeves.

Jewellery was a natural progression from primitive man's habit of decorating his body: at first he used colours and tattoos on the skin itself, then leather and bones, feathers, shells and mother of pearl. These pieces were not simply decorative, but were supposed to allay the wrath of evil spirits, to impress other tribes, to denote achievement, to make the rest of his group respect and honour him or to frighten potential enemies. Ornamentation became more complex and evolved into shapes and signs which identified an individual as belonging to one particular group.

With the advent of metallurgy, existing materials were supplemented by the use of metal, and man learnt that silver and gold were the two metals which did not discolour or otherwise affect the skin. These precious metals were therefore the most frequently used for ornamentation, and they increased in value to form an important part of a family's wealth.

Women became the guardians of this treasure, which was given to them on their marriage. Pieces made for weddings usually represent the very best work and designs, having a harmony of style characteristic of the area in which they were made and displaying a great number of decorative elements.

A bride may wear a huge amount of jewellery, concentrated on the upper part of the body where pieces surround her head and face, hang from her neck and ears and may completely cover the entire front of her body to the waist. She will have a waistband with a large clasp, bracelets, rings, pendants and silver shoes. In Djibouti, girls also wear special silver masks when they perform their traditional dance *Al-Malabu*. In the Al-Maharah region of South Yemen, amongst other places, the groom wears

Above left: *This Pakistani bracelet is decorated with various coloured beads and silver wire. The ornament is divided into many sections and covers most of the hand.*

The Algerian anklet (above right) *is engraved with a floral design and inlaid with plastic, which replaces the original coral.*

a sheathed dagger attached to a silver decorated belt, and he presents this, *Al-Mohanhan*, to his bride, increasing the three kilograms of weight with which she is already laden. A Touareg bridegroom offers his bride a silver dagger on their wedding night to protect her from evil spirits. Similar ceremonies survive in country districts all over the Arab and Islamic world.

The bridegroom must include in the dowry for presentation to his bride specific pieces of jewellery of previously negotiated value. In some of the oil states, such as Libya, Kuwait, U.A.E. and Saudi Arabia, silver dowries have been replaced by gold. In Baghdad, Aleppo, Homs, Karak, Riyadh and Beirut and many other Islamic cities, silversmiths are now leaving their profession because it is no longer sufficiently profitable. They are melting down existing silver pieces to be sold as bullion, and those who can afford it have started smithing in gold, to meet a new demand.

While city girls are given gold and precious stones, village girls' dowries are limited to silver. The majority of Arab and Islamic peoples still live in rural areas, and silver jewellery abounds there. In the desert and countryside women wear nose-rings, anklets and headdresses, pieces which are not often seen in the cities. In such areas the anklet is a large, heavy object, often hollow with beads inserted inside it. As a woman walks, the tinkling noise is supposed to attract the men's attention. In modern towns, where women no longer wear the veil, the traditional anklet has been replaced by a delicate gold or silver chain. This is just one example of how traditional styles are adapted to suit particular needs and the current social environment, so that the piece itself continues to be used, though in a new form.

The effect of religion and local beliefs on silverwork is clearly illustrated in the patterns and symbols of much Islamic jewellery. Some pieces carry religious inscriptions, such as *Ma Sha Allah* (God Willing) or *Ayat Al-Kurci* (The Verse of the Throne), and are often identified by the name of their inscriptions. There are also amulets, known as *du'a* or *hirz* in different countries. These talismans have many different functions: to protect the wearer from evil, disease and accidents;

THE FUNCTIONS OF SILVERWORK

"Ma sha Allah" is inscribed on this pear-shaped pendant (left) *which is part of a colourful Libyan piece.*

This ornament (above right) *called a sinn al-thib or "wolf's tooth" is worn on a child's head and is unique to Iraq. Real wolves' teeth have been used in this example, which is rare because plastic or other bones frequently replace them nowadays. It is supposed to have amuletic power and is held on by chewing gum or tar. The Iraqi bas bend amulet box* (left) *is worn fixed on the arm and is usually decorated on either side. In this example the well-executed inscription is a favourite verse from the Quran, which reads "nasrun min'allah wefathun karib".*

to bring luck; win the affection of the beloved; revive a husband's love; hasten the return of an absent member of the family; ease childbirth and bring boy babies; dispel envy or appease djinns.

The wearing of amulets is mostly confined to women and children, whose resistance to evil is thought to be weaker than that of most men. Iraqi children sometimes wear charms such as the *dahhasha*, *sinn al-thib* and *jnagh* for their magical effects. Beads, especially blue ones, are used in children's jewellery. Other charms are hung on horses and camels to repel envy and evil. Some of the symbols which the silversmiths use

17

ARAB AND ISLAMIC SILVER

Floral and bird decoration disguise the weight of this large Libyan anklet.

are depicted on this page.

The Arabs have always had an aptitude for mathematics and from their experiments with the line and the circle a symbolic art form developed. The geometric signs have deep philosophical meanings, but as time passed, ordinary people forgot their origins, although continuing to put them on amulets. Many silversmiths are also ignorant of their real meanings, but continue to use them because it is traditional to do so and because their customers continue to demand them. Only the genuine master craftsman ponders their significance as he employs this expressive vocabulary in his works of art.

While these symbols may still have a religious function in the villages, they are also commissioned in pieces for city women, who are deliberately regenerating the cultural heritage. The intrinsic beauty of these magical symbols is now becoming widely appreciated at a more sophisticated level.

There are some regions in which devout Muslims disapprove of the wearing of gold jewellery by men. There is no authority for this reaction in the Quran, but in the *hadith* of the Prophet it is written that "silk and gold are taboos to the men of my nation, permissible to its women." Therefore men in strictly orthodox regions wear silver betrothal rings instead of gold, and this is probably why silver jewellery is more widely worn by men, for instance in Al-Haqar and Oman. The Quran itself permits adornment, but states that moderation should

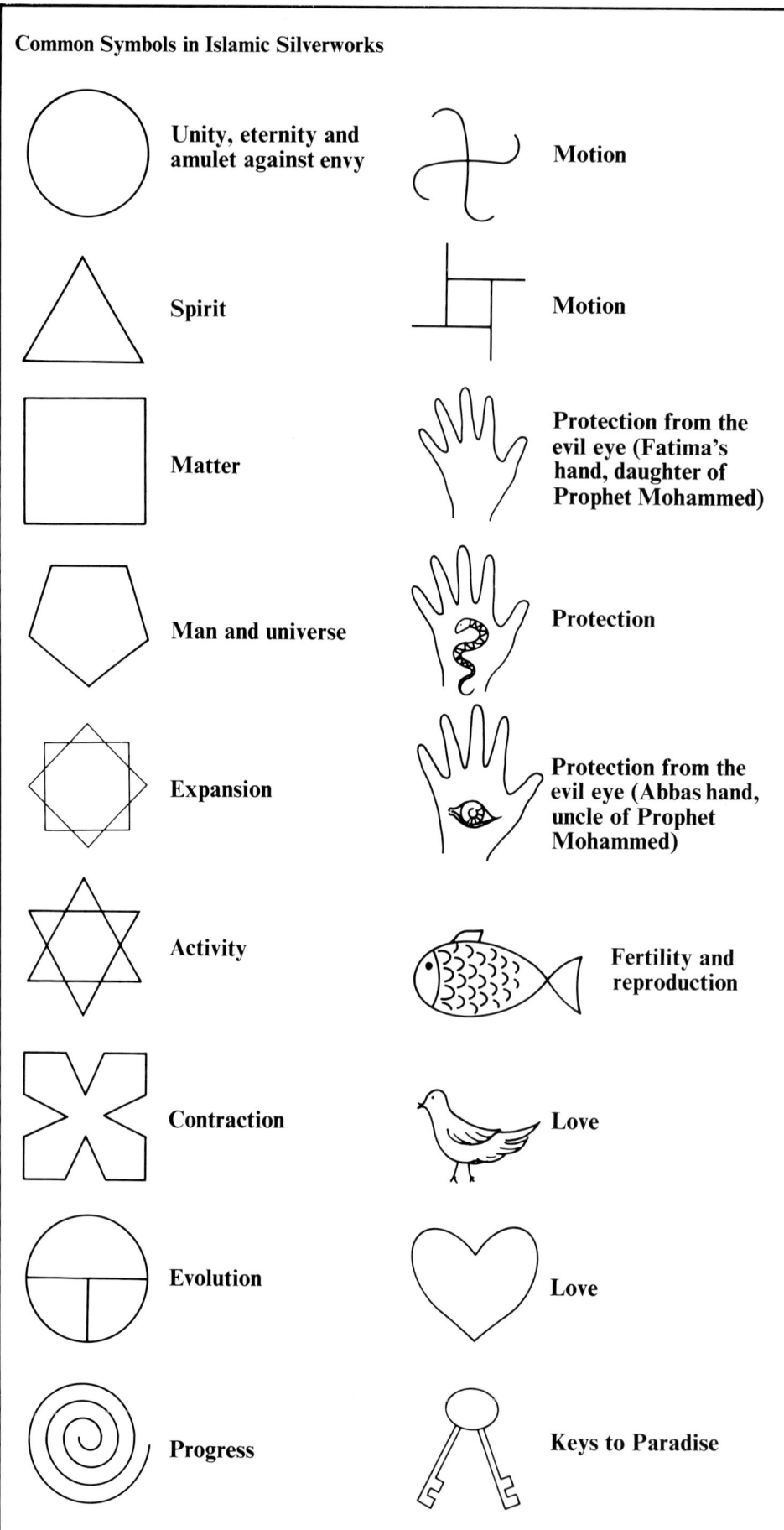

Common Symbols in Islamic Silverworks

Symbol	Meaning
Circle	Unity, eternity and amulet against envy
Triangle	Spirit
Square	Matter
Pentagon	Man and universe
Two overlapping squares (8-pointed star)	Expansion
Six-pointed star	Activity
X shape	Contraction
Circle divided	Evolution
Spiral	Progress
Swastika (curved)	Motion
Swastika	Motion
Hand	Protection from the evil eye (Fatima's hand, daughter of Prophet Mohammed)
Hand with snake	Protection
Hand with eye	Protection from the evil eye (Abbas hand, uncle of Prophet Mohammed)
Fish	Fertility and reproduction
Bird	Love
Heart	Love
Keys	Keys to Paradise

THE FUNCTIONS OF SILVERWORK

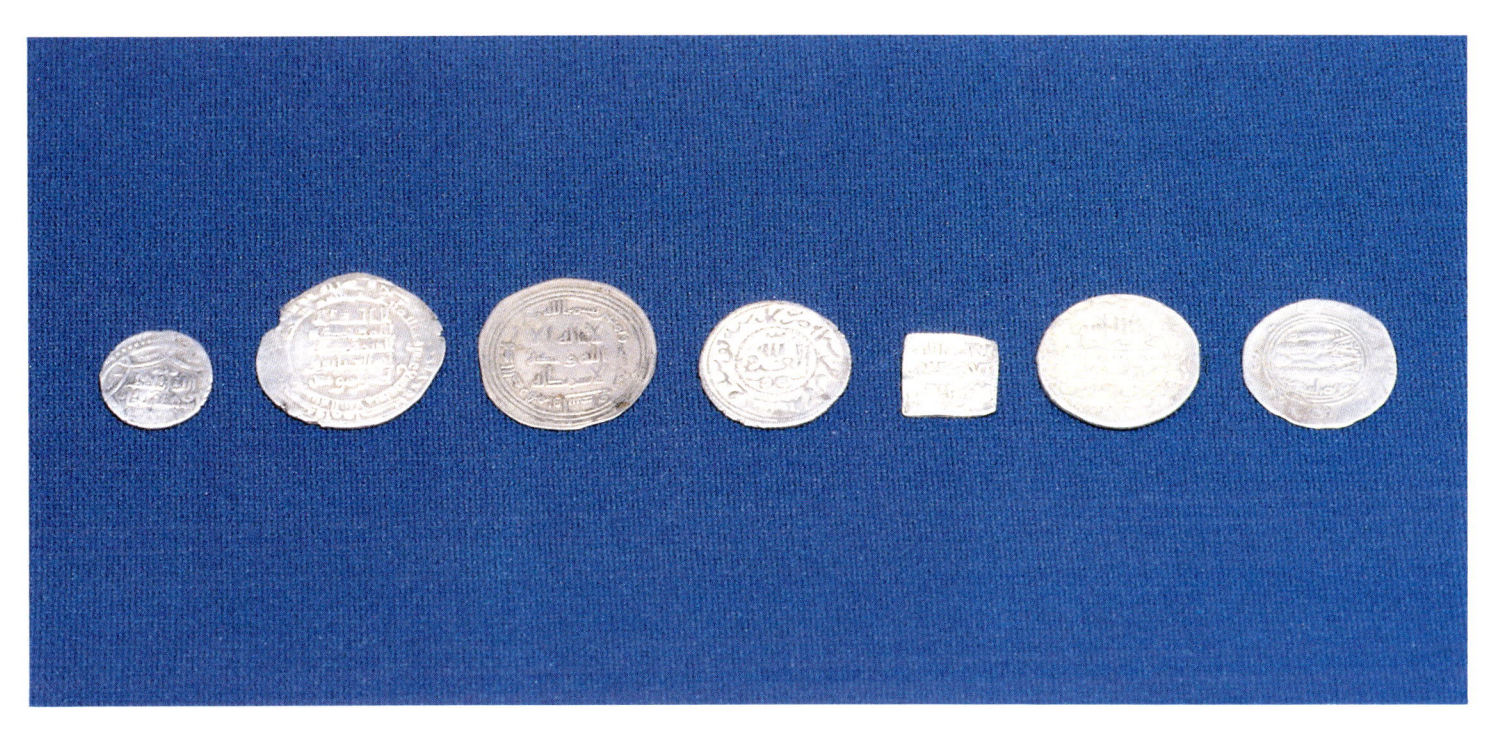

be exercised; so while verse 32 of *Al-Araf* reads:

Say, who has forbidden the decent apparel of God,
Which He has produced for his servants,
And the good things that He has provided for food,
Say, these things are for those who believe in
　　　　　　　　　　　　　　　this present life,
but peculiarly on the day of resurrection.
Thus do we distinctly explain our signs
Unto people who understand.

Verse 31 of *Al-Araf* states:

O Children of Adam, take your decent apparel
at every place of worship, and eat and drink,
But be not guilty of excess, for He loves not
those that are guilty of excess.

Goods were exchanged for gold, silver and bronze long before coins were minted. The Mesopotamians, Egyptians and the civilisations of southern Arabia used silver for barter thousands of years ago. Gold and silver coins were common in the pre-Christian era and Greek coins were made of silver before Alexander the Great brought gold from Persia. The Romans used bronze for coins in the fourth century BC, but later changed to silver because of its rarity value. Large quantities of ancient coins can be seen in museums, depicting various rulers and animals and bearing a variety of symbols denoting their value.

My collection includes antique silver coins found in oriental markets, originating from many countries. Some of them have been incorporated into pieces of jewellery, but in remote areas like North Yemen such coins are still in use today.

In many Arab homes there are pieces of silver with mundane practical functions as well as purely decorative ones. In the dining room there may be dishes, coffee pots and salt and pepper pots; the drawing room may contain vases, picture frames, cigarette boxes and samovars. Boxes for *kohl* and other cosmetics, silver *meel* for their application, toothpicks, earpicks and mirrors may be found in the bedroom. All these objects demonstrate a family's social standing and affluence. The most precious silver is brought out only on special occasions and for honoured guests. Then rosewater is shaken from a silver sprinkler over the faces and hands of the guests, coffee is sipped from silver cups and incense wafted from incense burners. The food may be served on silver dishes. The men of the family have their own silver possessions: seals, rings, belts and headbands, worry-beads, shaving equipment, soap-dishes and tooth-brushes, and weapons, such as ornamented rifles and the famous curved daggers and swords of Yemen, Morocco and Oman. Some of the old Yemeni daggers are decorated with *misned*, the ancient script of that country.

Camels and horses are often richly ornamented and may have decorative saddles, spurs, stirrups, bells, amulets and special anklets – another reflection of the wealth and standing of their owners.

Arabic everyday sayings stress the financial importance of acquiring jewellery: "Metals are for hard times" and "Jewellery for adornment and investment." By selling or pawning her jewellery, a woman can always realise

Above: *Various coins from different periods.* Left to right:
a. *Ilkhanid, about 1350 AD, Persian coin relating to Mongol period.*
b. *Abbasid period, relating to the Caliph Mukhteder, about 320 AH.*
c. *Ummayad period, minted in Wasit, Iraq, about 91 AH.*
d. *Turkish Seljuk dirham of Er Rum Khai Khusru I, 1210–1219 AD.*
e. *(Square coin) Almohades dynasty of North Africa and Spain, about 1165–1260 AD.*
f. *Husein I El Abbasi, King of Persia 1694–1722, from Tiflis in Georgia.*
g. *Umar ibn Al-Ala, Arab governor of Tabaristan, about 155 AH.*

funds to overcome a crisis in her life; so the possession of jewellery satisfies both a need for security and the wish to display her position. In Iraq, a woman will never sell her *khizama* (nose-ring) but keeps it until her death, when its sale pays for her shroud. Jewellery is inherited but also frequently given by the older to the younger generation at the celebration of such special occasions as engagements, weddings, births and circumcisions. Silver is also given by lovers to their sweethearts. Touareg girls in particular cherish these pieces and never sell them, regardless of the price offered or how desperately they may need the money.

Thus the purchase of jewellery has always had an economic motive. People are still disposed to buy gold and other valuable commodities to protect them-

ARAB AND ISLAMIC SILVER

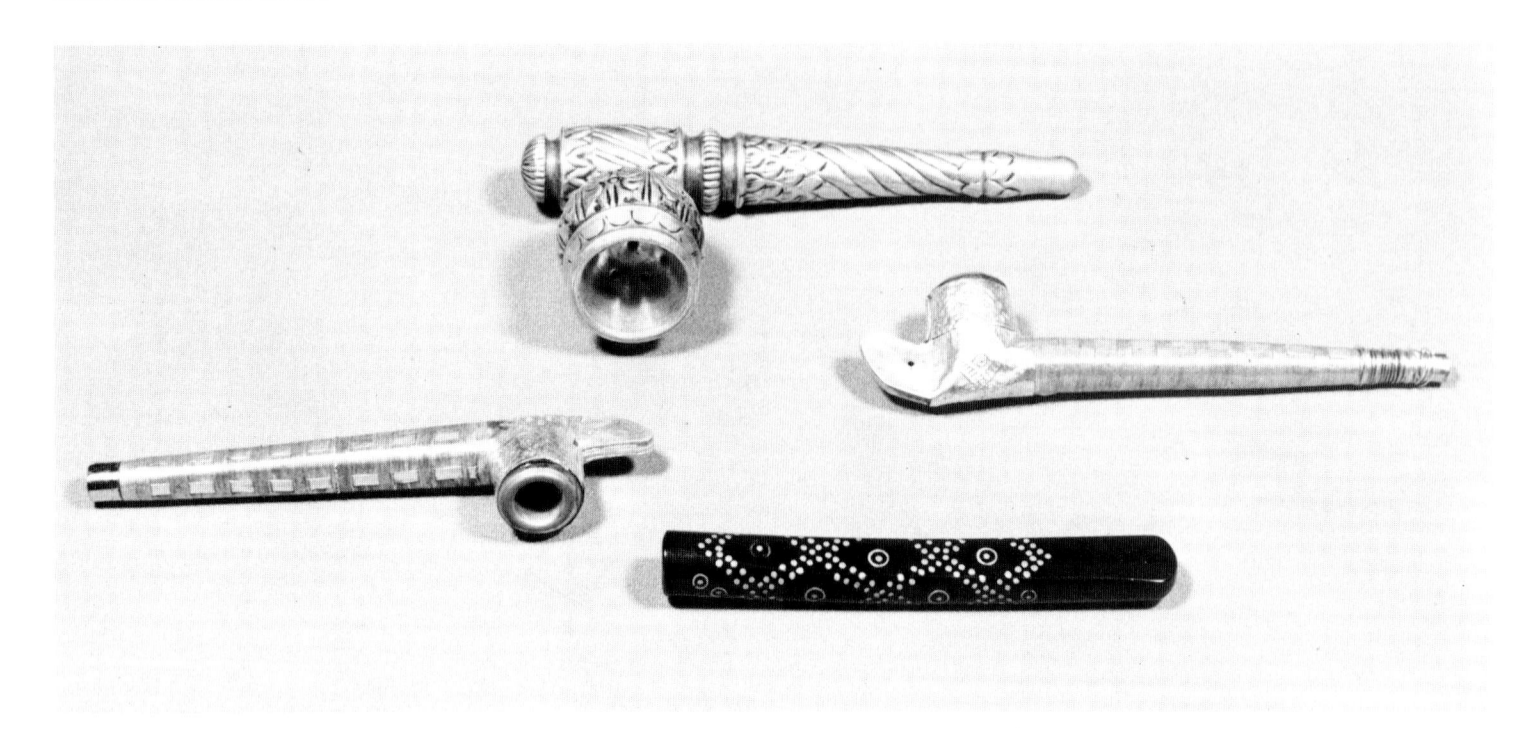

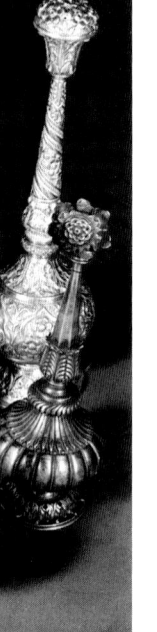

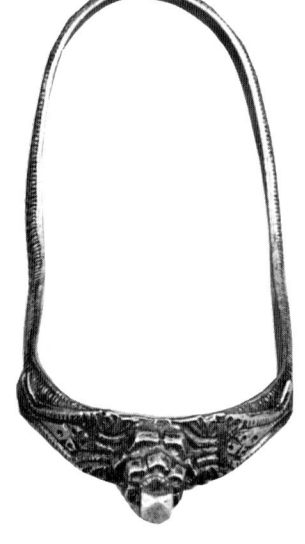

Rosewater sprinklers (left) *display different styles from Iraq, Pakistan and India. Four pipes* (top) *from Turkey, Oman and Iraq.* Above: *This ornate pair of Omani stirrups are made of a high percentage of alloy for strength.*

selves from the fluctuations of paper money. Jewellery is still deposited in banks or with wealthy organisations or individuals, money is borrowed against its value or it may be exchanged for other goods. In agrarian societies, wealth is measured by the number of animals in a man's possession, his acreage and his wife's and family's jewellery. Country women wear their everyday jewellery at home and on the farm, keeping their most distinctive and precious pieces for special family and social occasions. Sometimes a woman may borrow or hire another's finery to impress her neighbours.

It is difficult to assess the percentage of silver in a finished object simply by looking at it, but there are several techniques which may be applied. A small area can be treated with sulphuric acid or a piece of the metal rubbed with a touchstone. As the different colours emerge, an expert can judge the approximate proportion of pure silver. A hallmark protects the buyer from deception by describing the smith's wares precisely, but Arab and Islamic products often do not carry any detailed indication of their origin. Types of hallmarks vary from area to area. On Tunisian and Algerian jewellery they are small, square, triangular or rectangular. Libyan pieces carry several large ones, the size and shape of which are mostly related to the percentage of silver used. Omani silver, although characterised by excellent material and magnificent workmanship, bears no hallmark at all. In general, hallmarked silver commands a higher price. When oriental pieces contain other materials, such as stone, glass, ivory, leather or fabric, it becomes even more difficult to judge the real value of the metal.

Types of Silverwork

In this chapter I will set out brief notes describing the types of silver jewellery and objects to be found in my collection. The many names for the same piece originate in different countries or sometimes from different regions within a country. The careful reader will note a further complication – occasionally a name which is used for a particular design in one country will also describe an entirely different piece elsewhere.

These rings, pendants, necklaces, buckles and buttons (above) *come from Pakistan, Oman and other Middle Eastern countries. The buttons are worn on chains by wealthy Pakistani men on festive occasions.*

Headdresses

The most common name for a headdress is *Al-Iklil* but there are many individual types with their own names, such as *Al-Qulunswa, Al-Taj, Al-Jabeen, Al-Isabah, Al-Qobqob* and *Al-Taseh*.

Al-Iklil is a ceremonial headdress which covers all or part of the head for special occasions such as weddings. It may completely cover the head with an elaborate or simple raised crown or may consist of a band across the forehead with rows of silver discs, which is tied behind or fastened with a silver clasp. The forehead band is sometimes more ornately decorated and the hanging panels are shaped like fish, crescents, hands or waves, amongst which there may also be flower and star shapes, larger crescents and rings with rosettes or squares inside them. *Al-Iklil* may be enamelled, inlaid with agate or coral, or the entire design may be enlivened with the use of red, green or blue glass.

Al-Taj means "the crown" and is an ancient design of headdress denoting high status. There are many different varieties and they are worn by both men and women. *Al-Taseh*, otherwise known as *Al-Qurs*, is an elegant, round, ornately decorated piece of jewellery, inlaid with a central stone; dangling pendants are attached to its edge. It is lined and fixed to the head by a band of cloth, worn under the chin.

Al-Qellab appears in several shapes and consists of a woven silver mat, sometimes used to conceal a scar on the forehead; it is wrapped around the head and fastened by a silver chain or lock.

Hair Ornaments

Combs are worn to adorn the head and hair. They may be inlaid with stones and decorated with different engravings or can be quite plain and used only for practical purposes. Networks of silver, diamond or circular pieces linked by wire are sometimes fastened to the hair by hooks to keep it tidy. A row of bells may tinkle softly as the woman moves.

Pins for holding the hair back from the face may be fashioned in fantastic shapes with a stone forming the central boss, which is decorated by silver twisted wire. Long chains finished with bells hang to the shoulders on either side or both sides of the head. Another ornament which frames the face with linked diamond studs is worn over the head and held by a silver chain to secure the hair. Masses of triangular panels dangle from triple chains on both sides.

Earrings

Long ago in the Islamic world both men

This Moroccan head-dress (above) *is worn covering the front of the head, while the Turkish coins decorate the brow.*

and women wore earrings. Among the many names for different earring shapes are: *Al-Kharsah, Al-Allaqa, Al-Turk, Al-Minqash, Al-Meghawad, Ghohark, Um Al-Halaqah, Um Al-Wardah, Um Al-Shanasheel, Um Al-Digam* and *Tannah*. Some are round with toothed trimming, others are crescent, triangular or cone-shaped. Sometimes an earring consists of a ring with small roses or leaves suspended from it; alternatively the pendants are shaped like grapes or granular drops or they are interspersed with little chains. Most earrings are based on a ring with silver or stone pendants and are designed to be worn with pierced ears.

They may be so big and heavy that

ARAB AND ISLAMIC SILVER

Right: *Various necklaces from Libya, Oman and Afghanistan. The necklace on the left with wooden beads is Omani. The little one in front with coral and hollow silver panels is modern Iraqi. The necklace with orange and long beads and the one to the far right are old reconstructed Iraqi pieces. In the centre is a Libyan pendant. At the bottom right is an Afghani necklace with coral, coloured beads and bell-shaped pendants, held by chains which lead off the main hollow crescent. They are all displayed in a large Pakistani bowl which is extravagantly decorated with repoussé and floral design.* Below right: *This typically southern Libyan earring is decorated with wood, as an alternative to coral, and stamped seals. A typical Omani necklace threaded on rope instead of chain (below far right) in which silver balls and small decorative boxes are inlaid with copper and geometrically decorated with silver shots.*

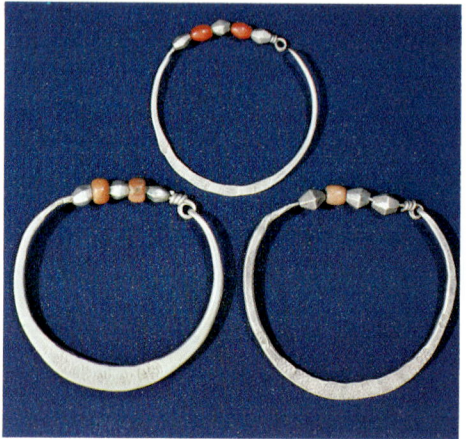

they have to be worn on the pinna to avoid stretching or tearing the lobe. Some earrings are so long that they play the dual role of earrings and neck ornaments. Sometimes women wear a headband which presses the earrings tight against the head to take the weight, which can be as great as 400 grams. These heavy rings carry many long chains made either from thick links or from twisted silver thread. Each chain is finished with coral or other stones or with differently shaped pieces of silver – crescent, semi-circular, conical or hand-shaped.

Some village women in Fezzan and Oman wear more than one earring in each ear and have three or more holes punched along the edge of the ear. This fashion has now reached the West, where it is followed by some men as well as by women.

Nose-rings
The collective name for nose-ring is *Al-Khazzamah* but there are many different types, such as *Al-Wardeh, Al-Arran, Shafi, Faridah* and *Al-Qaranfalok*.

When a girl reaches puberty her mother will make a hole in her nose, inserting a needle and thread through the side of the nostril. The needle is removed leaving a circle of thread which is moved round each day until the wound is properly healed. Then a piece of clove is inserted in the hole, after which the nose-ring will be finally positioned.

Al-Khazzamah is a little stud, sometimes inlaid with coral, turquoise and pearls. In some examples one small silver droplet or sometimes several will dangle from the ring. Occasionally a nose-ring is so big that it swings upon the woman's upper lip. They are mostly worn in the rural regions of Iraq, Arabia, Syria, Jordan, India and Pakistan, but city women in most places, excepting the Indian subcontinent, have abandoned them.

Necklaces
Necklaces or *Al-Qiladah* are one of the most important items of a woman's jewellery and are worn by country and city women alike. Several are often worn at once and in varying lengths; some fit tightly round the neck, while others hang to the waist. Some have coral, bead and ceramic decoration in different colours, which gives jewellery the same distinctive quality as some museum pieces which date to the ancient civilisations of Mesopotamia and the Nile.

The many names of necklaces include: *Al-Masbahah, Al-Ghardanah, Al-Qardol, Muqallad Leirat, Al-Jarrjarr* and *Al-Qalb*. *Al-Tawq* (known as *Al-Mekhnaqa* and *Al-Khannaqiya*) is a "torque" or necklace which surrounds the neck tightly. It is round and sometimes twisted, but more often consists of flat chain with silver beads or semi-circular or triangular pieces hanging from it. The pendants may be irregularly shaped and sized, but there is not commonly an outstanding central decoration. The piece may be plain at the back or may be fastened with a clasp, sometimes in the shape of a snake's head.

Abu Al-Qasab consists of several small silver cylinders suspended from a chain. *Al-Mohanhan* is heavy and worn by brides in Arabia; there are many bells or metal pieces attached to it which jingle softly as the woman dances. *Khait Louise* is made of string, which in some Omani examples may be as thick as rope, from

TYPES OF SILVERWORK

Left: *The Yemeni* shairiyah *with its hundreds of small silver pieces sewn on to material is reminiscent of chain-mail. This brooch* (below left) *is probably Turkish and displays characteristic crescent shapes at each corner engraved with floral designs. Below right: The filigree buckle inlaid with agate and enamelled is probably Moroccan.*

wearer from evil, danger, sickness and envy.

Although necklaces are generally based on these patterns, there are characteristic regional designs. The famous Kabyllie necklaces are inlaid with precisely cut enamel and coral. The chains are ornamented with spiral silver rings or with one or many rows of geometrically-shaped panels. The Libyan *Qardalah* is a fine composition of intricate stitch-like patterns, demonstrating a high level of silversmithing.

which original or imitation antique coins hang in great numbers. *Khait al-Hout* is a chain with silver-framed coral filaments for pendants. *Al-Mentishi* is made of linked coins with attached pendants.

Um Al-Hilal has a large engraved and stone-inlaid crescent pendant, which sometimes has additional smaller ones attached to its lower edge. The crescent is a major symbol in Islamic Art, can be seen on every mosque and is frequently used in jewellery throughout the Muslim world. *Al-Muhammediyah* has circular or square panels, on which the name "Mohammed" is sometimes inscribed. They hang in a row from a silver chain. This is a necklace which is mostly worn by children. *Al-Silah* means "weapon" and is worn like a bandolier with a number of engraved silver cylinders on a chain for further decoration. The best examples are to be found in Iraq and Syria.

Al-Lubbah is Yemeni, with hundreds of worked pieces fixed to, or hanging by rings from, a fabric pad. The top row consists of heavier rectangular panels, while the sides are decorated with an assortment of amulets, mother-of-pearl, buttons, coins and sequins. *Al-Shairiyah* is also common in southern Arabia and comprises many rows of worked silver plates alternating with silver bells. Each row of plates is differently decorated with silver shot and wire ornamentation.

Al-Hirz is a hollow piece of jewellery made for carrying the Quran or a *Surah* (the text of a prayer) or religious sayings; sometimes it may be empty. The Omani *hirz* usually consists of an ornately engraved cuboid or cylindrical box which is attached to a splendid silver chain with variously-shaped pendants hanging from its lower edge. In Iraq the equivalent is called a *Qab Quran* and is engraved with symbols and inscriptions to protect the

Pins and brooches

The most usual name for a pin is *Al-Mishbak* but individual styles are also known as *Ibzim, Khallalah, Qellab, Jnagh* and *Allaqah*. Brooches are used to fasten clothing in place and to secure accessories such as veils, sashes or shawls. They are often decorated with stars, crescents, triangles or circles and are mostly either inlaid with stones, like coral or turquoise, or enamelled and coloured. The latter type is most commonly seen in Kabyllie or Pakistan. Hanging chains are sometimes attached to pins, and these can be used to fix loops at the side of headdresses or to fasten the front of men's cloaks.

Brooches are often fixed to the front of the dress. Omani ones are frequently joined in pairs by a chain and have a central stone set into the circular, triangular or horseshoe-shaped ornament. Some are decorated with brass or gold

23

ARAB AND ISLAMIC SILVER

squares, with a row of chains finished with tiny bells. Such a *Mishbak* is tied to a child's hair and the bells jingle with his movements. A similar Iraqi piece is called *Jnagh*, and is worn by a child between the ages of five and seven years and then passed down to his younger brother or sister. It is a triangular ornament, engraved and inlaid with turquoise or with a piece of porcelain, and has small pendants. Sometimes it is pinned to the child's chest or fixed to his hair so that it swings on his forehead. Another silver pin is *Al-Dahhashah* which is similarly decorated and also worn on a child's chest. *Sinn al-thib* is a real wolf's tooth or a piece of bone or ivory encrusted with turquoise, rimmed with silver or gold and with pendants attached. It is likewise pinned to a child's hair, headdress or clothes.

Belts
Belts are known chiefly as *Al-Hizam*, but other names include *Al-Qayesh*, *Al-Nitaq*, *Al-Mihzamah*, *Al-Zinnar*, *Al-Hayassah*, *Al-Jaras*, *Hizam Leirat* and *Al-Kamar*. *Al-Hizam* is worn around the waist to hold the shirt down, while *Al-Zinnar* is the name given to the band of the head-dress which fixes *Al-Iklil* to the head.

The Indian *hizam* consists of beautifully woven silver threads and wires held by a pretty lock. Libyan belts are composed of one wide piece of silver with horizontally patterned areas which are engraved with different embossings, stipplings and geometrical figures. It has a striking clasp, known as *Mintaq* or *Mighlaq*. The Omani clasp is secured in the middle of the waist with the belt attached to it on both sides by hooks or leather straps. Boys wear it until puberty when it is replaced by a dagger.

The Algerian *mihzamah* has small silver panels engraved with floral or geometrical designs which are identically punched so that they can be neatly linked together by silver rings. *Al-Hayassah* is mostly worn by Iraqi children at their circumcision and is sometimes decorated with a central bell. *Hizam Leirat* is a chain of silver coins, and *Hizam Kamar* is composed of small silver pieces stitched to a fabric backing in fantastic patterns, which are particularly prominent on the clasp. Some of the *hizams* are inlaid with stones, such as coral or turquoise, or with coloured glass, or they are plated with gold.

Rings
Rings or *Al-Khatem* are worn on fingers and toes and are popular with both men and women. There are thousands of different styles of rings; some have coral, agate, turquoise or ceramic stones, while others are coloured with enamel. Some rings have small silver attachments and are most often ornamented with central pieces shaped like circles, squares, pyramids or domes, sometimes created from silver shot. Touareg rings are especially beautifully composed and well-known. Rings are only occasionally plain and undecorated.

Some seals carry their owner's seal engraved on them. As long ago as the civilisation of Mesopotamia, businessmen used them; they were made of stone, silver or gold. It is said that the Prophet Mohammed stamped his messages to the Roman emperor with a silver seal which was engraved with the words "Mohammed Rasoulullah" (Messenger of Allah).

Usually worn after circumcision, this Iraqi child's belt (bottom) *is decorated with ball-shaped beads and sometimes also bells. Below: These rings with floral patterns, enamelling and use of* tessarae *(mirrors) are Pakistani or Indian: the single-stone rings (e.g. the four in front) and the two gold seals come from Oman.*

Women sometimes wear as many as ten rings on one hand or symmetrical pairs of rings. The shape of each ring and its particular name depends for which finger it is made: *Al-Jubeira* is for the thumb, *Al-Shahed* and *Al-Marami* for the index finger, *Al-Khansar* and *Al-Habsah* for the little finger and *Al-Wassat* for the middle finger. A ring on the fourth finger mostly indicates betrothal or marriage. Rings also have many other names, such as *Mihbas Baqlawa, Hanash, Abu Al-Shanashil* and *Thalath Fusous*.

Women sometimes wear an ornate creation consisting of five rings, one for each finger, each attached to chains which cover the back of the hand, which is usually dyed with henna and tattooed. These are then connected to a larger piece of jewellery fixed to the wrist by a bracelet. In some examples of this silver ornament, commonly known as *Al-Khamsah*, but also as *Al-Shabbahah* and *Al-Kaff*, a bell is attached to each ring.

Some huge rings are not worn on the fingers but in the hair. In southern Morocco, for example, thick strands of hair are threaded through such a ring and clipped onto the crown or side of the head.

Bracelets
There are hundreds of different types of bracelets or *Al-Siwar*. The simplest ones are large rings round the wrist, but they are much more often decorated with stones, silver pieces and designs made from silver shot or with conical or cylindrical studs. Some bracelets do not join up and the free ends are shaped like mythical animal's heads. Dragons, snakes and deer are the most common patterns, probably introduced from Persian, Indian and South-East Asian jewellery. Other bracelets are fastened by silver clasps or large silver screws, which can be adjusted to fit the wearer. Some *siwars* are arranged in several rows with adjacent or overlapping designs and are worn round the wrist, forearm or upper arm, usually in symmetrical pairs.

Bracelets have many names such as *Maadhid, Radayef, Masayes, Hadayed, Qitar, Sabbah, Shathar, Janbar, Um Al-Sa'afah, Abu Al-Bankeh, Al-Safifah, Al-Hasiri, Btut, Dabbabah, Thoban, Mukaab* and *Muhabbab*.

Al-Habbasiyat is a child's bracelet which is sometimes inlaid with turquoise or other semi-precious stones. A remarkable bracelet is *Al-Dah*, which has prominent silver projections for decoration and is mostly found in Biskra and other parts of the Algerian Sahara. An *Amshloukh* is a famous Kabyllian bracelet inlaid with coral, plastic or coloured glass and coloured enamel. *Abu Al-Leirat* is made of chains with dangling coins and *Al-Melwi* is a twisted bracelet of thin or thick wire. *Al-Qalb* has a heart-shaped silver or stone central ornament with heart-shaped terminals. *Al-Zinadi* is snake-shaped and engraved and inlaid with turquoise, agate, coral or ruby for eyes. *Al-Sa'ah* is a bracelet used by men to attach their watches. *Damalij* is a broad bracelet which was probably originally designed to protect men's wrists in battle, but it is now only worn by women. *Shams wa gammer* or "Sun and Moon" is the name given to a Moroccan bracelet of alternating silver and gold panels.

This silver gilded and repoussé anklet (above) is probably Moroccan. Right: The hookah or nergileh *is Turkish or Persian and stands one metre high.*

Anklets
Anklets are famous in Oriental jewellery and have many names apart from the most usual, *Al-Khalkhal*, accorded to their various shapes and patterns, which include *Hijl, Jinjil, Abu Al-Qufl, Al-Ajwaf, Abu Al-Shanashil, Al-Mukhashkhish* and *Abu Al-Thuma*.

Anklets may be almost plain as can be seen in some Iraqi and Saharan examples or may be patterned with elaborate designs which look like embroidery. Anklets, like bracelets, may have free ends shaped like snakes' heads or be secured with ornate clasps. Some are composed of two rings, which may be worn singly or two different ones are worn on each ankle. Some pairs can weigh more than a kilogram.

Khalkhal sometimes consist of thick overlapping panels. They may be oval, circular or horseshoe-shaped. Their free ends may be pointed, ornamented or end in silver spheres or cube-shaped studs. Some are totally hollow and contain jangling pebbles, while others clang when touched by the other anklet. They are designed to attract the attention of passing admirers.

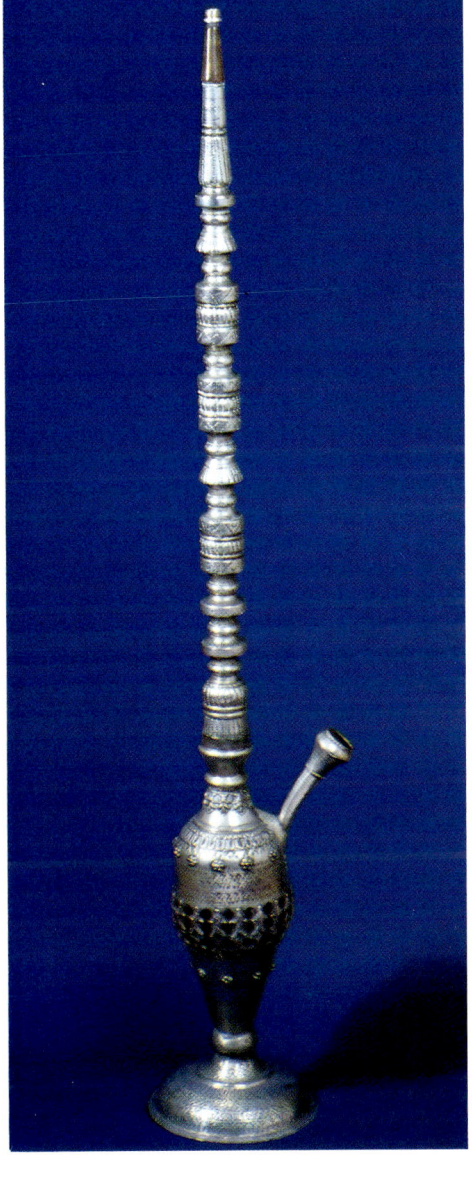

Jinjil have bells attached to them and are decorated with silver shots and *Abu Al-Shanashil* have silver locks and pendant bells as well. Both are worn by children in Iraq to tell mothers the whereabouts of their offspring. In Afghanistan they serve an added amuletic function.

Chains
The Arabic for a chain is *Al-Silsilah*, but it describes many different chains of many different types and functions. They are used most often to attach or join

other pieces of silver jewellery and to further ornament them. Some chains have rare designs, others consist of interlocking pieces of wire; some are made of similar small links as in *Al-Cha'ab*, while others have differently-sized links; some are doubled, others are fine or plaited.

Certain pieces of jewellery, like *Al-Suruh* which hangs down from the hair, headdress or clothes, are composed entirely of silver chain and silver pieces. *Al-Tulul* consists of five to twenty hemispherical silver pieces, all attached by heavy chains.

The proportion of pure silver in chains is usually less than in other jewellery. They need larger quantities of copper, zinc or tin to achieve a harder and stronger alloy, so that they can withstand strain and considerable weight.

Candlesticks
Early candlesticks were probably made of wood, but these mostly disappeared as Islamic culture developed. Candlesticks were so popular from early times that they were among the first objects to be cast in precious metals and to have attracted the skills of craftsmen. The number of patterns and designs employed to enhance their basic shape gave them great value. They were used both in the home and in mosques.

Candlesticks of both copper and brass from different Islamic periods can be seen in museums. Many are richly decorated and inlaid with silver, fashioned in the characteristic circular or cylindrical structure with a narrow socket, the whole like the body of a bell. They generally bear Arabic inscriptions in lettering kept simple to provide emphasis in the midst of so much ornate design.

When casting was introduced, the shape of the piece became more intricate to reflect more light. It seems that delicate eastern candlesticks grew so popular in Europe that craftsmen there were forced to produce similarly fine styles. From the candlesticks, various other shapes evolved such as candelabras, sconces and chandeliers. Islamic lamps carried Arabic inscriptions, divided into two – the top one from the Quran, the lower one relating to family life.

Tea and coffee services
The drinking of tea and coffee plays a significant role in Islamic societies. It is unimaginable that anybody should enter a Muslim home without being offered one or the other, for as the guest you honour the host with your presence and he welcomes you with the best that he has to offer. It is equally important that you, as the honoured guest, accept what you are offered. Islam is a teetotal society and has developed a ceremony in tea and coffee making. Large amounts of silver and creative energy have been directed towards this ritual throughout the centuries. Today a silver tea or coffee service is a prized possession and many families proudly display them as decorations in the home, using them only on the rarest occasions, such as weddings. They are also favourite gifts to newly-wed couples.

The variety of pots, kettles, samovars, urns, trays, sugar-bowls and tongs produced is a tribute to the attention silversmiths, past and present, paid and still pay to this custom. Craftsmen vied with each other in creating new shapes and designs to attract customers. Later styles were influenced by the exquisite masterpieces fashioned in porcelain by potters from the Orient, particularly China and Japan. Their designs filtered through to Middle Eastern and European smiths as trade opened up. Shapes began to change and there were many entirely new ones: the bullet shape, the bun shape, the round or polygonal shape and the inverted pear shape. Cup holders also vary greatly and some of them have fine filigree work interwoven, adding to already ornate designs.

The complete coffee or tea service is comparatively new in Islamic silver and there are no early examples to be found in museums. There are numerous examples of samovars, especially from Persia, and in many homes the samovar remains constantly alight in readiness for the visit of any guest.

Plates, dishes, trays, bowls and baskets
Islam possesses a wealth of plates, dishes, bowls, baskets and trays of all kinds, which have found their way into museums in larger numbers than any other metal objects. From such pieces we are able to determine the styles, skills and creative abilities of any particular period in history. The early influence of Sassanid craftsmen, who were among the finest ever known, was particularly beneficial; they developed every kind of technique to enhance these objects.

In various museums, one can see beautiful Islamic pieces of this kind, made of gold, silver, bronze, brass and copper, richly inlaid with silver and heavily decorated with human figures, animals, floral motifs, arabesque and the signs of the Zodiac. Understandably, pieces deemed worthy of display are either the oldest or the finest examples of designs and engraving. Nonetheless, these objects were generally functional, though probably used only on rare occasions. Their owners must have been men of great wealth or social importance.

These objects are made in as many shapes as there are decorative motifs. They are oblong, circular, round, hexagonal, octagonal or rectangular. The bowls and dishes have differently shaped bases. Some have hammer marks, others are fairly plain with almost no decoration and still others are engraved all over like other Islamic metalwork. There are fine edges and fluted rims of flowers, or animals or other motifs around a central composition. Some are decorated in rows, others bear relief decoration, or the subjects are divided into groups on a plainer background. Occasionally a simple floral, animal or geometric arabesque is spread over the whole piece.

This silver tumbler (above) *is probably Persian and used either as a vase or an ornament.*

TYPES OF SILVERWORK

These two vases (above) *are probably Turkish. This small fine silver box* (below) *has a block of agate along the top on which is engraved in Arabic script the names "Allah, Mohammed, Ali, Hussein, Hassan and Fatima". It is either Iraqi or Persian.*

Many are inlaid with gold and in some rich pieces one can find a combination of all these patterns. Many of them have Arabic writing inlaid into them, a common feature of much Islamic metalwork.

Such pieces still exist in Islamic homes today, but hardly ever display the exquisite workmanship to be found in museums. Trays are sometimes hung on walls for decoration, a bowl or basket may be used for fruit or nuts. The abundance of such objects further shows hospitality to be a strong Islamic tradition.

Boxes

Boxes have appealed to collectors for centuries. The myriad shapes, sizes and designs and the variety of woods and metals in which they are made testify to man's age-old fascination for the box. At first they were purely functional. Chests and trunks were made to hold possessions either at home or when people travelled. Prospective brides would collect and store treasures in them for their future married life. A lady's jewel box was one of her most treasured and private possessions. The richer the owner, the more finely the box would be made, and although the early ones were simple, they were often inlaid with gold, silver or precious stones.

The first small silver boxes were square or lozenge-shaped, only a few centimetres in diameter with a religious theme on the lid. People used them to carry amulets. Sadly very few early boxes have survived. From the introduction of these smaller boxes a unity of functional use and artistic creation developed. Many other delightful little containers for such things as oil, perfume and *kohl* appeared. The abundant demand for these boxes as gifts drew craftsmen to make them in silver with the same artistic inventiveness expended on larger boxes, which are often shaped like birds and animals and finely decorated. Many of these items were commissioned, and if a client demanded an unusual piece, the craftsman was given the opportunity to show off his talents and to develop and enrich his craft. Boxes of all descriptions displayed new ways of engraving and ornamentation: watch boxes, toothpick boxes and boxes for tooth-powder were all made in silver, and also wax boxes, scroll boxes, ink boxes, pen boxes with various patterns on them, tea boxes and spice boxes. Examples of the silversmiths' splendid ink and pen boxes can be seen in several museums.

Bigger containers for religious verses were introduced, made in various metals and displaying the many intricate designs of the greatest Islamic craftsmen. Incense burners, for example, were created in the shapes of animals, like the lion, or of birds; some had cylindrical bodies, some were domed. A water sprinkler, or a box used to hold water, more especially rose water, has a traditional function in Islamic society. It is used at weddings and other important festivities. Aesthetic appreciation and commercial demand encouraged silversmiths to develop unusually beautiful forms for sprinklers, many examples of which can be found in museums.

Modern boxes are much less interesting. No real innovation has occurred since the cigarette box, which is well represented in my collection. There are, however, a great number of reproductions of the best work. The silver box has developed down the centuries from small amulet-holders, and the original shape has been exploited to fulfil every personal and functional use man can devise for it.

Weapons

Arms-making and the art of Damascene

27

ARAB AND ISLAMIC SILVER

All these Pakistani incense burners (right) *open at the top and are decorated with exotic birds in the tradition of Islamic metalwork.*

flourished in nearly every great Muslim age – in Egypt, Persia, Turkey and Spain. Unfortunately almost nothing has survived from the earlier periods, although documents with minute descriptions exist, and from them we can recognise notable achievements in weapon-making. The rare examples which have survived are quite difficult to date precisely. Cairo and Damascus were great centres of culture and weapon-making during the thirteenth and fourteenth centuries, and the latter was particularly renowned for the fineness of its blades. Perhaps the most beautiful extant from this period are the weapons of the Mameluke Sultan Toman-Bey. The engraved arabesque style suggests that they were probably made in Persia and date from the fifteenth century.

Arms-making reached its zenith in Spain. The famous workshops of Toledo were already active in the ninth century. Other places, such as Almeria and Seville, later achieved almost equal renown. Again there are no surviving examples from these very early periods. Only late fifteenth-century pieces have so far been discovered, among the finest of which is the weaponry of Boabdil, King of Granada. The Boabdil pieces are distributed among several museums and in private collections in Paris and Spain. They are richly ornamented with silver filigree work, have coloured emblems blazoned on them, are inlaid with different colours of enamel and bear Kufic inscriptions.

Turkish arms merit special attention. They have a unique shape derived from the earlier basic shapes of the Turkic tribal traditions. Museums, such as the Berlin Arms Museum, the Invalides in Paris and the Old Seray Museum in Istanbul, house specimens of weaponry which date from the fifteenth and sixteenth centuries. Helmets are finished with a long spike, which offsets the chiselled silver arabesque motifs. Turkish sabres and daggers never achieved the same quality as those of Granada, but their distinctive curved form has always been much admired.

Persian weaponry is known to have been as fine as most other types of Persian metalwork. Very little survives from the golden age, but many documents have been discovered in Persia which describe their shapes and designs. The helmet of Shah Abbas in the British Museum and the sabres and daggers in the Louvre confirm the documentary evidence of the excellence of Persian craftsmanship in this field.

The variety and richness of ornament on North African arms is very great. Long rifles decorated with granulation, chiselling, inlaying, niello, enamelling, coral and ivory are typical of these tribal pieces. Wonderful geometric plaques and shapes are added, and powder horns are intricately worked in designs which blend with the individual shape of the weapon. Each tribe has its own distinctive design. Typical of North African work are the carved ivory, silver, niello and damascene pieces backed by velvet to give further colour and richness to the composition.

Coins
The Roman, Byzantine and Persian empires had a long tradition of coin-making prior to the rise of Islam.

The early Romans used coins not simply as a means of exchange for goods, but also as bearers of messages to be conveyed to the citizens of the Empire, recording events, such as victories and games, stamped on the reverse of the coins. The importance of coinage to the stability of the Roman economy is demonstrated by the early introduction of a sort of gold standard and by the fact that a young Roman would often be launched on his senatorial career by being put in charge of the mint, which was considered an apt testing ground of his ability. Gold, silver, copper and brass were used in transactions, although coins of differing metals were not exchangeable one for another, except through the medium of a money lender. Moreover, only gold coins were acceptable to the central treasury. The tax collectors had to find means of converting their takings into gold before dispatching them to Rome.

Later Roman coinage is more sober. It bore the emperor's head, often surrounded by a laurel wreath or a crown, and was simply inscribed with his name and the date of minting. The main denominations were the denarius, the solidus and the sestertius. Roman coins were widely accepted and became international currency, something like today's dollar. It was only when the Emperor Justinian II introduced the figure of Christ on to gold coins, confirming Byzantium as a Christian empire, that Roman coins became unacceptable to the Islamic world. The Persians did not mint gold coinage, preferring to use their gold supplies for fashioning metalwork, and were content with silver money. Until the fourth century, the only other coins minted in the area were those from the Kingdom of Axum, which circulated in parts of Ethiopia, Somalia and Yemen. These were quite stylised coins of gold, silver and bronze; some of the bronze and silver ones were inlaid with gold.

In pre-Islamic times, a silver ingot called the larin was widely used in the Arabian Peninsula. The larin derived its

Various coins (left) *from Arab and Islamic countries which are used as pendants or buttons in jewellery, worn with other pendants or, occasionally, as a single ornament. Each displays an Arabic inscription.*

name from the Persian city of Lar and was shaped like a fish-hook, reflecting the environment and commercial pursuits of early civilisations. The larin varied in length and size, and carried Persian and Arabic inscriptions. At first its use was confined to the Arabian Gulf area, but as trade routes were extended, it became common in the eastern coastal areas of India and in the Maldive Islands. It was a useful currency, for the larin could be divided into twelve sections. It could be cut according to requirements, and a portion split off and given in exchange for goods.

After the coming of Islam, silver remained the medium of exchange for some time, and, when new coinage was introduced, it was modelled on that of the ruling empire of the day, Byzantium. The Arabs also used the gold denarius of Byzantium and the Sassanian silver dirham, which circulated widely from Western Europe to the east Indian Ocean. The *Sacaca* was a kind of tax imposed on commerce and industry in early Islam. The levy was a weight of five *mithkal* of silver.

It was not until the end of the seventh century that the first real gold coinage was struck by order of the Ummayad Caliph Abd al-Malik, who commissioned an exclusively Islamic form of currency. Gold was used for dinars and silver was used for dirhams, which took their name from the Greek drachma.

From this time until early in the twentieth century Islamic coinage retained the basic features commanded by Abd al-Malik. It was inscribed with Quranic phrases and the motifs were geometric or similarly decorative without the use of human representation. Abd al-Malik's coins bear the *shahadah*, "There is no god but Allah and Muhammed is His Messenger." Later coins bore other inscriptions appropriate to the Muslim faith, such as the *Bismillah Al Rahman Al Rahim*, "In the name of Allah, the merciful, the compassionate."

At the beginning of the eighth century, Iraq was unstable because of risings against the Ummayad regime. Economic instability followed, and silver was exported in large quantities to the Arabian Peninsula; which caused an increase in the domestic silver prices. Tax collectors were hoarding the good dirhams and paying in low grade dirhams, which they had counterfeited. Old Sassanian dirhams were melted down for bullion and stored away or used for speculation. Then Al Hajaj, the governor of Iraq and a tough administrator, confiscated all the bullion, withdrew Sassanian dirhams from circulation and established the Arab dirham as legal tender, having decreased its weight by thirty per cent.

The historical record provided by Arab coins is of great value both to numismatists and to historians of Islam. The continuity, the precision of their dates and the inclusion of the names of reigning caliphs, emperors and sultans, as well as the year of the reign in which a coin was minted and its place of origin, are unusually informative. Coinage also demonstrates the development of silversmithing techniques such as pressing and engraving and the progress of Muslim decorative styles, since no other metalwork can be so precisely dated.

Through the centuries, smaller denominations of coins were introduced for various reasons. In the fourteenth century, the Ottoman Sultan Orkhan minted the first akce, a silver coin which only weighed one-third of the original silver dirham. The akce disappeared and was replaced by the para, which was superseded soon afterwards by the piastre, a larger coin than the akce. These rapid changes seem to have coincided with the growth of trade with Europe, for the piastre was of comparable size and weight to the thaler, a coin widely used in eastern Europe and particularly in Germany. A novel feature of Ottoman coinage was the *Tughrah*, an elaborate calligraphic signature of the Sultan, which was adopted as his emblem.

Arab-Islamic coins were a stabilising feature of Ottoman rule during the several hundred years when it dominated most of the Islamic world. Not until the decline of Ottoman power and the emergence of Ataturk's leadership did drastic changes occur. Ataturk's westernisation programme included Turkish coinage, and he began to mint coins displaying his own head. Other Muslim countries followed suit, and kings and rulers quickly had their features stamped on their currency in imitation of Western practice. As Arab countries gained their independence, however, representation was again forbidden. Today different emblems characteristic of their country of origin are depicted – for example the cedar tree on Lebanese coinage.

Famous Islamic coins, such as those of Turkey, Saudi Arabia and Yemen, and also the Maria Theresa dollar and the Napoleon, have been important components of jewellery. They were either melted down to be used in other pieces, or were themselves mounted as pendants or on pins and further decorated to form a new composition. Coins or their imitations are also widely used as necklace pendants or ring stones, notably in Algeria, Oman, Yemen and Iraq.

ARAB AND ISLAMIC SILVER

The Silversmith and his Craft

Silver is a noble metal. Raw and pure silver generally comes in cubic form, but is occasionally composed of crystals grouped together in rows, giving the appearance of a delicate metallic fern tree. It has a wonderful white sheen in its original form, but immediately turns black from sulphuration when removed from its gangue. Although darkened by sulphur gases in the atmosphere, and although silver does eventually corrode, it can resist oxidisation and corrosion for extremely long periods. When pure, it is too soft for use; so it is alloyed with other metals, such as copper. Bedouin women normally wear their silver jewellery over their clothes, because, being such a good conductor of heat, it would otherwise burn their skins in the desert sun. Because of its excellent workability and ductability, silver lends itself ideally to the creation of an endless variety of artistic designs.

The techniques of silversmithing depend on many qualities: patience, skilfulness, subtlety, creativity, inventiveness and an ambition to create a beautiful work of art.

Apart from large silverworking businesses, like those in Egypt, Algeria and India, most silversmiths' workshops are small and usually gathered in the old quarter of a city. Not all the craftsmen have shops where they exhibit and sell; some work in their own homes, others work in villages and bring their goods to be sold in cities, and others travel from place to place repairing jewellery. There are also those, like the Touareg, who wander through the deserts carrying their simple tools and crafting for the tribes.

Buildings – particularly the exteriors and interiors of temples – were decorated with silver and gold by the Greeks, Romans and Muslims. In the Gothic era, silversmiths would add a final touch to architectural work by ornamenting columns and ceilings, thus creating splendid compositions of structure, textures and colour. Reflecting this large-scale work, Gothic patterns emerged in silver objects and jewellery. I have similarly found that architectural elements, such as designs for walls and facades, appear on decorative daggers and jewellery in Yemen, where local historians relate that silverwork was frequently used for interior decoration.

It is interesting to note the existence of Christian themes in the Islamic world. Many non-Islamic craftsmen live and work in Arab and Muslim societies; Jews, Christians, Sabiites and others played an important role in the development of silvercrafts. In early Islamic times, their contribution was considerable because of the Muslim attitude to handicrafts of this kind. In nomadic conditions, the craftsman's efforts were despised as the lowliest of tasks, because they did not contribute directly to the livelihood of the members of the Bedouin tribe. Thus silvercrafting became the province of non-Muslims, although their products were commissioned by Muslims and fashioned to the requirements of Islamic society. Sometimes, however, the positions were reversed and Muslim craftsmen made objects in silver and other metals for Christian households, which demanded Christian themes. Even the Ayyubid metalworkers incorporated Christian elements and there are some interesting pieces in the collection which demonstrate the integration of Islamic and Christian designs. During the Abbasid period, Arab Christian women wore crosses and chains as necklaces. The court and wealthier classes were accustomed to a certain degree of luxury, which they were loath to abandon. Religious restrictions on using precious metals did not apply to those outside the Faith who worked under the Caliphate. Zoroastrians, Jews and Christians continued to make objects in gold and silver and these articles were acceptable, or at least less objectionable than if they had been made by a Muslim.

The craftsman's lot was changed largely by the Karmathians, a religious sect which was particularly active under the Abbasids. A whole range of reforms were attributed to their influence. Complex regulations were imposed to standardise workmanship, and guilds for each craft were established. A *muhtasib* or head of the bazaar police was installed, whose responsibilities included all areas of food supply and the supervision of craft standards. Although his judicial authority was limited, he became one of the most important state officials. The making of handicrafts of all kinds became a reputable profession, and artisans were accepted as respectable members of the community. Different grades of professional achievement came into being – apprentice, journeyman and master – and examinations had to be passed before a smith could progress from one level to the next. The craftsmen exchanged ideas and skills more efficiently as they were newly grouped in one place in the bazaar to facilitate the *muhtasib*'s checking procedures, and customers were enabled to compare and contrast silver products more precisely.

Then a new ruling was proclaimed which was exactly contrary to previous ones: cheaper raw materials were now forbidden for use in artistic products. Smithing in silver and gold began to be done by Muslim craftsmen; complete prohibition was relaxed into restrained acceptability. A new freedom of expression motivated artists to higher levels of creativity and a greater richness of decoration. Gold and enamels were used delicately in glasswork to give a finer and more precious appearance. Syrian craftsmen became supreme in this field, and the technique infiltrated Italy through Syrian workshops set up in Venice. The renowned Damascene style became enormously popular and was soon adopted by Italian artists. Finally freed from the Islamic ruling that handicrafts should be done by anonymous artists, craftsmen were now able to sign their creations. From these pieces we can identify the individual workmanship of Muslim masters and the techniques and methods of decoration known at the time.

The Sabiite work of Iraq is well known for its heritage of niello work. Jewish smiths worked in various cities such as Sana'a and there are numerous examples of the work of Christian Arabs in Palestine, Lebanon, Iraq and Syria. I have many icons, crosses and engraved boxes depicting religious buildings, with the use of filigree, granulation and engraved stones for decoration. One striking example is an amuletic silver box with an icon in the middle. Covered over with glass and with silver pendants on one edge, the whole creation hangs on a silver chain characteristic of the Iraqi area in which it originated. Such pieces

The pectoral (opposite top) *from the Rif area in Morocco is very heavy, weighing about a kilo. This parcel-gilt filigree silver casket* (opposite below) *may have been crafted either in Syria or Egypt at the end of the seventeenth century. A Persian box* (above left) *is beautifully embossed on both sides and decorated with pastoral scenes, birds and flowers. The Syrian head-dress* (above) *displays filigree and granulated decoration and also openwork which is inlaid with glass.*

were generally part of a bridal costume worn by Christian Arabs.

Another influence which made its mark on the development of silverwork was that of the pilgrims to the holy places of Islam, such as Mecca and Medina. They brought with them samples of their work, which they traded en route or sold to support themselves on arrival or gave away as gifts to other pilgrims. Silverwork is very often sold by Muslim families to enable their members to undertake the Haj, for they will make almost any sacrifice to make the journey to Mecca, which pilgrimage is one of the five tenets of Islam.

City silversmiths, unlike those in the countryside, frequently use modern machines and tools and new materials such as plastic. Some degree of mass production may be employed when such techniques as cutting, engraving or inlaying in quantity are used before the whole piece is assembled. The country craftsman, on the other hand, must be able to do everything himself with traditional tools. He knows the skills learned by his ancestors hundreds of years ago: annealing, hammering, cutting, moulding, casting, engraving, drawing, embossing, lacing and granulating.

Like other master craftsmen, silversmiths have apprentices who perform the preliminary work, leaving the final touches to their master's greater experience. Gradually they learn the secrets of the craft, and in time, they too will become master craftsmen, through whom the smithing tradition survives.

As one can see in *suqs* throughout the Muslim world, many Islamic silversmiths work without models or maquettes and a design is born and grows as the piece is worked. Thousands of different Islamic patterns exist and can be varied. A craftsman may develop a certain style which is recognisable, but will not repeat any piece precisely.

Craftsmen begin to learn their trade when very young, and in their early teens will already have grasped the essence of age-old skills and techniques and be capable of transforming a plain piece of silver into an ornate object. Their speed and accuracy is remarkable. I once saw a child of twelve at work in Karachi, using only a hammer and chisel, describe patterns of arches and flowers on a bowl in seconds. The decoration grew out of the metal as though it had always been there and the child was simply peeling off a covering which hid it.

The silversmiths of the past seem to have been motivated more by the desire to create a beautiful object than by profit. Nowadays even master craftsmen produce work of a lower quality for the profitable tourist trade. Thus, standards are sacrificed for money, and culture for personal gain.

Sometimes a silversmith will buy damaged or unfashionable jewellery cheaply for the metal, and will recondition or remodel it. If a piece is beyond repair, he may remove an undamaged part and use it in a new piece, or he might add new embossings or other decoration to an existing one. This sort of work is done for clients who are bored with their jewellery and want to impress their friends with new pieces. The expert can always identify these pieces by the variation in the quality of work and the age and colour of the silver.

Some smiths recognise that the intrinsic value of a piece may be lost in these amendments and refuse to do this kind of work. The value of silver jewellery is mostly in the originality of the artist's work and in its quality rather than in the weight and quality of the metal itself. Finely worked objects may be highly priced despite their low silver content.

In museums one can see that silver was once so highly prized that it was used to mount diamonds, rubies and other precious stones. My collection mostly displays semi-precious ones: coral, agate, amber, turquoise and coloured glass, which are usually in keeping with the value of the silver and blend well with its soft lustre. There are also pieces in my collection, crafted in the capitals and cultural centers of the Islamic world,

A fine nielloed silver bowl (above left) *with floral design which is probably Persian. Variously shaped Omani and Pakistani* kohl *boxes* (above) *for both men and women. The* meel *or applicator fits into a small silver case which is decorated with a pyramidical composition, and, to prevent spilling, the lid of the container screws on tightly.*

which are inlaid with precious stones. Sometimes the Bedouin will gather antique stones from archaeological sites on their familiar trails. When these are incorporated into jewellery, they give the pieces special value.

Silver jewellery is sometimes gilded or decorated with small studs of copper or gold to lend variety to the colour composition. Another form of decoration is the technique of flat or repoussé chasing, from which many patterns emerge: geometric designs, such as arches, vaults, and the traditional Islamic star pattern;

botanical patterns showing palm trees, lotus flowers, grapes and stylised leaves and flowers; zoological designs based on birds, fish and reptiles; and mythical creatures and parts of the human body, such as hands and locks of hair. Pastoral scenes of huntsmen or shepherds are also common. All these designs are to be found in other Islamic decorative arts.

A famous *hadith* attributed to the Prophet runs "The angels will not enter a house where there is an image or a dog." This idea is particularly reflected in Islamic art, and is accepted by silversmiths. Philosophers have interpreted this *hadith* variously, but the consensus seems to be that it derived from the need to prevent early Muslims returning to idolatry, since the early people of Arabia, like other desert and tribal peoples, were animists.

The creativity of the Muslim artist was limited, as a whole field of inspiration was taken from him – an area which has been an unending source of vision to artists in other civilisations, that of man and living beings and the interaction of man with his environment. The evolution of the Islamic way of life is made difficult for students to examine, because its representation of living forms, devised its own stylised medium and developed it to a level unequalled in other cultures, except perhaps that of the Hindus in India.

The effect of this was to introduce a unity of style to Islamic art, which in turn served to bring about closer understanding between the differing peoples and cultures of the countries which embraced the Islamic faith.

There are examples of the depiction of human beings, but they are so symbolic that the perspective is weak, giving the impression of flatness. An unreal quality

The filigree work on this Iraqi lady's powder box (above) *is inlaid with gold and also decorated with a picture of Ctesiphon. Elaborately decorated with floral designs and Arabic calligraphy, it is sometimes difficult to tell the difference between an imitation of an older piece and the genuine article, but this box* (left) *is probably the former, successfully achieved by a Syrian or Egyptian craftsman.*

customs, habitat and dress are nowhere depicted in a naturalistic way. Largely through pictorial representations we have come to appreciate such ancient civilisations as Egypt, Mesopotamia, Greece and Rome. To understand Islamic culture one has to learn a whole new vocabulary of symbolism, as Islamic decorative art, deliberately far removed from the pervades such representation. In the main, four types of decorative designs dominate Muslim art. We have mentioned floral and animal patterns; the other two are geometric and calligraphic. The predominant geometric patterns, such as squares, triangles, pentagons and circles, appear individually or together and their relationship with each other

ARAB AND ISLAMIC SILVER

creates the geometric whole. Arab and Islamic art is famous for its calligraphy, such as the Kufic, Naskh, Thulth and Farsi scripts, which were skilfully turned into decorative subject matter. The Quran is written only in Arabic and is read and known by heart in every Islamic country. So calligraphy has played a leading role in Islamic silver decoration and has been another unifying feature in the Muslim world.

These four main elements have given Islamic silverwork an unique imagery of patterns, an united frame and yet freedom of expression. Western artists have found a name for such patterns, particularly the floral ones – "Arabesque" – which suits the quality of movement, flowing lines and curves.

There are many similarities in objects, designs and decorative devices in silverwork throughout the Islamic world, despite numerous regional differences in the methods employed to create them. For example, the Quranic *hirz*, a square, rectangular or cylindrical box, is one of the main pieces of jewellery found from North Africa to eastern Asia. The crescent and flat triangular shape is a dominant theme from Morocco to the Caucasus. The use of amber, coral, coins and beads is to be found in North Africa as well as in southern Arabia and Afghanistan. The *tulul*, a series of chains and domed silver shapes, sometimes worn as clothing or on the back of the head, is to be seen as far west as Libya and as far south as Kuwait.

Regional differences manifest themselves either in the subject matter of decoration or in techniques. For example, niello is used with deep engraving in the Caucasus, and while the same method is prevalent in Iraq, it is done there on flat surfaces. The bell shape is common to much Islamic jewellery, but is found more abundantly in Yemeni or Omani pieces, which are distributed all over the U.A.E., particularly in the Al-Ain oasis.

There are very often inter-related influences in neighbouring regions due to the imposition of modern political boundaries where they had never previously existed between people of similar cultural history. For example, the Touareg range across the entire Sahara,

This beautifully-proportioned Turkish coffee pot (above right) *is engraved with floral decoration and the handle is dagger-shaped. This gilded Persian filigree basket* (right) *which holds confectionery is the work of a master craftsman.*

Minutely intensive floral and animal motifs of excellent Persian workmanship appear on his vase (above). *An Indian buckle* (above left) *with floral, animal and Arabic script designs.* Left: *This Iraqi sweetmeat dish is especially fine and unusually designed.*

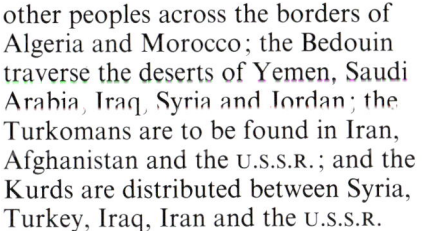

other peoples across the borders of Algeria and Morocco; the Bedouin traverse the deserts of Yemen, Saudi Arabia, Iraq, Syria and Jordan; the Turkomans are to be found in Iran, Afghanistan and the U.S.S.R.; and the Kurds are distributed between Syria, Turkey, Iraq, Iran and the U.S.S.R.

There has been a gradual but persistent decline in the art of silversmithing in recent times. The reasons are several. As the people of the Islamic world, particularly in the oil states, become more affluent and gain easier access to world markets, they are selling their traditional silverwork to buy gold, which is more universally valued and exchanged. This trend has been accelerated because old silver is light and soft, fragile and difficult to repair. The heavy designs of the pendants and chains are out of keeping with Western fashions, which appeal to the wealthy in the Middle East. In Morocco, Syria, Pakistan and India, modern metalworkers have begun to reproduce traditional designs in gold to meet popular demand, but the work is mass-produced and of inferior quality.

As we have seen, one of the main reasons for the absence of old silver pieces from past civilisations has been the melting down of silver. Today this happens on a huge scale as metal mania has gripped the world. We also use silver in many other ways – for photography, electronic appliances and, because of its chemical inertness, for surgery, such as the pinning of broken bones. There is a constant need of precious metals as raw material, and this, combined with speculation on world markets, often results in the large-scale melting of pieces. Many Islamic pieces are lost in the melting pot, for although interest is increasing, the rich collector is rare and the ordinary kind cannot afford to pay today's inflated prices. An Abu Dhabi silversmith told me a story about a dealer, who in the early '70s acquired large quantities of Yemeni, Omani and Gulf jewellery and melted all of it to be sent as ingots to Europe.

This practice has led the most respected and skilled smiths to use lower proportions of silver. By so doing, they prevent their pieces from being valuable enough to tempt melters, and their precious creations survive. Another reason for using low grade silver is to enable poor people to afford them. This may also have been the reason for gilding silver to give it the appearance of gold. Low grade silver is known by different names in different countries; in Iraq, it is called *wershow*. White metal is also used and is so like silver that only testing proves its low quality. In the Sahara, the Bedouin call it *meshur*. The artistic work in these pieces usually represents the same craftsmanship found in those made of precious metals. In my collection one can see the many different colours of metals added to silver for these purposes.

A few pressures exist to reverse the trend, as many people genuinely prefer the old styles of jewellery regardless of current fashion. One important influence is that of the Western tourist, who yearns to escape from the machine-made products of his technological society. But many silversmiths have now abandoned their craft and moved to other work for quicker profit; so it is increasingly difficult to find good and original old pieces.

ARAB AND ISLAMIC SILVER

The Revival of Folk Art and its Importance

Folk arts represent the heritage of a people's culture and the vicissitudes of its history. They reflect the local character of an area and its spiritual and material values and are most important to any study of Arab and Islamic civilisation. They impart a sense of pride in the work of a man's hands, deepen aesthetic reactions and forge links between a society and its past which give its members identification with their culture, society and homeland. In my view, it is vital that folk arts survive and to do so they must not only be preserved but developed within an Islamic framework and on a modern basis.

I have previously discussed this question in an earlier article, "Tradition and Modernity in Architecture" which was published in 1978.

"The restoring of the local heritage should be carried out in depth and should emanate from the influence of climate and nature and from the social and spiritual values which characterise a society. An understanding of these is a first requirement. They cannot gain by seeing their art from the viewpoint of Western and other societies."

In many Arab and Islamic countries, especially the oil-rich states, modern trends are destroying handicrafts. Handicrafts are among the greatest resources in China; in Switzerland, parts of watches are still made in homes and small workshops; in Japan, electrical components and electronic products are produced in similar environments. In countries like Greece, Italy and Spain, which have a well-developed tourist industry, national and regional organisation of traditional handicrafts is well known.

In the small towns and rural areas in the Islamic world where traditional arts and handicrafts were developed, they still provide the main earnings of whole families and supply their everyday needs. In Mzab towns in Algeria, for example, there is a weaving room in every home where the women weave bedcovers, carpets and rugs. In the city, women have to depend on products supplied to them from the countryside, from factories or from abroad. Thus the revival and development of handicrafts could provide significant revenues for raising the economic standards of rural people and help to reduce peasant migration to the cities by providing new jobs and making use of the working potential of the village women.

The success of development projects in handicrafts depends on government encouragement in several areas: drawing up a feasible plan of action, financing, making raw materials available, establishing training centres and sponsoring the marketing of products.

In some places interest in handicrafts is reviving, for instance in Tunisian earthenware, the Iranian and Indian carpet industries and in Egyptian copper and brassware, which are already appreciated worldwide. The revival often starts at grass roots, but government sponsorship, encouraged by the interests

This imitation Kabyllian necklace (above) shows the traditional crescent form incorporated in a modern piece.

of the tourist industry, has been of great importance too, notably in the establishing of annual markets for local products. Similar efforts could promote a revival of high-quality silversmithing.

However, the authorities in some Arab and Islamic states are increasing their efforts to develop traditional crafts and are establishing special centres for handicrafts. One such project is the first women's handicraft centre in the U.A.E. which was set up in cooperation with UNESCO. In 1973, a Crafts Council was established for the preservation and promotion of the many handicrafts of Jordan and dispenses generous aid to craftsmen of pottery, olive wood, mother of pearl, embroideries and to silversmiths.

Silversmiths cannot create new works

THE REVIVAL OF FOLK ART AND ITS IMPORTANCE

Algerian ornaments (above) *aptly demonstrate modern craftsmen's skills in reproducing traditional designs.*

if raw materials are only available by melting down older products. In some countries silversmithing would have ceased entirely if official efforts had not been made to purchase metal for the needs of the country and its craftsmen. There is now an abundance of silver in world markets and with the increased demand for its products there should be an optimistic future for the craft.

The biggest problem is the lack of technical training centres and teachers, but this could be overcome by establishing vocational training centres offering specialist courses given by master craftsmen. The programme should be an integrated one and should include theoretical and practical lessons on the technology of metals, the history of traditional arts and courses on composition and design. In addition, general courses should exist to eliminate illiteracy and raise the level of education.

Eventually, trained teams would visit remote villages to give expert advice to the craftsmen in their homes and shops, and to help with any problems of financing or obtaining raw materials.

There are few researchers in the field of silversmithing in the Arab and Islamic countries. The training centres would therefore conduct researches in the field and record statistics on all old work found in order to begin the compilation of complete historical records. Researchers would discover and study the characteristic designs of individual silversmiths and reveal the cultural relationships, historical background and meanings and purposes of the various symbols and decoration. The training centres would also be experimental centres for all traditional crafts.

It is important to recognise and preserve the distinct regional character of handicrafts. The experience of other countries which have developed local crafts for the tourist trade thereby providing themselves with wider markets, would be of great value to Arab and Islamic countries. Permanent and seasonal exhibitions in major centres of the world are no less important. This idea has been implemented in Algeria, where the National Exhibition for Mzab Handicrafts is organised annually in Ghardaia and is always well attended. The establishment of an Islamic Arts Centre would enable all these projects to be coordinated in every subscribing country.

By these means our inherited arts and crafts would occupy their proper position in the world arts and crafts markets and a new advance in handicraft development could be encouraged.

ARAB AND ISLAMIC SILVER

North Africa and Spain

NORTH AFRICA AND SPAIN

MEDITERRANEAN SEA

- Benghazi
- Beida
- Tobruk
- Al Mansura
- Gaza
- Port Said
- Alexandria
- **Suez Canal**
- **CAIRO**
- Siwa
- Asyut

EGYPT

- Aswan

RED SEA

- Port Sudan
- R. Nile
- Albara
- Omdurman
- **KHARTOUM**
- Asmara
- Massawa

ERITREA

SUDAN

- **DJIBOUTI**
- Berbera
- **ADDIS ABABA**

ETHIOPIA

SOMALIA

- **MOGADISHU**

39

ARAB AND ISLAMIC SILVER

While the Islamic faith was readily accepted by the people of North Africa in the seventh century, the rule of the Eastern Caliphate was resented by them. Culturally there is a certain uniformity of influence in the different regions of North Africa. In Egypt and fertile areas of the Mediterranean littoral, most Arab communities are descended from peoples who were part of Graeco-Roman civilisation. They include the Algerians, Moroccans, Tunisians, Tripolitanians, Cyrenaicans and Egyptians, amongst whom were many town dwellers and farmers.

These favourable areas bordering the Sahara also gave rise to the civilisations of Ancient Egypt, Nubia and Ethiopia and to the tribal culture of the Saharan groups, such as the Berbers and the Touaregs. Contact between the people of Arabia and those of the Sahara existed long before Islam. Commerce and trading in this great desert is older than recorded history.

Religious practices grew up similar to other desert religions, animal and idol worship succeeding animism. Islam filtered into the North African desert through traders. The Somali people were amongst the first to adopt it, and as the Muslim faith became an integral part of their culture, they acted as missionaries when they travelled to Kenya, Ethiopia and what is now the Republic of Djibouti. The Somalis themselves retained some aspects of their indigenous religions within the faith, and ancestor-worship is still quite usual.

Ethiopia had much in common with the more fertile regions of southern Arabia. The Amharic and Tigrina languages displayed similarities to southern Arabian Arabic, and contacts with the Yemeni area were maintained from the time of the kingdom of Saba'a. But Ethiopia regarded herself as being at a superior cultural level to neighbouring countries, and, seeing Islam as the faith of nomads and merchants rather than of sophisticated town dwellers, clung tenaciously to other religions such as Judaism and Christianity. Nubia too remained predominantly Christian until the fourteenth century, as the Nubians tried to maintain a cultural independence from Egypt and the Sudan. Nevertheless the cultural influences from these two areas were strong and are visible in the evolution of Nubian Art.

The Nubians dwelt outside the boundary of the First Cataract, which was the limit of Pharaonic rule for much of the early period of Egyptian civilisation, when an agricultural community grew up along the banks of the Nile. They not only built houses and magnificent tombs, but possessed the gold mines which later impelled the Egyptians to establish their rule over part of Nubian territory. Nubian Art influenced Egyptian Art, although it was largely eclipsed by the achievements of the Pharaohs. Fine enamelling for jewellery was developed with rich blues, green and reds inset into complicated designs of geometric patterns and human figures with winged arms. Trade in ivory, ebony, incense, gold and ostrich plumes flourished, and the Nubian Art and techniques of metal-working were learned by the Egyptians. This tradition emerged in the work of the Copts, who became influential smiths in the court of the first Ummayads.

The spread of Islam across North Africa was achieved by a pincer movement. Islamic ideas permeated the southern areas through early converts, and the tribes adopted Islam quickly. In the northern areas, the Muslim religion was imposed more by conquest. There the Berbers and Kabyllies were the most urbanised groups, although with a strong sense of ethnic identity, and they resented the turmoil of constant invasions. At first the Arabs were regarded as simply another wave of conquerors to be repelled.

The armies of the Caliphate reached Egypt early in the history of Islam. They advanced swiftly as far as Tunisia, where they encountered a mixed ethnic population with a predominantly Berber heritage. The Phoenicians had settled in the area in 1100 BC and built the city of Utica. Subsequent empires had risen and fallen but the stubborn independent Berber strain persisted and fought against Arab rule for some considerable time.

The Arab commander, Okba bin Nafi, established a settlement at Kairouan. Strangely, although the Berbers' resistance had been fierce, they eagerly converted to the Islamic faith, much as their kinfolk had in the south. The simplicity and logic of its creed appealed to them, as did the belief in posthumous rewards for a virtuous life. Religious tolerance still permitted Christian and Jewish communities to thrive harmoniously in this region. The Berbers finally became the Arabs' main allies. Baghdad allowed them some measure of autonomy and they lived contentedly within the Islamic sphere of influence.

Much fine architecture is to be found in Tunisia reflecting the people's conversion and adaptation to Muslim life. Under the Aghlavids, the Muslim Berber rulers, mosques and palaces were built. Kairouan became a holy city and there the first mosque was erected on the site of Ibn Nafi's first camp. It was followed by many others. Kairouan became a centre of Islamic scholarship and was the springboard for the Arabs' westward thrust across North Africa and into Spain.

Handicrafts developed in traditional Islamic styles, and the strong influence of the Abbasids can be seen in ninth-century architecture and the decorative arts. The *menber*, or pulpit, of the Kairouan mosque is decorated with characteristic Abbasid floral and geometric designs. Wrought-iron craftsmanship is evident in the picturesque village of Sidi Bou Said. In later periods, when the Islamic Caliphate seemed to them to have become decadent, there was a strong Berber movement for a return to the purity of Islam.

Before we examine the glories of Islamic Egypt we must turn to the history of the Arabs in Spain. They first set foot on the Iberian Peninsula early in the eighth century AD. "El-Andalus" was their name for the entire peninsula, but it referred primarily to the provinces of Granada, Seville, Cordoba and Jaen. The fertility of the area had attracted Phoenician, Greek and Carthaginian settlers. It fell successively to the Romans, Visigoths and then to the Arabs. These many influences gave the original Iberian inhabitants a colourful and varied culture unlike any other. Geographically, and in many ways historically and culturally, attached to the continent of Europe, Spain is also aloof from it. The Romans influenced her literature, administration and language, fervent Catholicism dominated Spanish history and her empires, while her arts and crafts, architecture and social life were strongly influenced by Islam.

Andalusia became an important part of the Caliphate. Cordoba, particularly, grew in authority and oriental grace. The edifices built in the Andalusian province are some of the finest Islamic monuments. They include the mosque of Cordoba and the Al-Hambra in Granada, which still stands today. In this period Andalusian culture was remarkable as a focus of many artistic skills. Many superb surviving examples illustrate the importance of artistic expression in the evolution and expansion of Islamic civilisation.

One important feature of Andalusian Islamic Art is that many of its works are signed and dated. The mixture of representational and symbolic expression denotes the blend of Muslim and pre-Muslim elements and the relationship between Islamic and European ideas. Much of the engraving was of courtly subjects and of hunting scenes decorated with floral, animal and human figures. Sculpture, pottery, textiles, carving on ivory and many kinds of decoration, were all exquisitely worked in Cordoba, Al-Zahra, Valencia and Cunia.

Andalusian culture did not fully emerge until the rule of the last of the Ummayads, Abd al-Rahman. This poet-warrior escaped from Damascus when the Abbasids came to power, and, arriving in Andalusia, made his way in triumph to Cordoba, where he installed himself as the "caliph of Islam," in competition with the Baghdad "usurpers." His independent Western Caliphate was challenged by the rebellious inhabitants of the Iberian Peninsula, and continual unrest and wars marked his reign. It was not until the reign of his son, Abd al-Rahman II, that Cordoba attained a settled prosperity and became the centre of a flourishing civilisation.

Artists, poets and craftsmen flocked there. Music, learning and the arts were established in the Islamic tradition. Eastern fashions of coloured silks and ornate hair styles enlivened the court. Iberian Christians complained, not of Muslim rule, but that their children so admired Arab eloquence, freedom, tolerance and culture, that they imitated Arab ways too fervently.

Spanish and Moroccan culture influenced each other notably after the fall of the Fatimid Caliphate and the rise of the Murabitin Dynasty, in particular under Youssef Ben Tashfeen, who ruled both Morocco and Islamic Spain at the end of the eleventh century and the beginning of the twelfth. Many magnificent architectural examples testify to this mutual influence in such places as Cordoba, Zahra, Granada, Toledo,

The remarkable Moroccan earrings (above) *were made in Tetouan. They are enamelled, decorated with glass, and have hollow gilded clasps.*

Malaga, Palma, Marrakesh, Sicily, Malta, Ibiza and several other places.

The numerous minor artistic objects of this period have largely disappeared, presumably destroyed during later wars between Muslims and Christians, but the few which still exist are of rare beauty.

Ivory masterpieces and jewel and perfume boxes survive in various museums – the Victoria and Albert, the Metropolitan, the Louvre, the Madrid. There are also ceramics, for which the Cordoba Caliphate was famous, displaying gold and lustre sheen on plates, ewers, cups and so on. As for metal-working, there are bronze and copper pieces such as candlesticks and incense burners, but very little silver has survived. There is a box in the cathedral of Kherona (Corona) which Al Mustansar commissioned for his son Hisham in 970, and a small perfume bottle with a lid and chain is to be found in Cordoba, dating from the year 1003. Three small bronzes, with gilded and floral decoration and Kufic inscriptions, are displayed in the Saint Isidro Museum at Lyon.

Some Andalusian jewellery has been found – for example, a piece dating from the beginning of the eleventh century which was discovered in Zahra and now forms part of the Walters collection in New York. Animal and floral and geometric designs are frequent; so are arches, horseshoe shapes and stars, the stones being inlaid with glass. Forms and decorations have been inherited through the generations and still survive in Moroccan silverwork today.

At the National School of Minor Arts in Tetouan in Morocco, Andalusian patterns are evident not only in the silverwork but also in wood, plaster, leather and copper crafts.

The swift spread of Islam westwards affected Egypt as well, although it was not until after the Abbasid period that Egypt became a prominent cultural centre. Having conquered in 641, the Muslim general Amr ibn Al-As began to build a town on the site of his camp, naming it Al-Fustat ("the tent," although the word may be derived from the Latin *fossatum*, an "earthwork"). The site of Al-Fustat is now included in the district known as Misr el-Atika or Old Cairo and was Egypt's capital for many years, when that country was a province of the Baghdad Caliphate. A mosque was built there and was famed for being the first religious building in Egypt.

It became a city of great beauty according to contemporary chroniclers, who wrote glowingly of its shaded streets, gardens, handsome seven-storeyed buildings and crowded markets. Ibn Hawqal and the Persian Nasir Khusro described the wares in detail – irridescent pottery of such intricate delicacy that one's hands were visible through it, expensive green transparent glass, rock crystal and tortoiseshell.

Early Muslim Art was influenced by the Abbasid style introduced by Ahmad ibn Tulun, whose mosque is the most celebrated example of the architectural achievements of this period. Plaster decorations with calligraphic, floral and geometric designs were created in impressive new styles. Wood engraving, pottery with shining lustre and weaving patterned with stylised human images, animals and floral motifs, all reached a very high standard.

Al-Qahira (Cairo) was treated at first only as a resort. The capital was at Kairouan. But when Caliph Al-Mo'ezz decided to make Egypt his centre, he chose Cairo for his new capital. The arrival of the Fatimids transformed it architecturally into a resplendent city, and this dynasty made the strongest impression on North African Art.

Another historian, Makrizi, describing the luxury of the courts of the early Fatimids, wrote of the amazing palace of the Caliph, which comprised hundreds of rooms, including the Emerald Hall with marble pillars and the great golden pavilion, where the Caliph presided over celebrations, seated on a golden throne behind a golden screen. Innumerable courtyards with marble fountains, exotic birds and animals, high ceilings encrusted with exquisite gold ornamentation and curtains hung with pearls complete a picture of fabulous wealth.

Under the Fatimids, the mosque and compound of Al-Azhar was dedicated to learning. Theology, law, tradition, Arabic grammar and rhetoric were taught and the mosque became one of the greatest theological and educational centres of the Islamic world. Other mosques and palaces were built with similar intricacy of workmanship, whose main features were decorative frescoes and honeycombs.

A new period of stability and prosperity, religious tolerance and economic development, marked the rule of the early Fatimids, who remained dominant for 200 years. Docks and ships were built to increase international trade, which in turn promoted the sale of handicrafts. Peace permitted arts to flourish in every field, and Egypt competed with Baghdad for leadership of the empire. The extravagance of the Caliphate is legendary, but it created a new impetus for artistic achievement. Metalwork was produced in gold and silver, and Fatimid smithing was superb. Ewers, vessels, bowls, sprinklers and incense burners were made for everyday use. Ornamental pieces were finely worked and richly decorated with floral and calligraphic designs, inlaid with precious stones and enamelling.

Carving and engraving on wood and ivory developed; some pieces found at Al-Fustat depict whole scenes illustrating court and palace life. Weaving was of high quality and even today Egyptian cloth is renowned. Some lustre-ware pottery and glasswork decorated with enamelling and gold have been discovered signed by the artists. This denotes the work of a master, for his patron would have requested a signed piece only if his creation was to be offered to the Caliph or to an individual of great importance in the empire. The illumination of texts was another beautiful art form enhanced by skill and innovation at this time.

The rule of the Fatimids declined into riot and revolt under the Caliph Al-Hakim as dramatically as it had once risen. His dynasty was doomed after a reign of repression, famine, mass destruction and extravagance.

The subsequent Ayyubid period restored a measure of peace to North Africa and had some influence on contemporary Islamic Art, evident in the *madrasahs*, mausoleums and castles of the period. Silverwork flourished again and Eastern designs, from such centres as Mosul, were adopted with their calligraphic, animal and stylised human motifs. The Ayyubids ruled between the twelfth and thirteenth centuries. New methods of metalworking from Andalusia, Iraq and Syria filtered into North Africa. The crusader armies encountered the superior craftsmanship of the East, and the trade opened up between the Islamic world and Europe, via Sicily, brought a gradual interaction of ideas between Christian and Muslim artists. Just before the Renaissance, Islamic master craftsmen were well established in Italian cities. Arabesque was introduced into Europe

The Egyptian bowl (above) *displays typical Islamic smithing styles of embossing, calligraphy and flower patterns.*

at the end of the fifteenth century, and by the sixteenth century European masters, such as Francesco Pelligrino, Peter Flotner and Hans Holbein, were influenced by its themes.

Sheer size characterised the next period of the North African Caliphate. The Mamelukes, still centred in Egypt, built enormous monuments and encouraged masters of stone carving, plasterwork and wood engraving. Star patterns were popular and used abundantly on their *madrasahs*, mausoleums and palaces. A new technique of inlaying wood with ivory or mother-of-pearl was perfected.

The handicrafts of the Mamelukes benefited from the influx of craftsmen fleeing for sanctuary in Egypt and North Africa from the Mongol invasions, bringing with them technical skills and innovatory themes. Many of the Mosul artists moved to Egypt or to Syria. They set up workshops and metalworking developed rapidly. New artefacts appeared – candlesticks, candelabras, pen-holders and armour, all fashioned in metals for the rich. The technique of silver inlay improved. The crafts of weaving, pottery and glass-making were revived. There was progress too in the illumination of manuscripts, as Qurans were produced with coloured drawings, floral designs and gold patterns. The name of the owner was signed alongside that of the craftsman, and the book was further embellished with a calligraphic dedication to the ruler.

The emergence of the Ottoman empire brought Islamic rule in North Africa to a close, as the centre of Muslim power retreated east. The Ottomans were content with loose promises of allegiance and left the North African countries free to choose their own rulers. New imperial forces came later from Europe. But North Africa belongs to the Islamic world today, for despite years of European rule Islam has remained its unifying force. Its traditions are Muslim.

To sum up, the crafts and metalwork of North Africa were enriched by the contributions of masters and artists from more sophisticated civilisations; notably, in the fifteenth century by Andalusian craftsmen and in the sixteenth by an influx of Turkish craftsmen.

Although there are hundreds of types of silverwork in Morocco, three main styles emerge in the silver jewellery of the cities. The areas of Fez and Tangiers produce jewellery which is intricately worked, with delicate pendants reminiscent of Andalusian ornaments. The jewellery of the Meknes area is famous for its use of geometric designs on simple filigree backgrounds. Abstract floral decoration is often enamelled in the favourite blue of the region. On the coast above Agadir, the Essaouira area produces jewellery with extensive floral network decoration, which is sometimes enhanced with enamelling on a coloured background.

The dominant feature of rural Moroccan jewellery is the amulet, generally symbolising the desire for fertility and growth. Fibules and pectorals are especially renowned in the Rif, Tiznit and Terudent areas. These and other items are worn on blue clothing in the south and on white in the north. Jewellery is mainly worn by women in Morocco; the men carry silver daggers in scabbards inlaid with gold and sometimes with coral, and ornamented with floral decoration.

Until the beginning of this century, Constantine, Algiers and Tlemcen were the main centres for jewellery-making in Algeria. This craft survives today in various other parts of Algeria, such as Tamanrassit, Bou Saada, Biskra and Ghardaia, and in villages like Beni Yeni, which is the best known, and Aet Al-Arba'a. There are striking differences between the Kabyllie silverwork of the North and the Saharan and Touareg work in the south, but a few similarities are discernible, owing to the continuous movement of the tribes. Kabyllie bracelets, anklets and necklaces are big and heavy, but lemon-yellow, violet and turquoise enamelling give them a lively and colourful character, while mosaics add to the oriental effect. The coral studding is reminiscent of work found in Palestine and Jordan. Touareg work is much more simply designed, with plain geometric shapes such as squares, pyramids, cones and cubes. These abstract patterns give the jewellery a dynamic heavy appearance. Touareg jewellery is sometimes engraved, but not typically studded with stones. The Kabyllies live high in the Atlas Mountains or in the coastal areas, and their work may be said to reflect the colours of their environment. The Touaregs, on the other hand, are a people of the Sahara, where the hardship of life in an endless sea of sand has shaped their consciousness. Their work reflects the vastness of their surroundings.

The island of Djerba lies off the coast of Tunisia near the Libyan border. One can see efforts being made there to keep the traditional crafts alive. The suqs are divided into different areas for different trades. Weavers, potters and basket-makers supply both domestic and tourist demand. Metalworking is popular, and old techniques of working precious metals are being revived.

In Tunisia, as in many other North African countries, there are marked differences between city and rural communities; differences which are reflected in much of its jewellery. City women love pearls and gold or silver-gilt pieces, while in the country traditional plain silver is used.

In many tribal areas, silver has long been considered a symbol of truth and purity, while gold was associated with vice. There is a story of a Touareg

This Moroccan pendant (above) *is inlaid with red glass and nielloed. A Kabyllian brooch* (right) *is worked on both sides of the ornament known as* tebsimet.

ARAB AND ISLAMIC SILVER

Enamelling

One of the finest Kabyllian necklaces with various pendants characteristic of Algerian jewellery; enamelled and decorated with coins, this unusual design with striking yellow enamel work demonstrates the perfectionism of some smiths.

Enamelling is one of the oldest ways known to decorate objects and give them an attractive and colourful finish. It is also, despite a variety of techniques, one of the simplest. It is the application of glass powders of varying colours to a design on metal. It can be used on almost every metal – gold, silver copper, brass. The powder is fired under heat to make it adhere.

No one knows where or when enamelling began. Some Mycenean jewellery dating from 1300 BC shows evidence of the use of a vitreous blue substance, but it is uncertain whether these early examples were actually "enamelled" or whether pieces of crushed glass were inserted into them. Later ornaments from the Caucasus region, dating from 900 BC show more definite traces of real enamelling. Enamelling was certainly known to the Ancient Egyptians; the beautiful sarcophagus of Tutenkhamen shows its use on gold. Tutenkhamen lived at about the same time as the Mycenean pieces were made, so it is possible that the Myceneans copied the art in a cruder way from their more civilised contemporaries.

Inheriting it through the Myceneans, the Greeks refined the technique, which then spread across the world with the Greek conquests. Alexander the Great is known to have taken many craftsmen with him to the East.

Early examples from Europe and North Africa, now in the British Museum, demonstrate that enamelling was known in these areas during Roman times.

Enamelling is known as *meenakari* in the Indian subcontinent, where it has been popular since early times. The Mughals excelled at the craft and today enamelling is to be seen in the silverworks of Lucknow, Rampur, Jaipur and Kashmir.

Various methods of enamelling have been developed. *Cloisonné* is the name given to the thin wire divisions on the basic object which delineate the proposed pattern. Each section is then filled with the appropriate enamel powder. This is a popular method in Chinese and Japanese pieces, where enamelling was revived in the last century. *Pliqué-à-jour* is related to *cloisonné* but the effect is of a stained glass window; it is usually done only with precious metals while *cloisonné* is normally used on the baser metals. The attraction of *pliqué-à-jour* is that the enamelling has no backing, but is transparent so that the light catches the colours.

Champlévé is one of the oldest ways of enamelling. Literally the word means "raised plain", and this describes it exactly. Depressions are made in the metal by engraving or carving before the enamel is added. Ancient Indian jewellery is a fine example of this kind of work. Another method is *baisse taille*, where a coating of wax is used and the design imprinted into it before the powder is positioned. Generally this method is rare and is used only on heavy gauge metals.

Every area of the world has used and developed its own form of enamelling. We tend to think of it now more as an oriental craft because of the popularity and wide variety of *cloisonné* objects, but this is not accurate. In Europe, enamelling was very popular in the eighteenth century and the Limoges enamels are beautiful. Limoges developed a form of enamelling like a painting. The powder was ground very fine, then mixed with oil and applied to porcelain and metal objects in a great variety of ways.

Today the markets have plenty of fine enamel works from all over the world; and despite being basically a glass material, enamelled pieces have survived in large quantities through the years in almost perfect condition. They fetch very high prices now both in the auction rooms and in shops. Enamellers themselves have never achieved the kind of recognition that metal workers have received, but, in their own fashion, with the most delicate craftsmanship, they have transformed quite ordinary-looking objects into beautiful and desirable collectors' pieces.

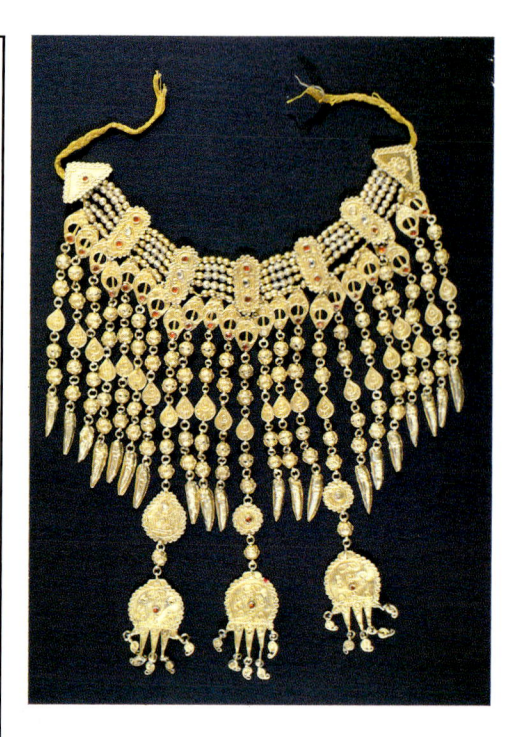

Above: This fine Libyan kerdala *covers most of a woman's upper body and jingles as she moves. Red crystal and white beads appear on the main piece and five rows of imitation pearls are finished with hollow pendants. The words "Ma sha Allah" (God willing) are embossed on the longest pendant.*

chieftain who abhorred gold and never touched it with his hands, preferring to use a stick to count the tax collected in gold coinage from his people.

Much Tunisian jewellery was originally functional. Buckles and pins, for example, were designed to keep clothes in place. Over the centuries, however, increasingly ornate examples were produced. Bracelets might also be used as protective weapons, with large pointed pieces or stones inserted into them. Fierce tribal and clan traditions survive among the desert people of Tunisia.

If gold was disdained by many of these people, it nevertheless retained its peculiar attraction and symbolic power through the centuries. In Tripoli, for example, the Caramanlis passed a law forbidding gold anklets to be worn by anyone outside the Royal Family. But in the cities many pieces were made in silver-gilt, a process introduced into North Africa from Spain during the Middle Ages. In the more traditional styles of Tunisian jewellery filigree and enamelling are also widely used, as they are throughout North Africa.

Some Libyan jewellery is completely covered with gold which makes it shine and gives it the appearance of solid gold. One of the favourite decorative symbols in Libyan work is the amuletic image of 'Fatima's hand'. (Fatima was the Prophet Mohammed's daughter and his cousin Ali's wife). Libyan craftsmen also use the crescent shape very widely in their pendants. They try to simplify the decorative elements whether there be floral or animal motifs. Libyan jewellery is generally stamped and one complete piece can sometimes be composed of twenty or more separate parts strung together, each bearing its own stamp. The hallmark itself sometimes becomes a decorative feature.

Characteristic of Sudanese work is its use of calligraphy mixed with simple floral designs covering small areas of the piece. Sudanese silver, especially from the first half of the twentieth century, is famous for its typical filigree work, displayed especially in boxes and baskets.

These differences illustrate the tribal and urban divisions of arts and crafts in North Africa. While coastal towns and cities developed techniques and skills which were influenced by, and exported to, the outside world, the groups of the interior have retained simpler and more traditional styles. It is therefore in these latter regions that one can see the genuine designs of ancient masters. There are a few differences in ornamentation between the rural groups, such as a varying use of stones and a heavier or lighter look on a silver piece; but most basic ornaments have common features.

In the rural and desert areas men and women still proudly wear ornaments which distinguish them as members of their group. Some may have plain bangles, others wear heavy amber necklaces with silver plaques of varying shapes and amulets for good fortune. In Siwa, an Egyptian oasis, the local jewellery includes heavy pieces so large that they cover women from head to waist. Armour embellished with silver decoration is a sign of virility – as it is in Peshawar, Yemen or Kurdistan; a man must be seen to be ready to protect himself. A feature of many tribal groups is the lovely combination of colourful strands of cloth mixed with silver chains which hang to the shoulders from a headdress. Arab women who still wear the veil have richly decorated silver pieces or coins attached to it. The desert women tend to wear their silver jewellery at all times, even when performing the most arduous tasks. Occasionally when travelling, they may remove some of the pieces, putting them on the saddles of their animals or round the creature's neck, adding to the silver ornamentation with which it is already laden.

Islamic customs, such as tea and coffee drinking, reflect North Africa's identification with the Islamic world. This ritual can last for several hours, and many of the pieces – coffee pots and samovars – are made of silver.

A wedding is an especially important

Above: *Fine filigree work is common on Sudanese cigarette boxes. A cylindrical box from Omdurman* (below left) *displays typically Sudanese simple floral decoration and Arabic calligraphy.*

occasion in North Africa from Morocco to Libya, whether held in a city or a small tribal village. The festivities may continue for more than a week. Ceremonial pieces reflect both the local heritage and the Islamic cultural tradition. The bride is adorned from head to foot. Diadem headdresses, with fine cutwork chiselled into delicate patterns, have small jewels set in them. A row of articulated plaques across the forehead support hanging tresses of silver chains and baroque pearls, which flow to the waist and are then attached to the bridal gown with jewelled pins. Circular gypsy-style earrings made of precious metals and jewels are also worn. Silver belts fashioned with the same decorative techniques are either attached to articulated pieces or sewn onto a fine cloth backing. A necklace of silver chains with numerous plaques of different shapes, interspersed with amulets, completes the effect of this rich ornament. The bride's appearance expresses the family's social standing and she will receive many silver pieces as presents to add to the wealth of the new home. Berber women tattoo their faces and hands, a tradition still prevalent even among modern city brides, who mark their faces with delicate lines in symbolic observance of old tribal customs.

ARAB AND ISLAMIC SILVER

This Moroccan piece (right) *is decorated with a crescent solid inlay, an Arabic inscription, decorated star and hollow pendants, old coral and old coins. Bottom: Enamelled and inlaid with plastic which is a substitute for old coral, this Algerian hayasa is a* jebeen *from Kabyllie.*

46

NORTH AFRICA AND SPAIN

This Libyan silver gilded head-dress (left) *is worn either on the forehead or on the side of the head or fixed on clothes, but the two ends are never joined.* Below: *An Algerian* jebeen *displays open work engraving and decorative use of glass beads and French coin pendants.* Bottom: *There are large openwork engraving and small geometrical designs to be seen in this Libyan forehead decoration.* Overleaf: *An excellent example of Libyan work, this fascinating* jebeen *is mainly worn for weddings or formal occasions.*

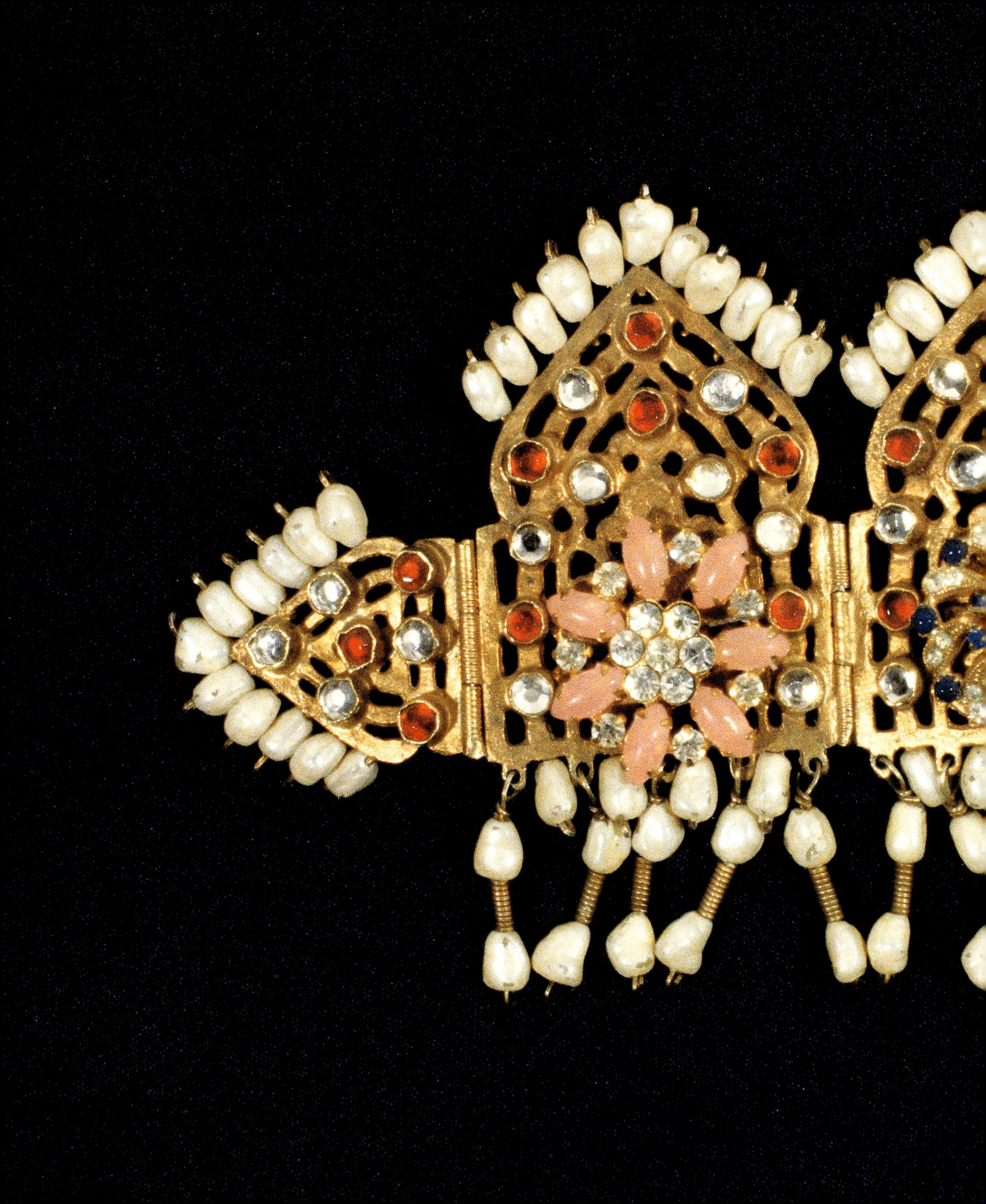

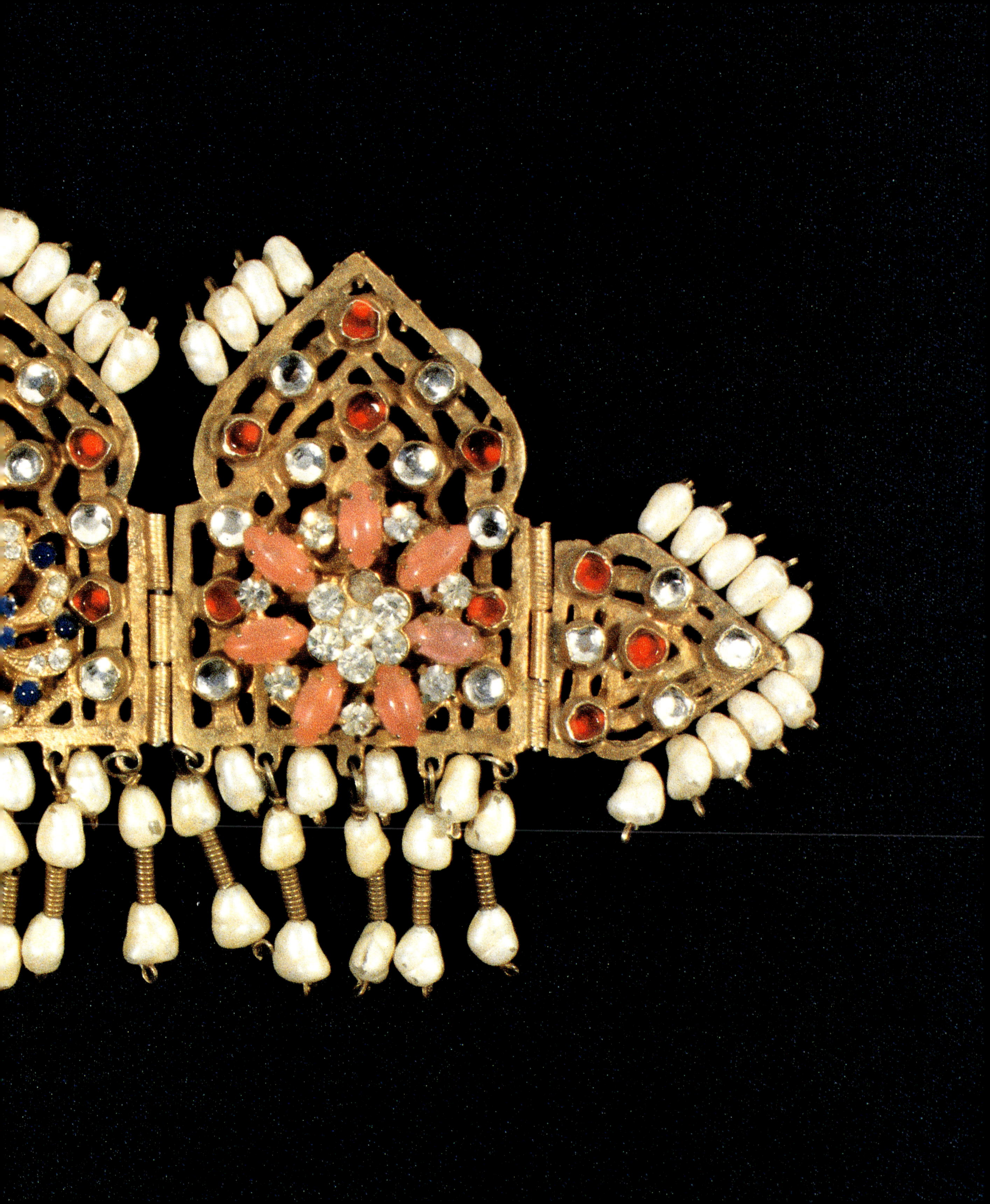

ARAB AND ISLAMIC SILVER

Another kind of Libyan pendant (below) *displays an eight-pointed star which is simply engraved and inlaid with glass.*

This lavish Libyan body ornament (right) *displays the* tulul *style (which is Arabic for hills or sand-dunes).*

Suruh, *which is Arabic for flowing, is the name given this Libyan head-dress* (below). *This piece is often worn in pairs on the hair and rarely on clothes.*

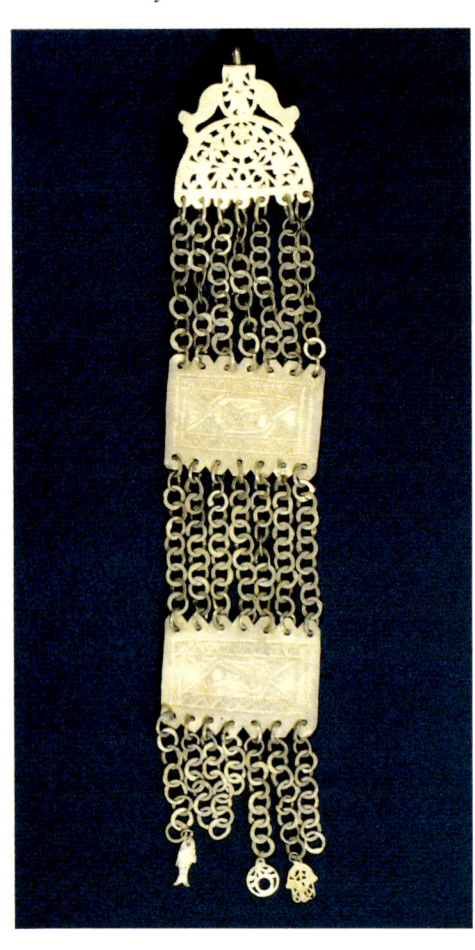

This Libyan body ornament (opposite) *has threaded balls inlaid with various stones, coral, beads and glass.*

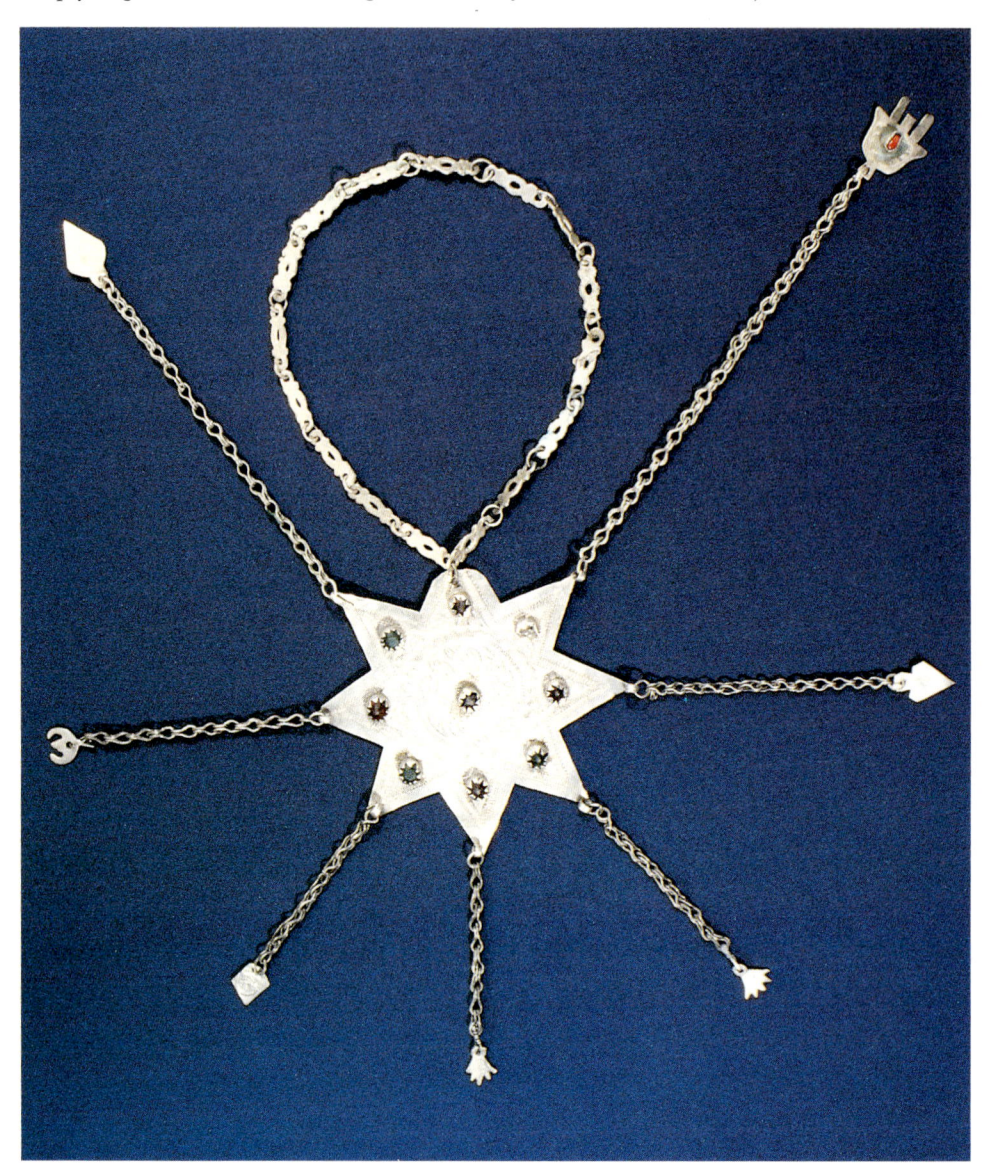

50

NORTH AFRICA AND SPAIN

51

ARAB AND ISLAMIC SILVER

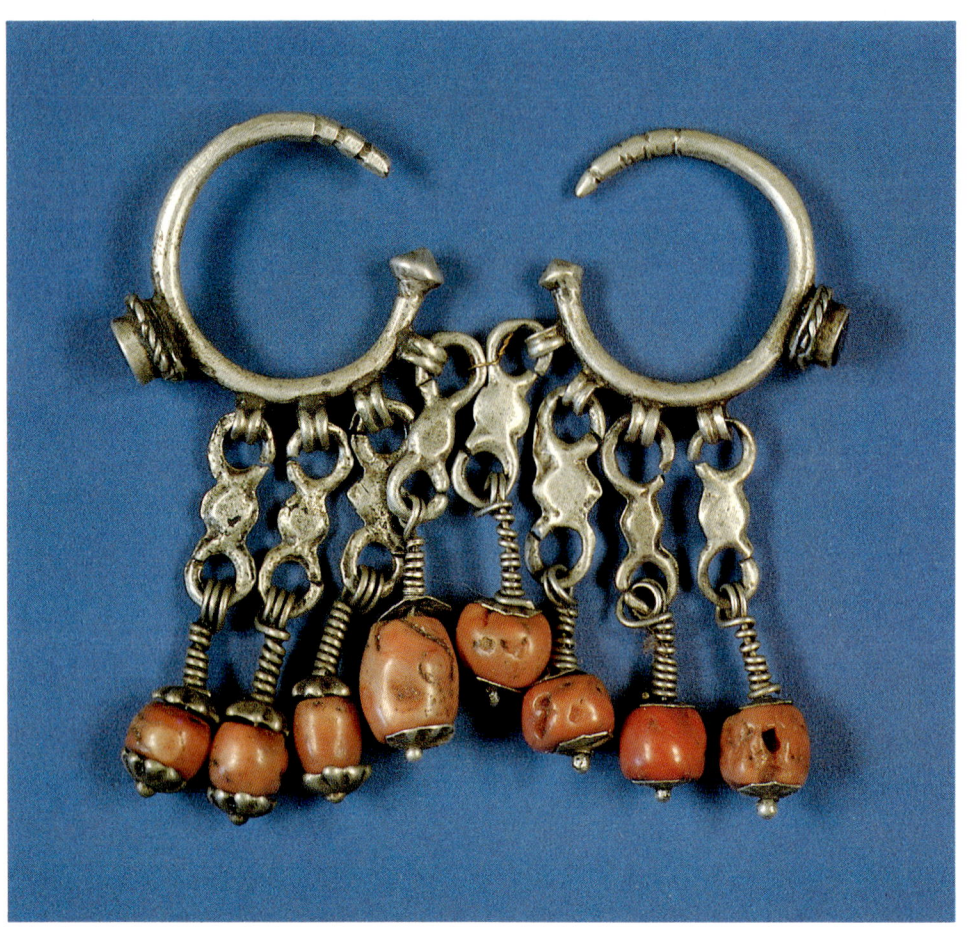

Top: *This is an odd example of a Moroccan piece in which the clasp is missing. The main disc of this breast decoration* (above) *which is probably Algerian is decorated with silver balls and edged with a twisted silver wire design. In this characteristically Moroccan brooch* (right), *pendant chains are supported by red beads where there was once real coral.*

NORTH AFRICA AND SPAIN

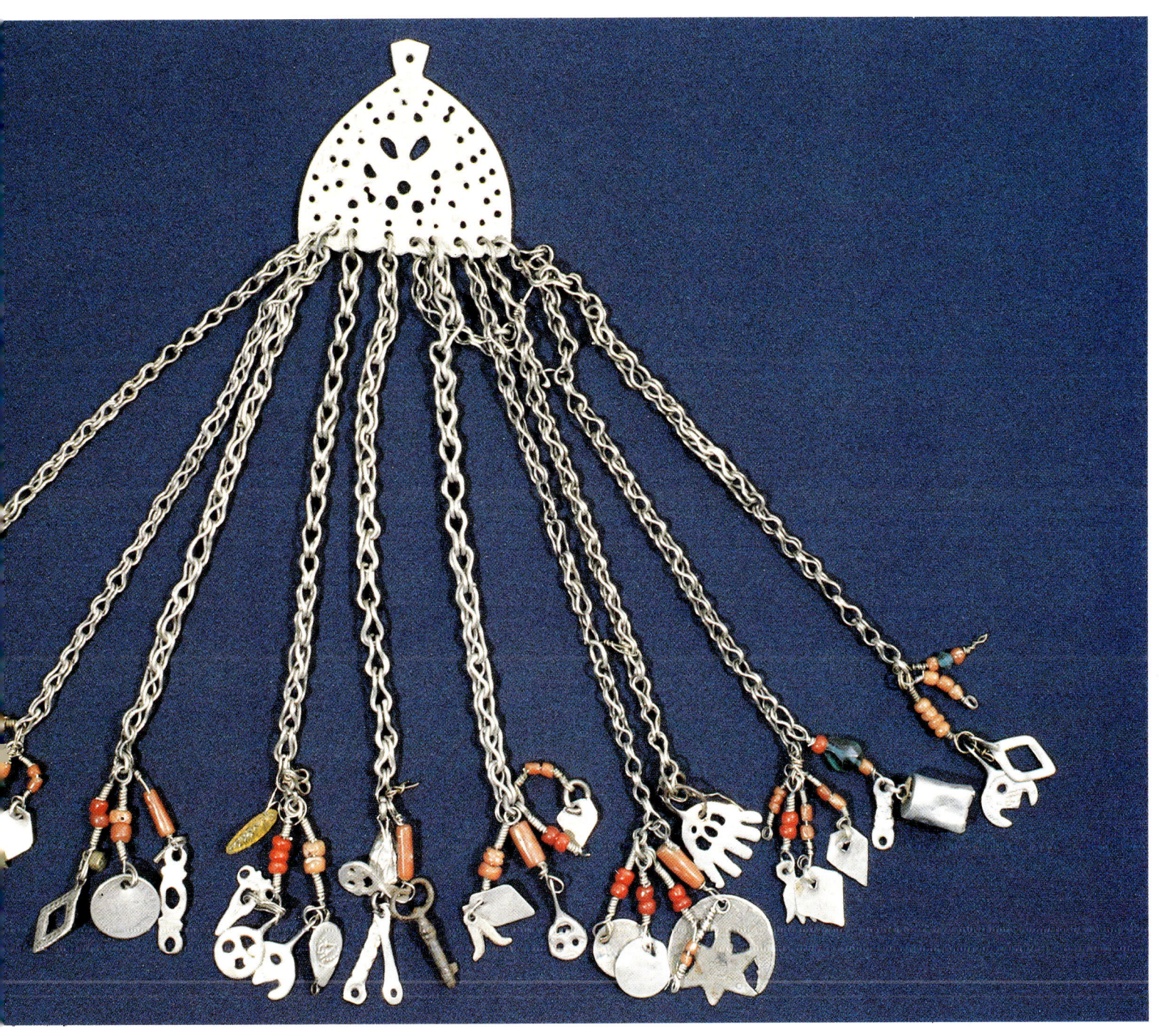

This Libyan pendant (above) has long chains and little pendants which include keys, beads, coral, coins, crescents and other silver shapes. The calligraphy on these two matching Algerian brooches (left) reads "Algeria", and they were originally panels of a belt.

ARAB AND ISLAMIC SILVER

NORTH AFRICA AND SPAIN

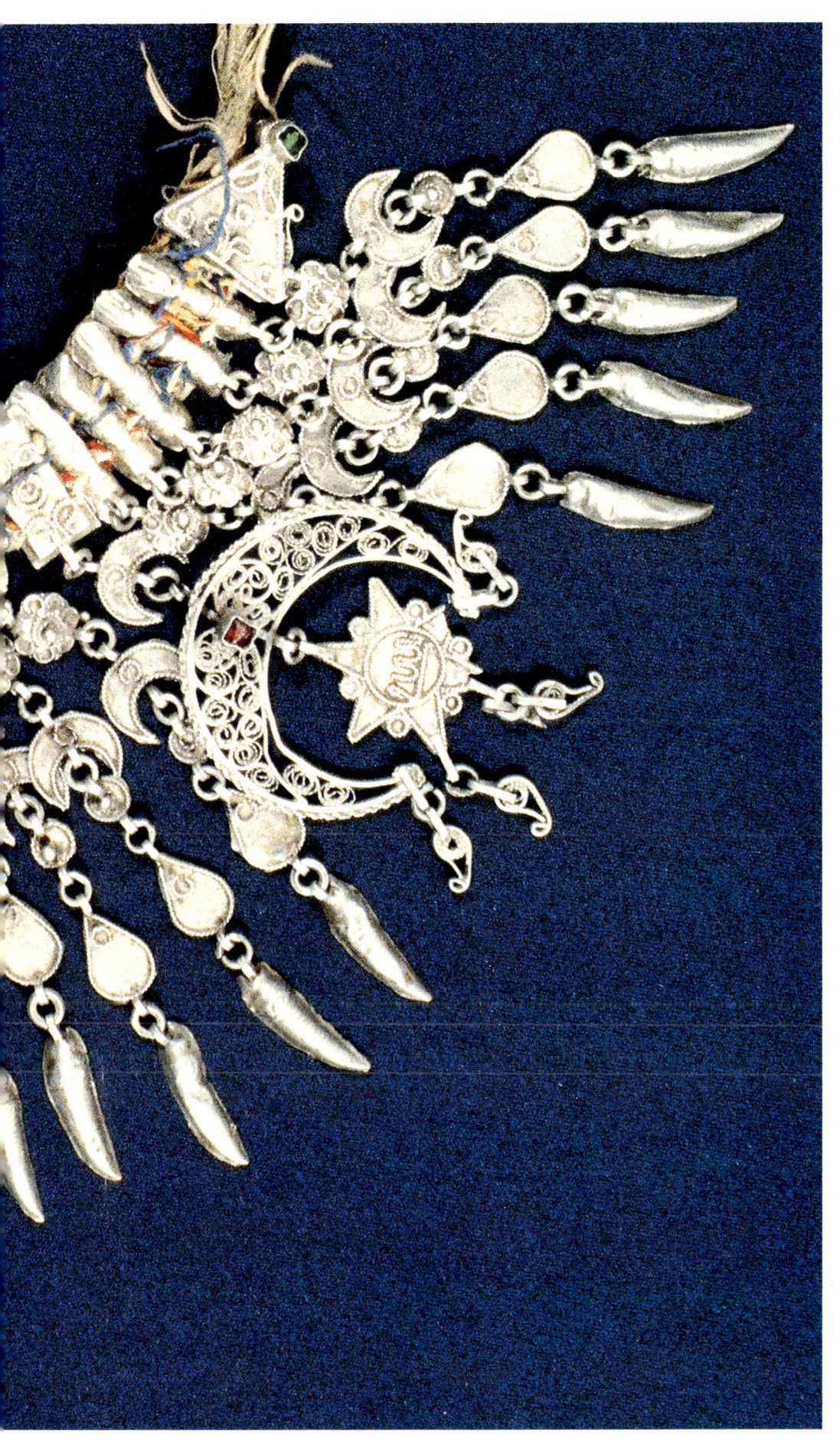

Left: *This Libyan composition is complicated and remarkable. The three main crescent-shaped pendants which carry heavy openwork are ended with hand and star pendants, made of solid silver.*

ARAB AND ISLAMIC SILVER

The pectoral from Tiznit (above) in southern Morocco is engraved and enamelled and studded with glass and silver enamel balls. This Libyan body decoration pendant (right) is worn like a brooch. Engraved with floral decoration, crescent, star and simple openwork, this large, typically Libyan, pin (far right) forms part of a body ornament.

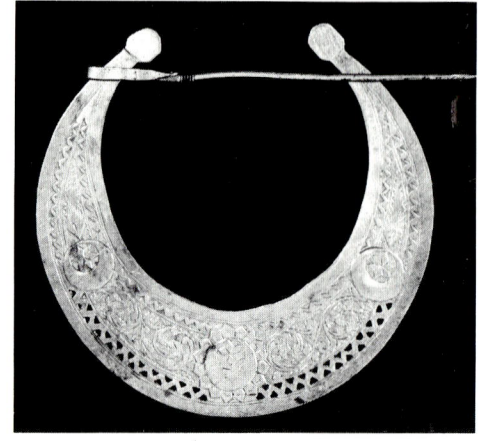

NORTH AFRICA AND SPAIN

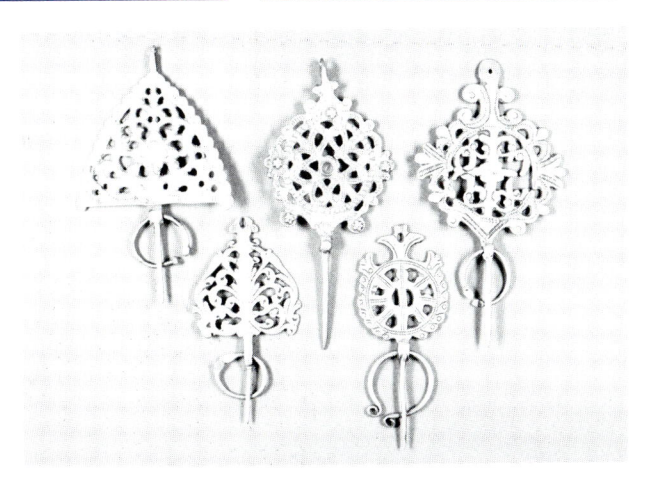

A characteristically Moroccan brooch (above) *is pear-shaped. Two pins fix this south Algerian pendant* (left) *to its wearer's clothing. Many Algerian pendants* (far left) *display openwork and floral designs of different kinds.*

ARAB AND ISLAMIC SILVER

Far right: *An Algerian brooch inlaid with glass and enamel.* Centre: *A Libyan silver brooch inlaid with a pottery bead which may be part of a larger piece of jewellery. This Libyan body ornament* (below) *consists of five* tulul *joined to a heavily engraved and chased silver disc.*

58

NORTH AFRICA AND SPAIN

59

ARAB AND ISLAMIC SILVER

Right: *The simple openwork decoration on floral-designed main panels, crescents and Fatima hand pendants are typical of many Libyan earrings. This earring* (below left) *demonstrates filigree and granulation work in Algerian jewellery and ends with half a silver ball. The considerable weight of this Libyan earring* (below right) *may force its owner to wear it above the ear. Equally typical of middle and southern Algeria, these Libyan Saharan earrings* (bottom) *carry symbolic designs and jagged edged decorations.*

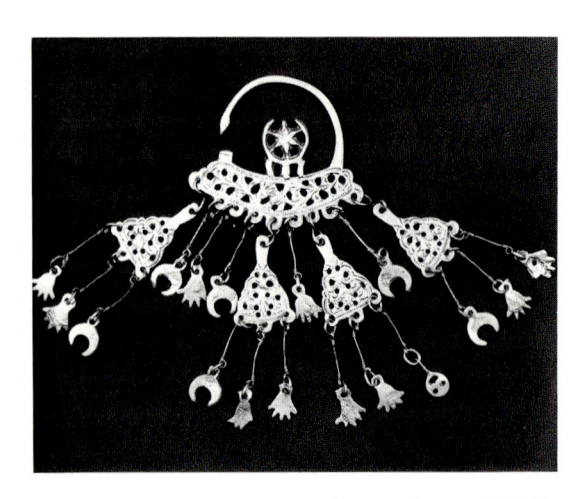

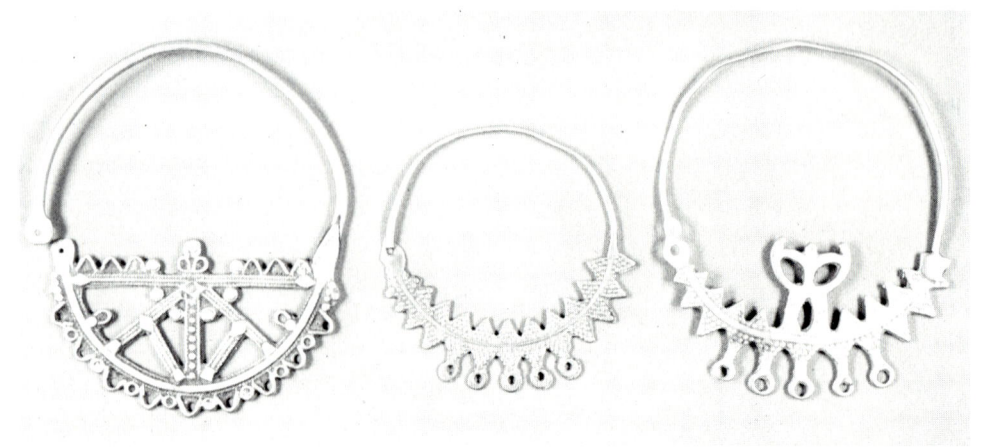

Above: *An impressive Saharan design of necklace found in Tamanrasset and Insalah in Algeria, but characteristic also of other Saharan regions.* Far left: *Another Algerian Saharan necklace which was found in Ouargla, is also typical of the Saharan central area from Sudan to Mauritania. The continuity of pattern in the south Algerian necklace* (left) *gives the entire ornament a flowing design.*

ARAB AND ISLAMIC SILVER

An Algerian Kabyllian necklace (top right) *with typical pendants and inlaid coral. This style of Libyan necklace* (top left) *with hand and crescent shaped pendants fixed to a chain is frequently found in bracelets also. Rare and delicate engraving, akin to sculpture, makes this south Algerian necklace* (above) *specifically Algerian/Saharan. The Algerian torque* (above right) *is made from twisted silver wires ended with solid embossed flowers as fastenings. The cylindrical body of this Libyan necklace* (right) *was originally an amulet holder which can be opened from one side only.*

62

NORTH AFRICA AND SPAIN

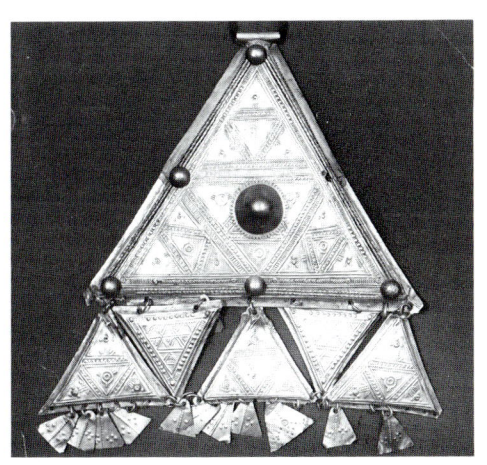

This Libyan embossed piece with bell-shaped pendants (top right) *is inlaid with red beads. The central ornament of this Libyan necklace* (above right) *is simply chased with silver wire. The lower part of the piece displays the distinctive Libyan pendant designs of Fatima's hands and crescent shapes. The Kabyllian Algerian piece* (above) *is worn either as a brooch or as part of a necklace and is inlaid with four coral stones and rich enamelling. Left: A characteristic Touareg necklace or* terwit *is a large piece of impressive size with geometrically balanced decoration.*

63

ARAB AND ISLAMIC SILVER

An akd *or* Beni Yeni *necklace* (above) *is a prized possession in Algeria. Various hollow enamelled boxes or* hirz *are usually decorated with coral, which is sometimes replaced with plastic. Inlaid with four stones and inset with silver balls, openwork engraving, geometrical and floral design, this necklace* (right) *comes from south Algeria.*

NORTH AFRICA AND SPAIN

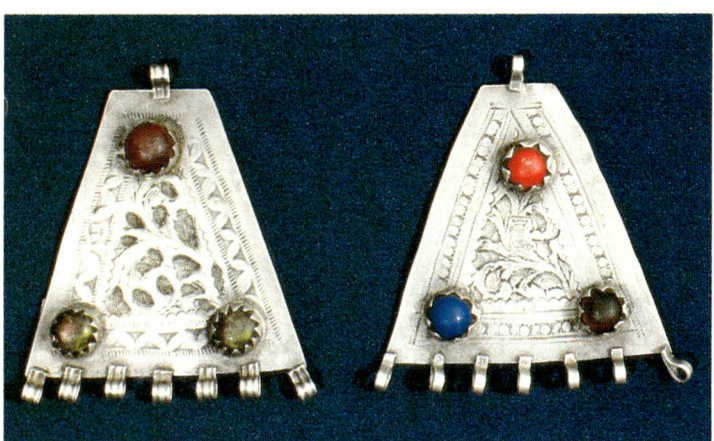

Above: *An Algerian necklace incorporating old French coins of various eras. The pendants are missing on the Libyan ornaments* (left) *which display a simple chasing technique, floral designs and various coloured beads.*

65

ARAB AND ISLAMIC SILVER

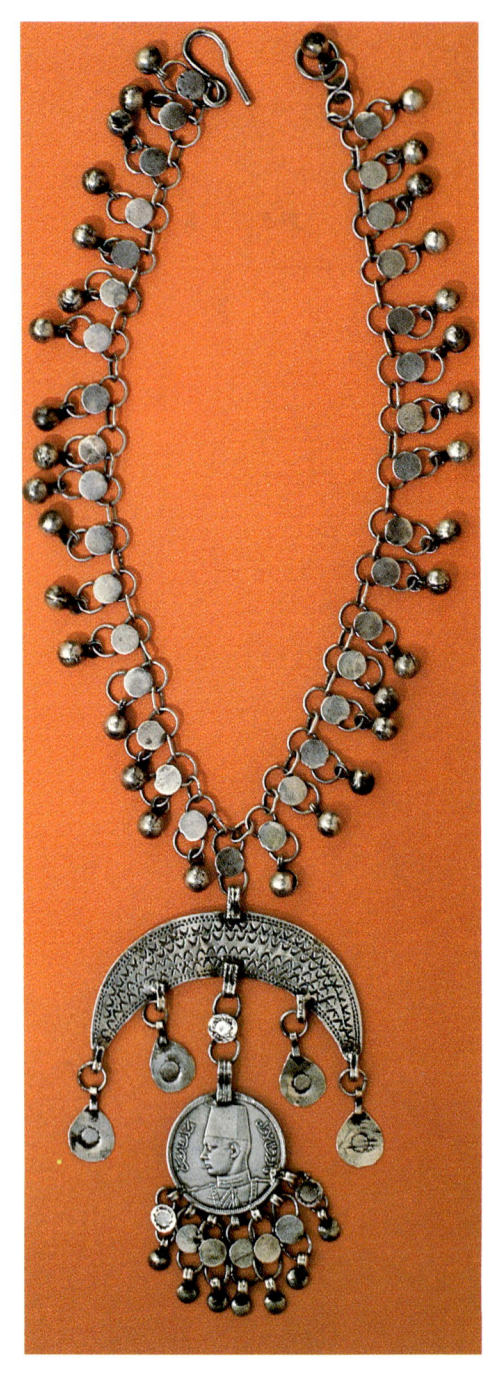

Above: *An Egyptian city-style necklace with a crescent joining coins of King Farouk's time with pendants. Touareg necklaces* (right and opposite) *from the Hoggar area based on amulets and strung on thin black leather string (rather than chain) which is characteristically used in Touareg jewellery. Far right: The tassels and the big geometrical patterns on this necklace are typical of Touareg jewellery.*

NORTH AFRICA AND SPAIN

67

ARAB AND ISLAMIC SILVER

Right: *An ornate Libyan belt which is made from one sheet of silver crudely chased by hammering to make very simple designs, both geometrical and floral. It is characteristic of pieces from old towns like Tripoli, Misurata and Benghazi. The buckle of this Algerian belt* (below right) *is the most arresting part of the ornament as is typical of belts from the Islamic world. It is inlaid with coral and French coins.*

68

NORTH AFRICA AND SPAIN

Delicate interlocking panels make this Algerian belt flexible for the wearer. It is typical of silver found in north-western Algerian towns like Oran and Tlemcen, but also in bordering northern Moroccan towns.

ARAB AND ISLAMIC SILVER

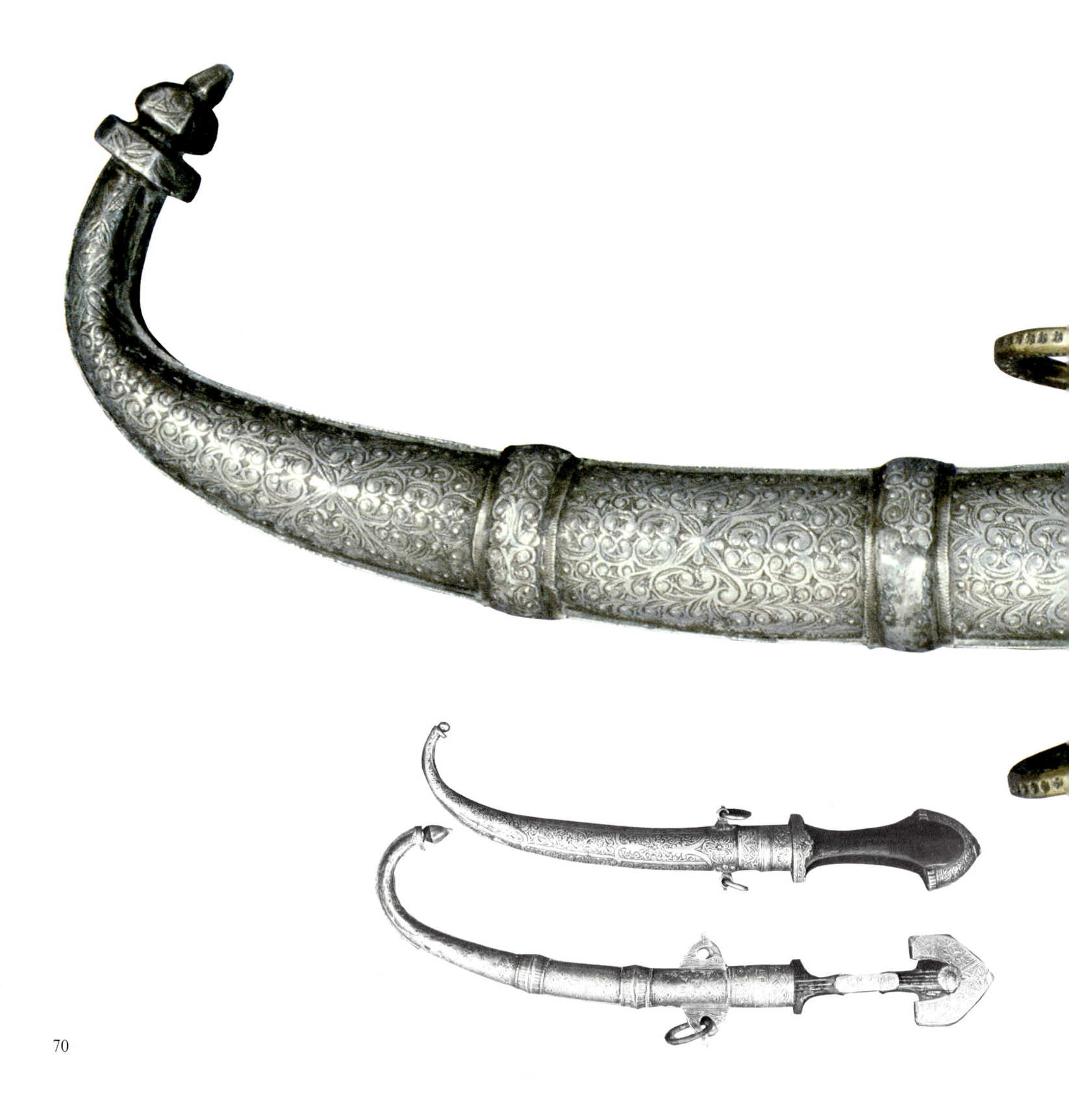

70

Opposite below: *Various floral motifs decorate different patterns of Moroccan daggers.* Below: *Moroccan daggers are frequently beautifully chased and partially enamelled. The rings attach the weapon to a belt which is most comfortably worn with the dagger point in an upward-thrust position.*

ARAB AND ISLAMIC SILVER

This simply chased southern Libyan ring (right) *is inlaid with plastic and beads and the holes indicate a missing pendant. An imitation Kabyllian bracelet* (below) *is decorated by silver wire which separates the various areas of enamelling and is inlaid with silver balls of different sizes.*

NORTH AFRICA AND SPAIN

Top right: *Repoussé work of clear geometrical forms is characteristic of the modern Touareg bracelet. Two patterns of Algerian bracelets* (top left) *display an attractive floral decoration: the left-hand one has filigree work and is inlaid with beads; both have safety chains. The Libyan cylindrical bracelet* (above) *which is made from a large sheet of silver, hammered into shapes as floral and simple repoussé work. The perfect lines of this bracelet from Niger* (left) *are exceptional.*

73

ARAB AND ISLAMIC SILVER

*Hammering, chasing and repoussé work are characteristic of Libyan bracelets. The examples below are gilded all over.
Bottom: This Egyptian pumice stone holder is decorated with Egyptian subjects e.g. the Sphinx, in repoussé. There are beautiful shell-shaped side panels on the lock of this heavy Moroccan anklet (top centre) which is of elaborately worked silver, enamelled and inlaid with glass.*

NORTH AFRICA AND SPAIN

The main locks of these delicate Algerian bracelets (above) *form the focus of these ornaments but actually do not open. These solid silver snake-shaped bracelets from Algeria* (left) *have simple embossing decoration.*

75

ARAB AND ISLAMIC SILVER

NORTH AFRICA AND SPAIN

The beautiful round seal box (left) *has the name of King Farouk of Egypt engraved in Arabic on the lid. This Egyptian cigarette box* (below) *is engraved with floral,* *geometrical and fish shapes.* Bottom: *Specially commissioned and enamelled with the name of its owners, this Egyptian jewel-box has a shell-shaped lid.*

77

ARAB AND ISLAMIC SILVER

Moroccan Quran holders (right and opposite) *may hold an amulet or Quaranic verses and their tops slide open. They are attached to a necklace or a belt and, when they are as large as the one opposite, are usually worn across the body, over one shoulder and under the opposite arm. Below: This heavy filigree box with floral design is probably Sudanese. The central part of this Egyptian box* (bottom right) *is a plaited star design inside which "Egypt" is inscribed. Another Egyptian box* (bottom left) *is covered all over with floral design and has a tapering base.*

78

NORTH AFRICA AND SPAIN

ARAB AND ISLAMIC SILVER

Architectural arches and dome patterns appear on these Nigerian silver bowls.

80

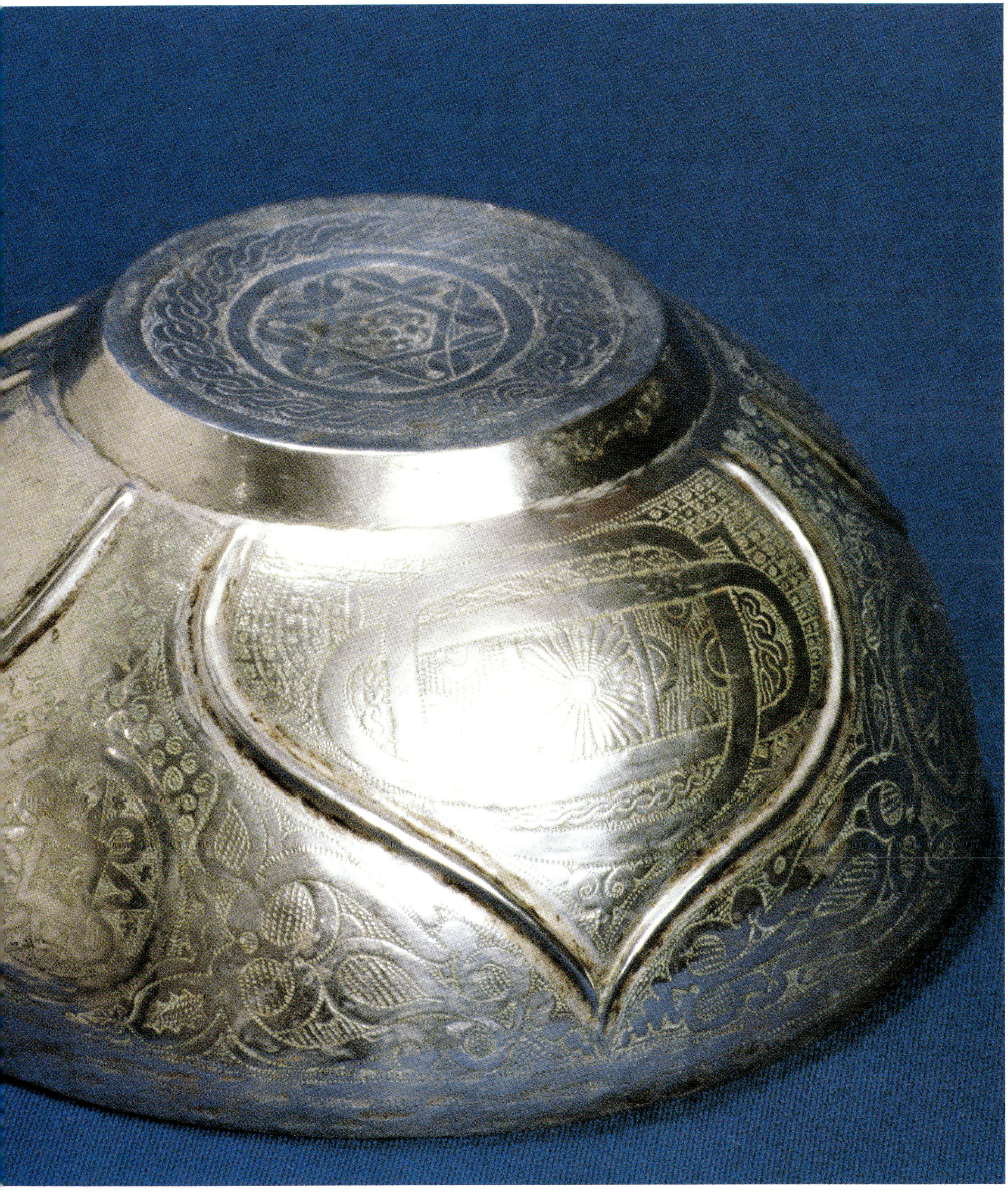

ARAB AND ISLAMIC SILVER

Above: *A Nigerian tray which is decorated with embossed patterns of a plaited design is typical of Nigerian silver work. It is unusual for a Muslim tray, such as this Egyptian example* (right), *to have silver decorative design only in the centre.*

NORTH AFRICA AND SPAIN

Above: *This Egyptian bowl displays several characteristic Islamic smithing styles – embossed decoration, calligraphy, flower and star patterns in complicated designs. This Egyptian dish (left) is engraved all over with floral and geometric decoration and inside the central flower-shaped design there is an Arabic calligraphic inscription.*

ARAB AND ISLAMIC SILVER

A remarkable Egyptian tray (above) displays Arabic calligraphy and also has an eight-pointed star in the centre inside rose-shaped decoration inside two squares inside two circles with plaited decoration outside the whole, with a floral design and ended with scallops.

Embossed decoration and calligraphy are displayed on this Egyptian tray, seen above.

ARAB AND ISLAMIC SILVER

The Arabian Peninsula

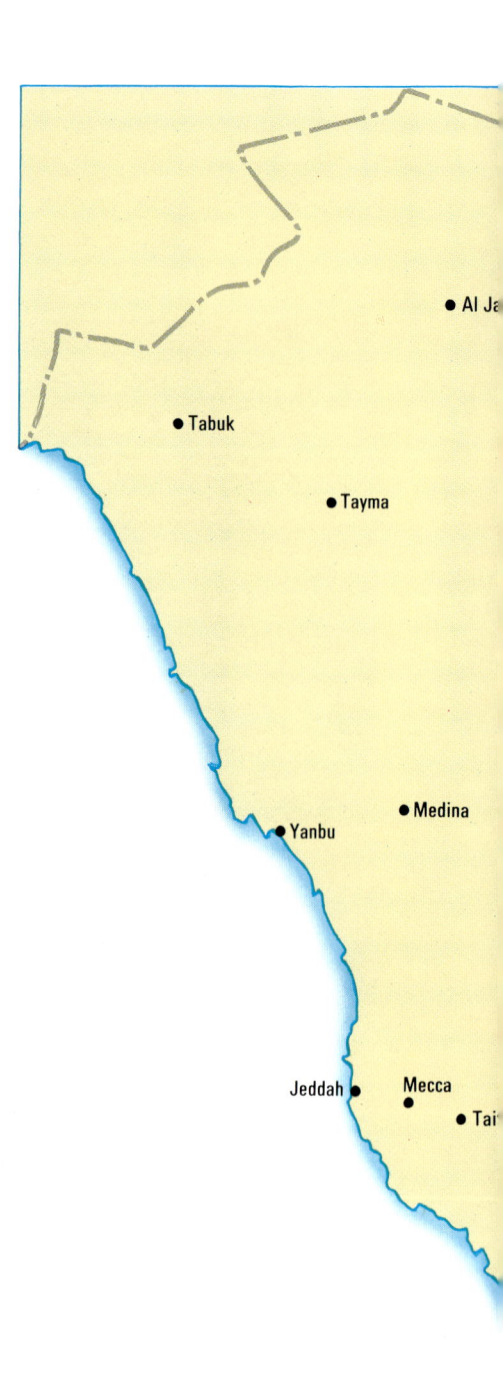

• Al Ja

• Tabuk

• Tayma

• Medina
• Yanbu

Jeddah • • Mecca
• Tai

RED SEA

THE ARABIAN PENINSULA

ARAB AND ISLAMIC SILVER

The Arabian Peninsula is a strongly marked geographical unit, defined on three sides by sea – to the east by the Arabian Gulf and Gulf of Oman, to the south by the Indian Ocean, to the west by the Red Sea – and on its northern side by the deserts of Jordan and Iraq. This isolated territory covers more than one million square miles. It is divided politically into several states, the largest of these is Saudi Arabia. To the east and south lie much smaller countries. Along the shores of the Arabian Gulf and the Gulf of Oman, there is first the State of Kuwait, with two adjacent patches of neutral territory, then, after a stretch of Saudi coast, the island of Bahrain and the Qatar Peninsula, followed by the United Arab Emirates and the larger State of Oman. The People's Democratic Republic of Yemen occupies most of the Peninsula's southern coast-line. To the north, facing the Red Sea, lies the Yemen Arab Republic.

For many centuries trade routes have flourished in the Arabian Peninsula, by sea through its ports and by land along the caravan trails. The great desert of the Rub-al-Khali, in the centre is a rainless unrelieved wilderness of shifting sand, almost entirely without human habitation: but the coastal regions, western Saudi Arabia, Yemen, Oman, eastern Saudi Arabia and the Gulf area long ago developed civilisations which were in touch with peoples far beyond the Peninsula. Today these areas are considerably developed, and many of the old cities have become international centres.

The spice trade was vital to the wealth of these early kingdoms. The Romans called the region Arabia Felix (fortunate or happy Arabia) because it was the source of exotic riches – frankincense, myrrh, gold, silver, pearls, silks, ivories, and spices; things which were coveted in the Roman empire. But Rome was not anxious to dominate the caravan routes in the great deserts or to conquer the ports, so the tenacious and hardy people of the Peninsula developed their civilisation untroubled by conquests. Their country neither threatened nor attracted foreign powers.

Earlier chroniclers recorded the fabulous wealth of the ancient kingdom of Saba'a in Yemen which lasted from 950 to 115 BC. Its notable buildings, its fine crafts and the serenity of its people were all commented on by visitors to this comparatively isolated land. The fertility of the soil created by the Marib Dam, which must rank with the Egyptian

Above: *A necklace displays Yemeni crafting characteristics in the use of hollow silver balls and amber.*

pyramids as one of the great technological feats of antiquity, produced lush fruits and spices, and the frankincense and myrrh shrubs, reputedly so difficult to cultivate, grew in abundance.

Saba'a's reputation and the fascination which it held for contemporary civilisations can be judged by the stories of the epic journey of her Queen to the court of King Solomon, which is recorded in the Quran, the Bible and the Talmud. She ruled from a magnificent throne surrounded by courtiers decked in silks, jewels and skilfully worked precious metals. She travelled with a great train of camels bearing spices, gold and jewels.

Saba'a itself was situated in the heart of Yemen, but the area was divided into four kingdoms which coexisted in relative harmony. The Sabaean civilisation declined with the coming of the Himyarites, who established their centre at Sofar. They never achieved comparable levels of technological competence. The great dam was not maintained and burst several times, until it finally collapsed in the first or second century AD. Yemen's commercial wealth declined along with its culture. The people began to spread north when the Himyarite kingdom was conquered in the early sixth century by the Abyssinians who in turn were overthrown by a Persian invasion in 575.

During the seventh century the country accepted Islam. The Shafi'ite Sunnis established their power in the Tihama (the coastal region) and the Zaidis, a moderate branch of the Shias, held the highlands. During the ninth century the

Zaidi Imam Yahya al-Hadi ila'l-Haqq founded the Rassid dynasty of the Yemen.

Despite the disappearance of these many ancient kingdoms and the diaspora of their inhabitants, the country has inherited unusual traditions and a complex social structure of tribal organisation. The customs of each tribe are based on a code of honour, and each jealously guards its autonomy. Until recently the tribes were linked by their allegiance to the Imam, but they retained rights of self-determination. There were no written laws; the structure and standards of each group depended on oral traditions.

Yemen's isolation has produced a characteristic indigenous culture. Each area is strikingly different from the rest. Colour and style, strength and richness of decoration are common features, however, in the architecture of Sana'a, Mukalla and several other towns.

Its silverwork has similar features and is no less individual, although various semi-precious stones, such as cornelian, coral and amber, are used in jewellery throughout the whole region. Granulation is a typical feature of Yemeni craftsmanship, adding to the ornateness of its compositions.

The great Queen of Saba'a also ruled Oman, which may have been the home of the Phoenicians, those legendary sea-farers whose origin remains obscure. It was certainly a major trading centre between the East and the early kingdoms of Mesopotamia and Egypt. Its strategic importance on the Indian Ocean and at the entrance of the Arabian Gulf is still vital and its sea coast extends for over 1600 kilometres.

The area is traditionally linked with the Iraqi legend of Gilgamesh and the Flood. It was supposedly part of a fabled fertile region where Indus Valley migrants came to settle, over four thousand years ago. Oman was probably the land of Magan, mentioned in Sumerian tablets with which cities like Ur of the Chaldees traded in the third millennium BC. The province of Dhofar produced frankincense in vast quantities, which was shipped to markets in Iraq, Syria, Egypt and the West. Roman geographers mention a city called Omana and another called Portus Moschus, which may have been Muscat.

Masirah was known to Pliny as the Island of Turtles. At various times Oman came under the influence of the Himyaritic kingdoms of south Arabia and of Iran, to which the introduction of the *falaj* irrigation systems is probably attributable, although legend attributes it to Sulaiman bin Daoud, or Solomon.

The people of Oman came from two main stocks, the Qahtan, who immigrated from south Arabia and the Nizar, who came in from the north. Oman was one of the first countries to be converted to Islam by Amr ibn al As, who later converted Egypt. The Omani peoples today trace their ethnic origins to this Azd tribe. Apart from these groups, there are smaller tribal units who have preserved their own identities and traditions.

The Omanis of the tribe of Al Azd played an important part in Iraq during the early days of Islam. They subsequently embraced the Ibadhi doctrine, which holds that the Caliphate in Islam should not be hereditary or confined to

Above: *The great central circular pendant, which is heavily granulated and set with a turquoise coloured stone, provides a wonderful example of Yemeni skill*

any one family, and in the eighth century AD established their own independent Imamate in Oman. Though subject to invasions by the Caliphate, Iranians, Mughals and others, Oman has largely maintained its independence.

During the tenth century Sohar became one of the largest and most important cities in the Arab world. Omani mariners, like those from Basra and other Gulf ports, travelled as far afield as China. Sohar, throughout various declines and recoveries, continued to be a major port until, and indeed after, the Portuguese conquests. When the Portuguese under Albuquerque arrived in 1507, on their way to India, they found the Omani sea-

ARAB AND ISLAMIC SILVER

The hand-shaped pendants in this Omani piece (above) *are symbolic of protection against evil and also of the five tenets of Islam. Above right: Geometrical and floral patterns are the traditional decoration on an Omani silver* khanjar.

port under the suzerainty of the King of Hormuz, himself of Omani stock. The towns of Qalhat, Quryat, Muscat and Sohar were all then thriving and prosperous.

The arrival of the Portuguese in the Indian Ocean radically changed the balance of power. Portuguese and, later, British and Dutch traders dominated the region. It was not until 1650 that the Imam Nasir bin Murshid of the Yaruba dynasty effectively turned the Portuguese out of Muscat and the rest of Oman. By 1730 the Omanis had conquered the Portuguese settlements on the coast of East Africa, including Mogadishu, Mombasa and Zanzibar.

In the first half of the eighteenth century the country was ravaged by civil war until Ahmad bin Said was elected Imam and founded the Al Bu Said dynasty which still rules Oman.

There has always been so much communication between Oman and the rest of the civilised world that the designs and techniques of metalwork display similarities to those of Persia, Iraq, Egypt, Asia Minor, India, Greece, Morocco, even China. The historical relationships between Oman and Zanzibar and between Yemen and Djibouti, Somalia and Eritrea are manifested by the Arab influence which survives in the traditional silverwork of East Africa.

In Oman today, one can still find pieces of horn, bone or wood, glass bottle-stoppers and dried seed pods, set in silver and attached to elaborately designed necklaces. They represent the vestiges of an age-old belief in the amuletic properties of silver, but are now mainly used for teething babies. Apart from these symbols of the past, very little of Oman's silverwork contains added ornament, except an occasional piece of coral or glass which has been finely cut to enhance an earring or bracelet. Generally the metal itself is decorated with diamond shapes and bells and silver plaiting. The quality both of the metal and of the workmanship is excellent.

One of the main centres of silverwork in Oman is Nizwa, which ranks with Mosul and other famous Islamic metalworking centres. As late as the 1920s and '30s, silver was dispatched from England to the Nizwa workshops for final embellishment. Today much of the raw silver used there comes from China. The other main centres for silverwork are Bahla, Rostaq, Ibri, Sur, Muscat and Matrah. Each centre has its own particular patterns and compositions; for example, those of Nizwa feature geometric designs, while those of Rostaq are better known for their floral decoration.

Characteristic of Oman is the *khanjar* or dagger, which is so much a symbol of masculinity that every man wears one with pride. It is a distinctive piece which differs from other daggers in the Peninsula. The sheaths have a sharp right angle. Ceremonial ones for the rich are made of gold or a mixture of gold and silver. The plainer ones are of leather, but even on these there are usually traces of silver decoration. The finest *khanjars* have seven rings – two to serve as belt-holders, the other five for ornamental strands. The upper part of the handle is generally flat, except for the Saidi examples worn by members of the Royal Family, which are much more ornate. The *khanjar* is always worn attached to a belt of woven silver thread. A leather pouch holds a small knife positioned behind it, which is also decorated with an ornate silver handle. Other weapons, such as Omani swords and rifles, are also finely decorated with silver ornamentation.

At feasts or other celebrations, rich Omani families use silver plates, dishes and bowls and uniquely-shaped coffee pots. This coffee pot and the minute cups which make up the set play an important role both at the beginning and at the end of the meal. Sprinklers and incense burners are also significant. The sprinkler, often made of silver, is brought in and scented water is sprinkled across the room to dispel cooking smells and perfume the air. The burner is then laid in front of the guests for the same purposes and also for their personal use, so that the smell of food does not linger on their clothes. This ceremony marks the end of the feast when it is time for the guests to leave.

It is quite difficult to ascertain from which region a piece of Omani silver originates. There are some general distinguishing factors: for example, the works of the interior seem to have retained more of the ancient styles of Mesopotamia and Asia Minor than those of the coastal areas. Northern Omani work differs slightly from that of the south; the former appears to resemble Persian and Indian styles, while that of the southern area has more affinity to Yemeni work. Much more research is needed to explain the origin, patterns and designs of Omani silverwork.

With the coming of Islam, which was readily accepted by the Omani people, new designs were introduced and merged successfully with traditional ones. Like much of the Muslim world, Omani culture is tribal, but there are some slight differences attributable to the fact that Oman has long been a commercial nation and her early inhabitants were city-dwellers rather than tent-dwellers. Despite the foreign invasions to which she was subjected and her traditions of seafaring, Oman displays a more settled quality than the other countries of Arabia.

Saudi Arabia itself is the home of the Bedouin, whose traditions reach back to the earliest civilisations of mankind. They provide one of the purest Arab links with "the cradle of civilisation." Our present knowledge of Bedouin culture is very limited, but recent archaeological discoveries within the kingdom have proved beyond doubt that Bedouins influenced the cultures of Sumer, Babylonia and Assyria. The ancient Kingdom of Saba'a, which has already been described, can be said to typify the advanced level of civilisation that the early Bedouins had attained. Interaction between them and the people of Mesopotamia is well documented.

The nature of their environment has served to perpetuate the belief that Saudi Arabia is a land of nomads. Even some recent historians who have good reason to know that the country has always contained cities and permanent settlements continue to propagate this myth.

By the end of the sixth century the Hijaz cities of Taif, Mecca and Medina were influential; and when the southern regions fell under the control of the Sassanid rulers of Persia, this area grew in independence and importance as a trade route between the Byzantine Empire, Egypt and the East. From the fifth century onwards Mecca was dominated by the Quraish tribe, through whose extensive commercial activities outside influences made themselves felt.

The Prophet Mohammed himself was a member of this tribe, and so powerful was the appeal of the Islamic religion he preached that not only was it widely adopted, but even the language of the holy book, the Quran, has left an indelible impression on the speech of all the peoples who subscribed to it. Mecca acquired an unique status as a place of pilgrimage for the whole Muslim world.

The Bedouin love poetry and the spoken word. They are an open people, whose hospitality is legendary. As a guest you honour their dwellings and they will always share what they have. Time is of little importance to them, and they do not hurry at all in their commercial dealings. They will sit for hours in the *suqs* haggling over the price of goods. Barter is an essential part of Bedouin life and culture. It is important that both the buyer and the seller should not only be satisfied with the eventual exchange but that they should have demonstrated their ability to barter – to each other and to other members of their tribe.

To be adept at this personal style of trading is admirable to a people whose way of life revolves round basic needs. The desert produces little; their diet

ARAB AND ISLAMIC SILVER

consists mainly of dates and milk products. They rarely eat meat. Bedouin wealth lies in livestock, textiles, pottery and silverwork, all of which are transportable. Even the semi-nomadic Bedouin who settled in the oases and river valleys retained these traditional ideas of wealth.

Some silver and some woven products are fashioned into household objects to be sold and traded, but most are specially commissioned for an individual. Bedouin tradition holds that jewellery has only one owner. It is so much a part of that person that it must be melted down at his or her death or sold off in the *suqs*. Silver jewellery is enormously important in Bedouin life as the means by which a Bedouin woman can display her wealth and independence. The jewellery is commissioned for her by her husband and given to her as a dowry. Once given, it cannot be retracted but remains exclusively hers. She will carry it with her for the rest of her life. It is an expression of her husband's love, and as such is admired at her wedding ceremony where she will sit on a rostrum so that the wedding guests can view her new wealth.

The histories of Kuwait, Bahrain, Qatar and the United Arab Emirates (U.A.E.) are similar inasmuch as their pearling industry and prosperous trading activities made them all obvious prizes for the territorial ambition of outside powers. Bahrain's history stretched back to the earliest days of mankind, for there is plenty of evidence that the islands were inhabited by primitive man. In the last century archaeologists discovered the vital links that Bahrain had with the Sumerians in south Mesopotamia four or five thousand years ago, and that Bahrain was almost certainly Dilmun – the Sumerian land of immortality and enchantment. Apart from this mythological importance, Bahrain was also a trading entrepot between the cities of Mesopotamia and of the Indus. Dilmun's influence spread up the Gulf Coast as far as Kuwait and seems to have brought some prosperity to areas like the oasis of Al-Hasa in Saudi Arabia. In Kuwait there was a flourishing community on the island of Failakka from 3000 BC to 1200 BC. It had close connections with the cities of the Tigris and Euphrates, and became a trading outpost for the Dilmun civilisation.

Some archaeological sites in the area which now makes up the U.A.E. have been tentatively dated to 5000 BC. It seems that the area had trading links with Mesopotamia and with the Indus Valley and may well have served as a staging post between the two civilisations.

Remains of decorated pottery unearthed at Umm al Nar, an island close to Abu Dhabi city, are similar to finds in Baluchistan, Sind and the Indus Valley. Relics of a settlement dug up at Hili near Buraimi, which have been dated to the third millennium, indicate that at the time the people probably had closer connections with the Indian subcontinent than with Mesopotamia. The inhabitants of Hili were wealthy enough to employ craftsmen capable of cutting stones in geometric patterns. Excavations at Hili and nearby Al Ain have provided evidence that a vigorous and sophisticated society may have flourished in the vicinity in about 2500 BC.

This Saudi dagger of silver and copper (above) displays silver wire decoration, granulation and floral designs. The handle is inlaid with solid silver balls.

The Greeks appear to have settled briefly in the northern part of the U.A.E. when they took over areas of the Gulf shortly after the death of Alexander the Great at the end of the fourth century BC. Hellenistic relics have been found at Mileiha and Umm al Qawwain indicating that the Greeks took advantage of the shelter provided by the deep creeks which existed on the coast. Other finds show that Ras al Khaima was probably a busy seaport, which may have had connections with the Kingdom of Saba'a in Yemen during the early years AD and have been used as a watering place for ships transporting incense from the southern Arabian Peninsula.

Islam came to the area during the Muslim expansion across the Peninsula

THE ARABIAN PENINSULA

Above: *Two designs of Omani bracelets.*

soon after the death of the Prophet Mohammed in 632 AD. At this time the U.A.E. region appears to have consisted of a network of permanent settlements inherited from its early history. Arab historians in the eighth century mention Ras al Khaima (then called Julfar) as a port used by the Caliphs of Baghdad as a base for their entry into Oman.

By the tenth century the port had become an outlet for trade from Al Ain, and for a while the northern parts of the Emirates fell under the control of the Hawala tribe, whose domain stretched into Oman. The tribe lost its command of the Emirates early in the sixteenth century when the entire Gulf area first came within the orbit of spreading European power.

To European traders the Gulf area was increasingly important because it provided a vital link between the sea route to India and the Far East and the overland route to Europe via Basra. The first Europeans to invade the Gulf were the Portuguese, but they soon lost their ascendancy to the French, Dutch and British, all of whom were struggling for control of the region. By the middle of the eighteenth century the British emerged with practically unchallenged supremacy among the European powers in the Gulf. Eventually in 1820 a General Treaty was concluded between Great Britain and the Arab tribes of the Gulf, followed in 1853 by a Treaty of Maritime Peace in Perpetuity.

It is only comparatively recently that the Gulf region has been able to free itself fully from colonial power, for it was not until the 1960s that the British Government announced a total withdrawal of its forces. Kuwait, Bahrain, Qatar and the U.A.E. became independent countries. Just at the same time the Gulf states were beginning to exploit the huge reservoir of oil lying beneath their territories. Within a few years, largely because of their new oil wealth, the Gulf countries had begun to have a powerful influence on world events.

Today foreigners outnumber the indigenous population of the Gulf area – in the U.A.E. the ratio is as great as four to one. Silverwork is more in demand than any other traditional craft, and shops which sell it have opened in all the major cities in the region. They display original pieces, either obtained from rural areas or imported from such countries as Pakistan or India, or from the European markets.

Silversmiths from different areas on the Gulf littoral work in Kuwait and Bahrain; Pakistani and Indian smiths work in the U.A.E. So one may, for example, find typically Iraqi work with a Bahraini signature. The movement of the tribes and the strength of traditional Islam are also reasons for the great mixture of silverwork to be found in the Gulf area. Omani, Yemeni and Saudi pieces are widely distributed there.

The new oil wealth has stimulated a demand for gold, and many shops have opened which sell gold pieces in imitation or traditional silverwork. These are mostly brought into the Gulf states from Syria, Pakistan and India.

The growing interest in silverwork has prompted some states to support their museums by purchasing old silver. The Al Ain Museum in Abu Dhabi, for example, contains Bedouin jewellery, daggers and other pieces, mostly obtained from the Buraimi and Omani areas.

ARAB AND ISLAMIC SILVER

This fascinating Omani hairdress (right) *is also found in Abu Dhabi and holds the* chaddar *in place. It is known as a* burkhoh *and is made of dark violet material decorated with imitation gilded coins.* Below and bottom right: *Decorative Yemeni hair ornaments.*

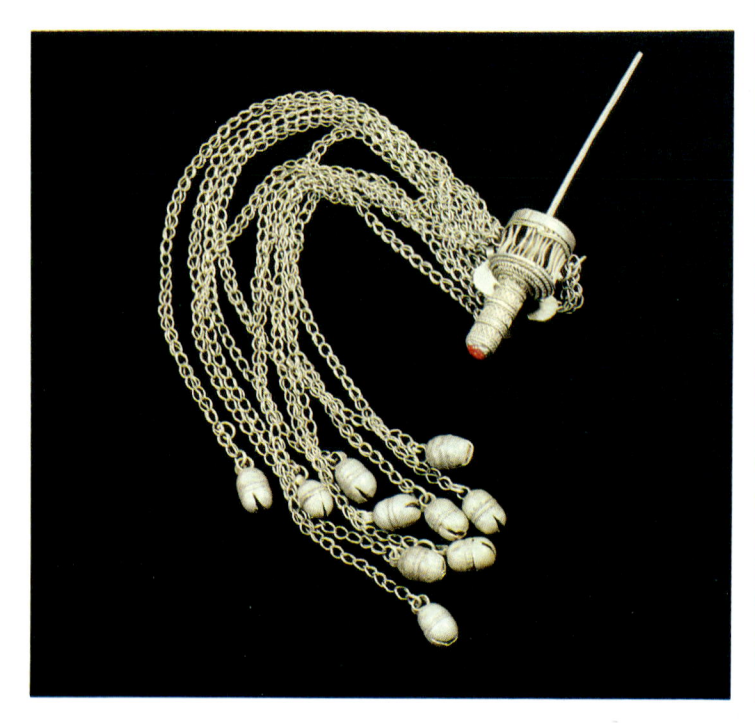

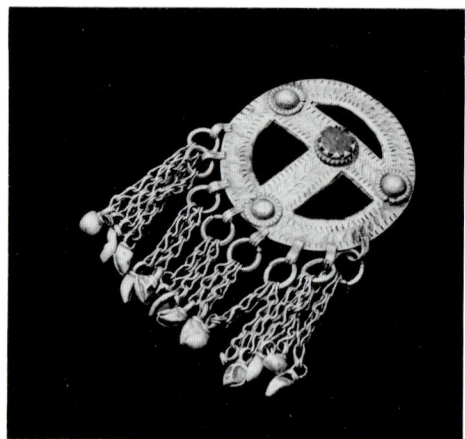

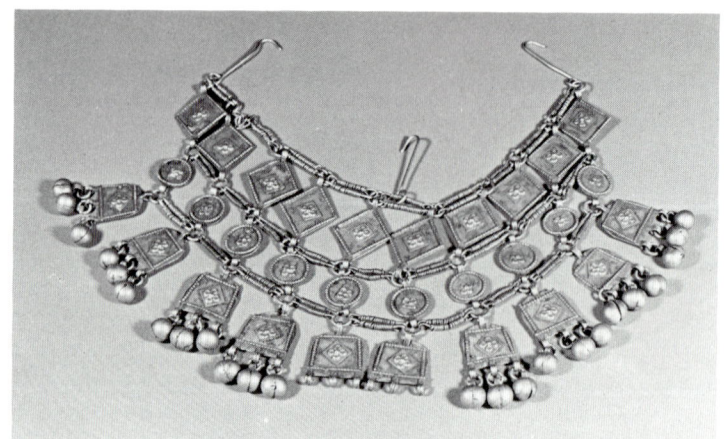

Above: *Worn to hold the hair in place, this Omani decoration is inlaid with silver balls and a central red plastic seal.*

THE ARABIAN PENINSULA

These different patterns of Omani earrings (below) *represent various types of workmanship.* Below centre: *This hair ornament, or* iklil *and two bracelets come from Yemen. The various panel shapes are inlaid with agate and coral.*

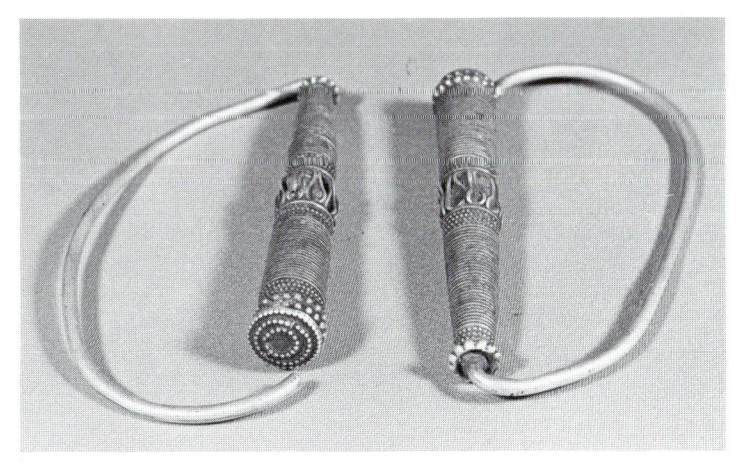

These Omani earrings (above) *have openwork, granulation, and silver wire decoration. The bodies are hollow but still heavy. This Omani hairdress* (above right) *is to hold a veil in place: as in some Indian and Pakistani jewellery, chains are sometimes the main decorative item.*

ARAB AND ISLAMIC SILVER

This Yemeni triangular piece (above) *is inlaid with coral and red agate with bell-shaped pendants and the main piece of the Yemeni necklace* (right) *is also inlaid with three red agate stones.*

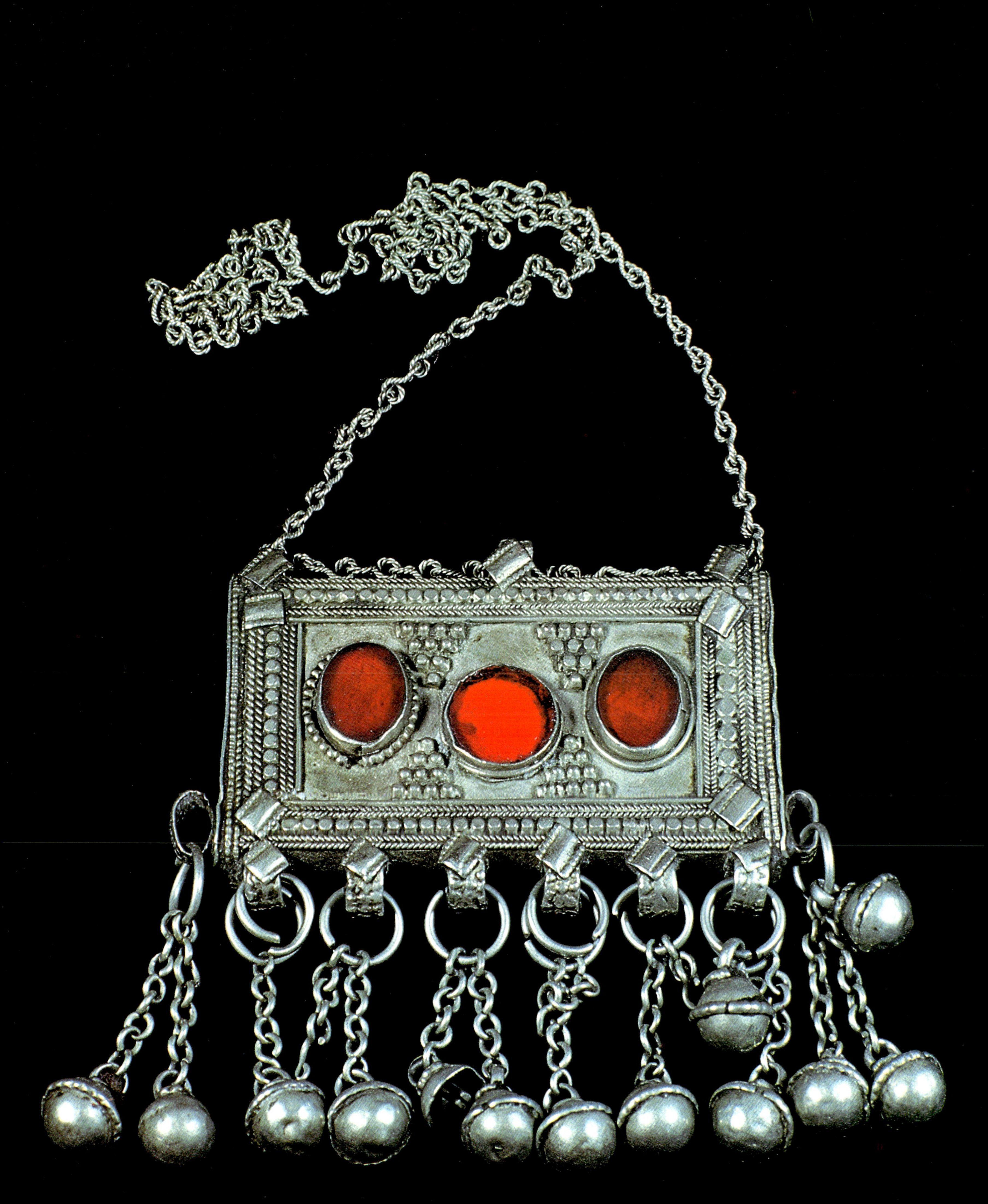

ARAB AND ISLAMIC SILVER

Reminiscent of Algerian workmanship, this Yemeni necklace (right) *is decorated with coral and with silver dome-shaped studs. Another popular style of Yemeni necklace is shown* (above).

THE ARABIAN PENINSULA

This typical Omani necklace (left) has bell-shaped pendants and is inlaid with embossed copper. **Below:** *The main body of this Omani composition is finished with pyramidical silver shots and this design probably came from Greece. Alexander's army and his general, Nearchos, explored the Gulf and some Etruscan and Cypriot jewellery displays exactly this pattern employed in brooches, pendants and rings.*

Left: *Red plastic and red wooden beads ornament this Omani necklace.*

99

ARAB AND ISLAMIC SILVER

This impressive Yemeni necklace (above) consists of beautifully balanced and proportioned panels with silver shapes soldered on to a plaited chain. Right: Unusually, this heavy Omani necklace has no particular focus.

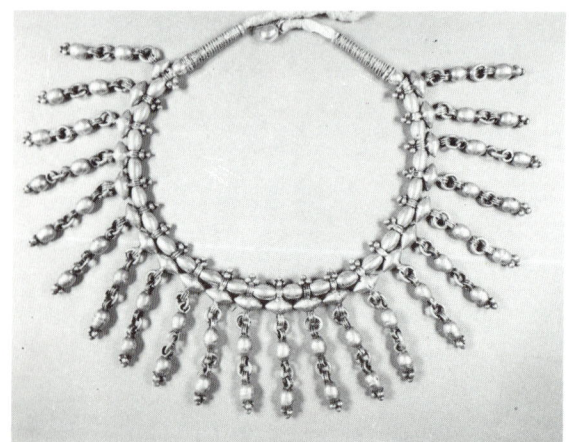

Above: *A typical example of a Bedouin Yemeni necklace, which is nevertheless extremely ornate, with silver pieces fixed to material and displaying pendants, coins and balls. The ornate Yemeni necklace (left) has a large crescent as a medullion disc which is heavily granulated with solid balls and stippled decoration.*

ARAB AND ISLAMIC SILVER

Above: *The heavy silver connecting beads are angular with silver wire twisted round each, characteristic of Yemeni jewellery. This delicate Yemeni work (right), known as* shairiyah *creates a necklace of hundreds of small pieces of silver sewn on to material with no space between them, looking like chain mail.*

THE ARABIAN PENINSULA

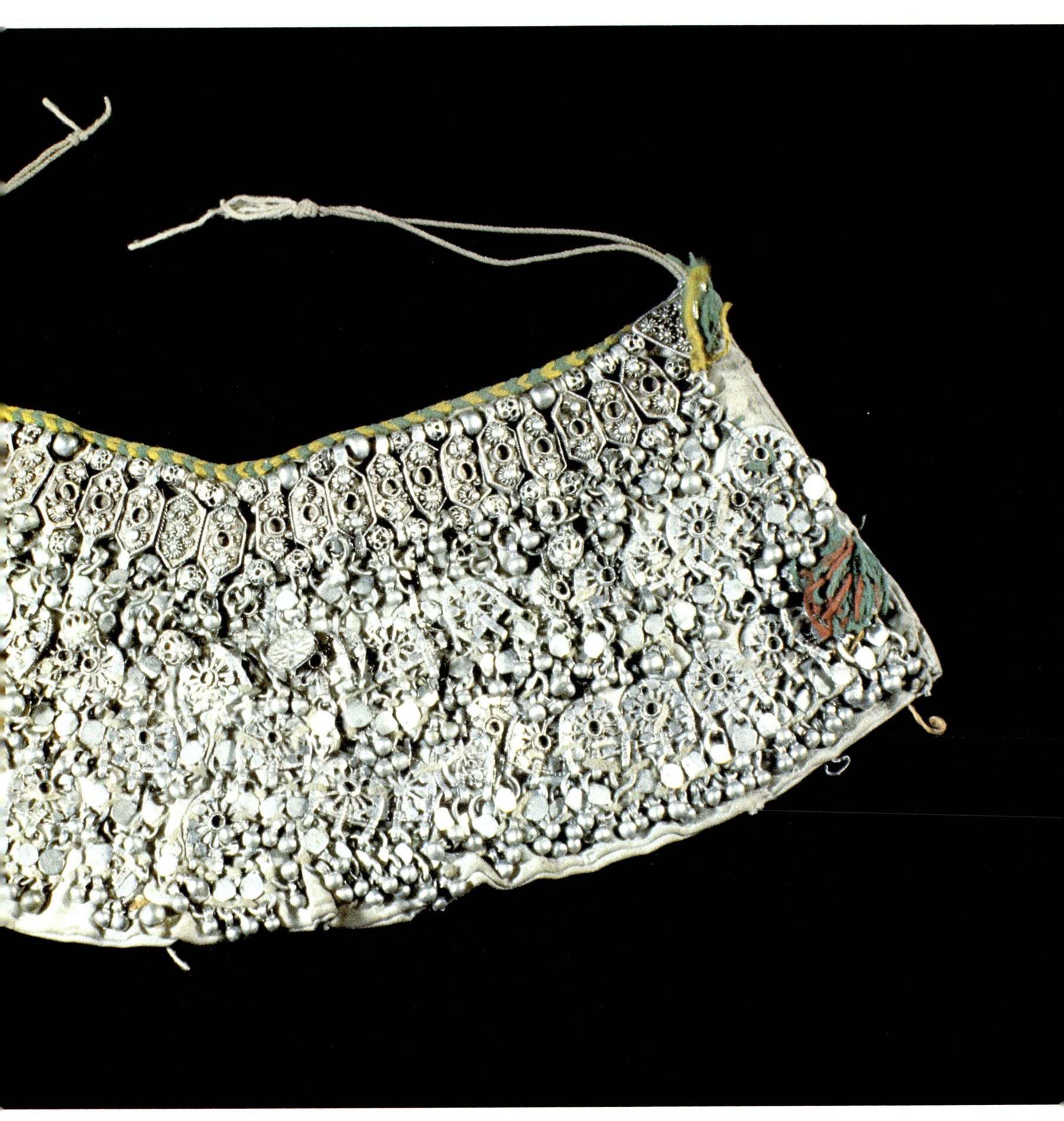

ARAB AND ISLAMIC SILVER

104

THE ARABIAN PENINSULA

The main four panels of this Yemeni necklace (top) *are inlaid with red agate. The rectangular panels show silver and green beads. Another Yemeni necklace* (above right) *consists of similar panels which are inlaid with silver balls, whereas the chain of the final example* (above left) *has silver and coral beads. Opposite: Coral, amber and agate are all more remarkable in this Yemeni necklace than the silverwork and are threaded on rope.*

ARAB AND ISLAMIC SILVER

The main part of these two Omani pieces (top left) are triangular, inlaid with copper and decorated with coral and beads. Top right: *These triangular pieces were originally used as head-dresses but are now normally attached to chains and thus converted into necklaces. The pendant in this Omani necklace (above left)* is a silver disc which is simply chased and decorated with Arabic calligraphy. Above right: *Three silver hollow panels are joined by light silver balls and bell-shaped pendants in this beautiful Yemeni necklace.*

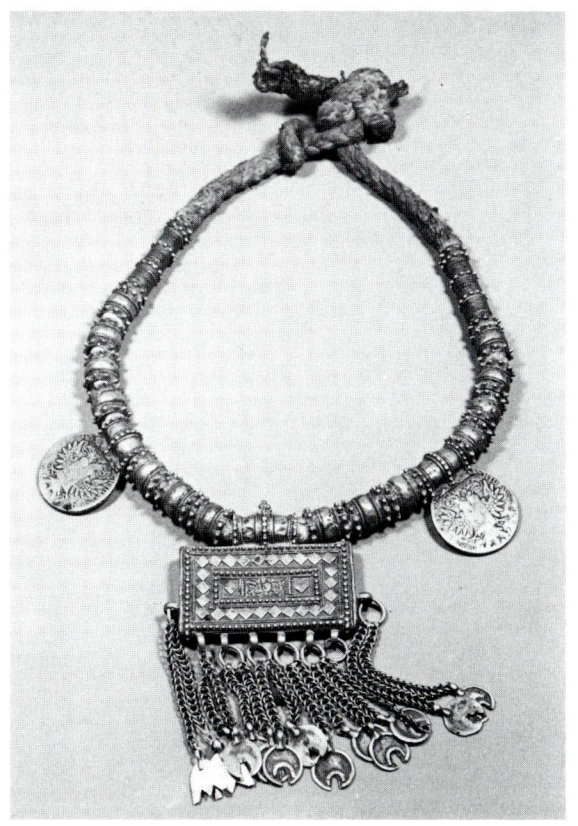

THE ARABIN PENINSULA

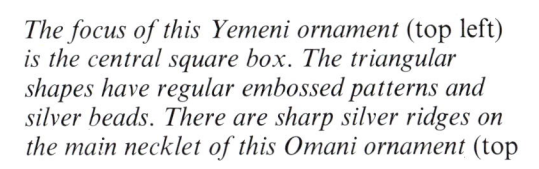

The focus of this Yemeni ornament (top left) *is the central square box. The triangular shapes have regular embossed patterns and silver beads. There are sharp silver ridges on the main necklet of this Omani ornament* (top right) *with two coins (thalers) and an amuletic box with granulation work edged with small silver shots. Above right and left: Both sides of a typically Omani necklace in which coins, both genuine and replica, are set.*

ARAB AND ISLAMIC SILVER

The main decorative devices on this Yemeni necklace (right) are granulation and hollow but heavy silver balls. Another Yemeni necklace (below) displays various shapes and small bell-shaped pendants.

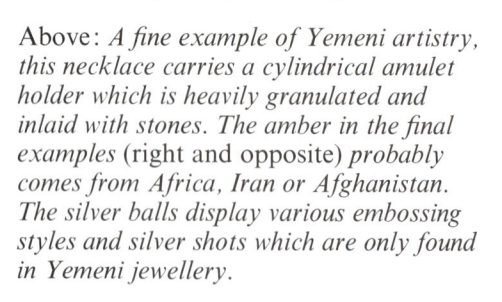

Above: A fine example of Yemeni artistry, this necklace carries a cylindrical amulet holder which is heavily granulated and inlaid with stones. The amber in the final examples (right and opposite) probably comes from Africa, Iran or Afghanistan. The silver balls display various embossing styles and silver shots which are only found in Yemeni jewellery.

THE ARABIAN PENINSULA

ARAB AND ISLAMIC SILVER

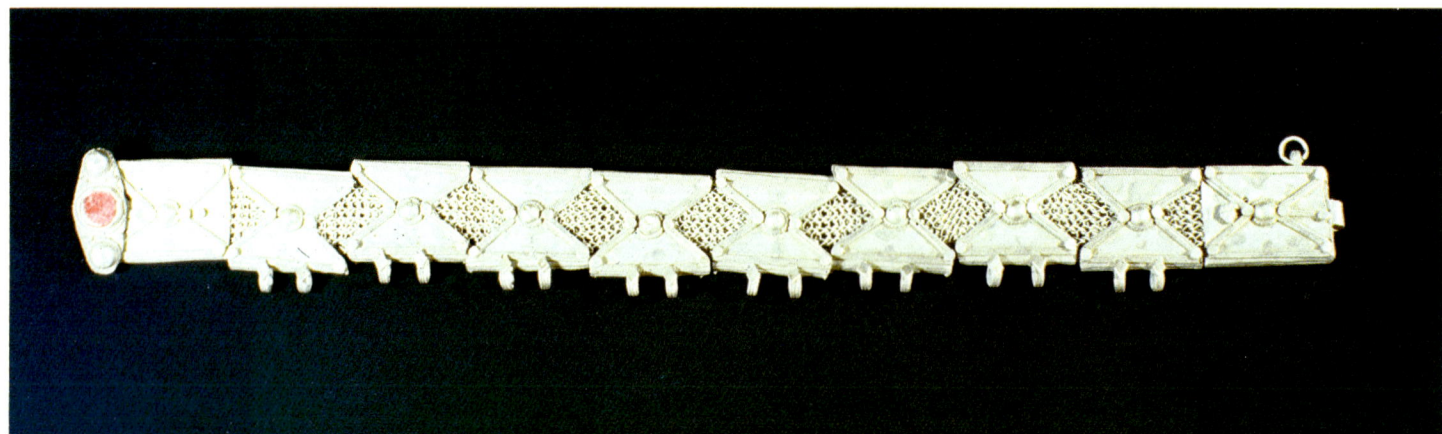

This Yemeni breast decoration (top) is divided by twisted silver wire into four parts, each of which is decorated with a dome shape ended with a pyramidical composition. In this style of Yemeni belt (above), regular panels inlaid with silver balls alternate with chains.

THE ARABIAN PENINSULA

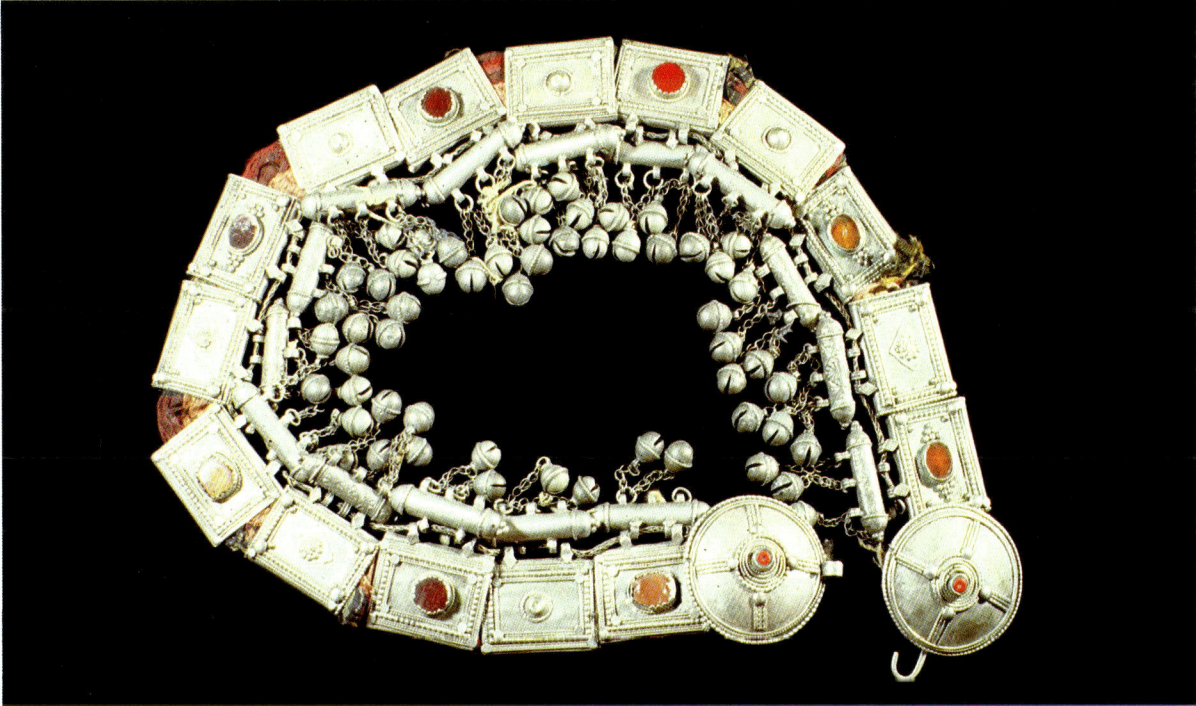

Top: *Boxes, arrow and circular shapes, links and a chain form this Omani belt. This heavy Yemeni belt* (above) *is finished with cylinders and bells which jingle when dancing or walking.* Left: *Another Yemeni belt with its panels, openwork and repetition of floral design and various sizes of hollow balls is characteristic of the nomadic style.*

111

ARAB AND ISLAMIC SILVER

THE ARABIAN PENINSULA

In these Omani gilded silver daggers (left and overleaf), *the ornamental use of silver and of leather is equally impressive.*

ARAB AND ISLAMIC SILVER

THE ARABIAN PENINSULA

ARAB AND ISLAMIC SILVER

A complicatedly shaped Yemeni dagger (above) displays deep granulation and openwork and has a monumental end with an Arabic inscription on the handle which is also inlaid with two coins. Gilded and decorated with engraved openwork, embossing and Arabic calligraphy, this belt (above right) displays excellent Yemeni workmanship. The Yemeni belt (below right) supports an ornately granulated khanjar *which has various amulets inlaid with coral, agate and beads. The handle of this Omani dagger (below) is wooden with silver flower decoration; the big rings have both decorative and practical roles.*

116

THE ARABIAN PENINSULA

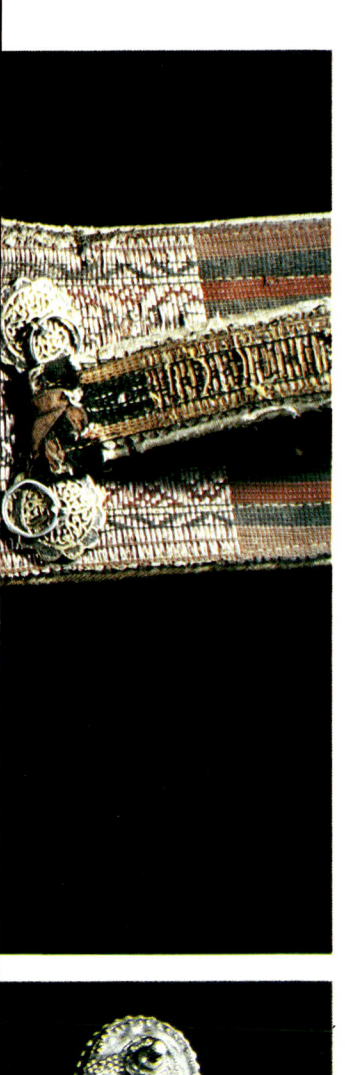

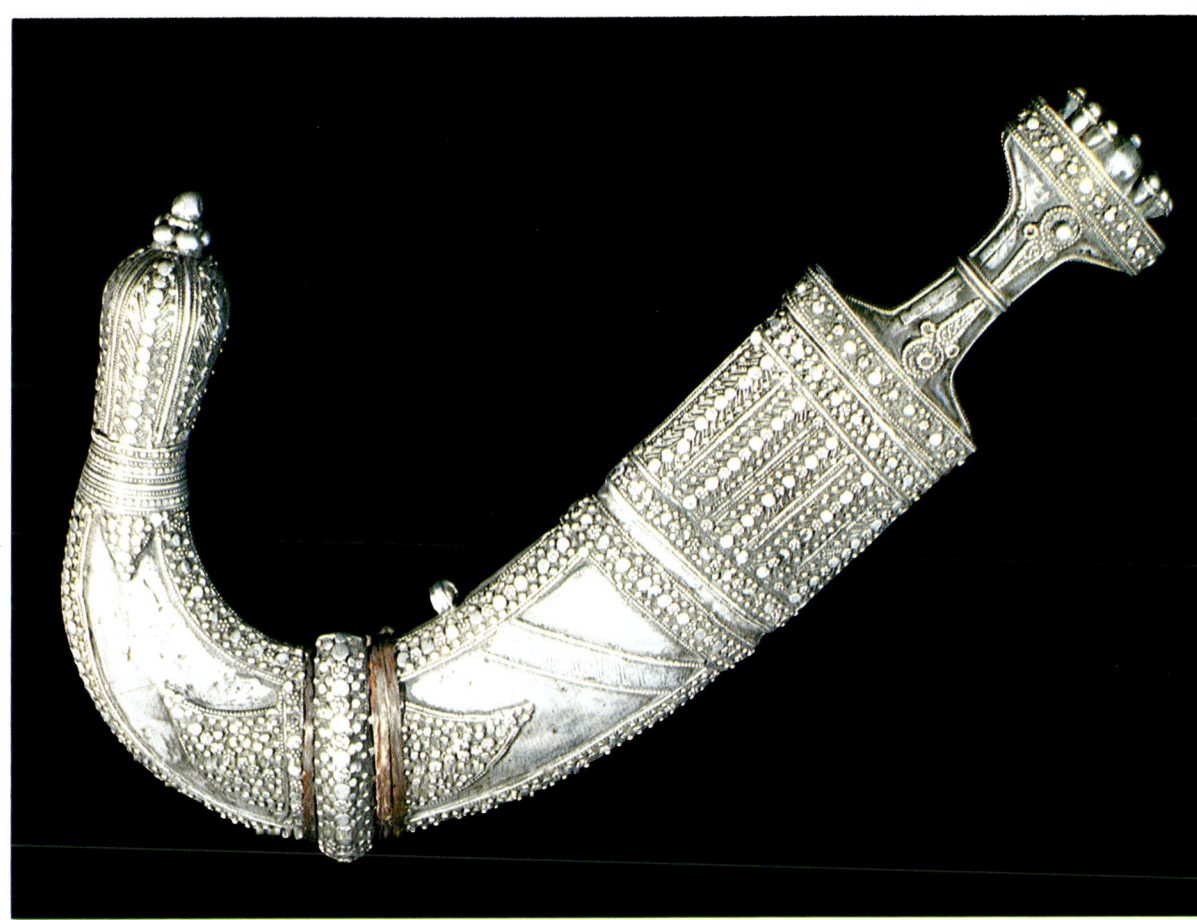

(Above) *The ornate Yemeni dagger represents a particular type which is only found in southern Arabia.*

117

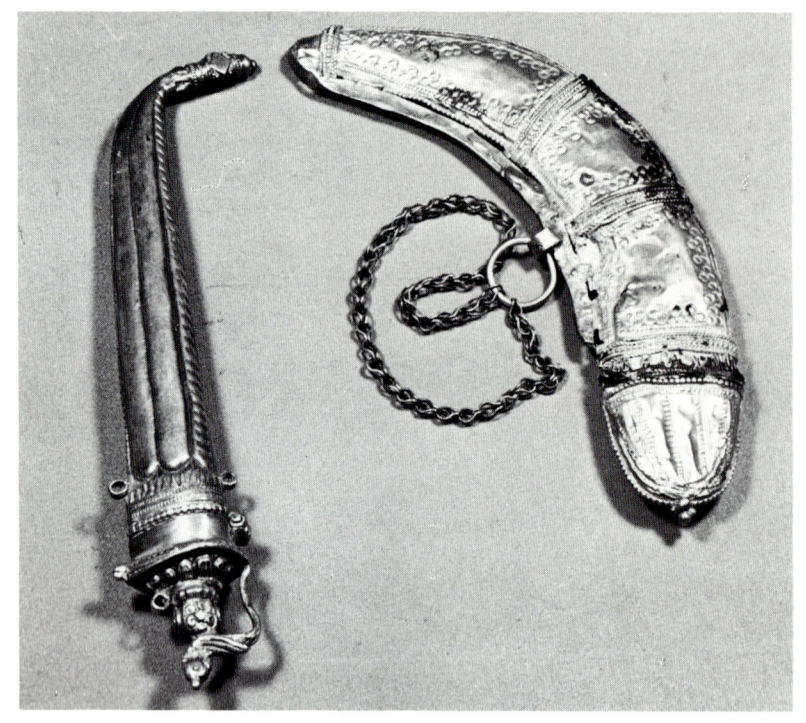

ARAB AND ISLAMIC SILVER

The Arabic inscription on this Yemeni khanjar or dagger (above left) reads "malboos al-hana" which means "enjoy wearing it". Top right: *Behind his khanjar, a Yemeni will often also wear a knife in an ornately decorated sheath.*

118

THE ARABIAN PENINSULA

Opposite: *These two examples of Omani powder flasks or* talahiq *open at the top and hold gunpowder. They are worn hanging on a strap across a man's back. The lever to the right of each flask releases the powder.*

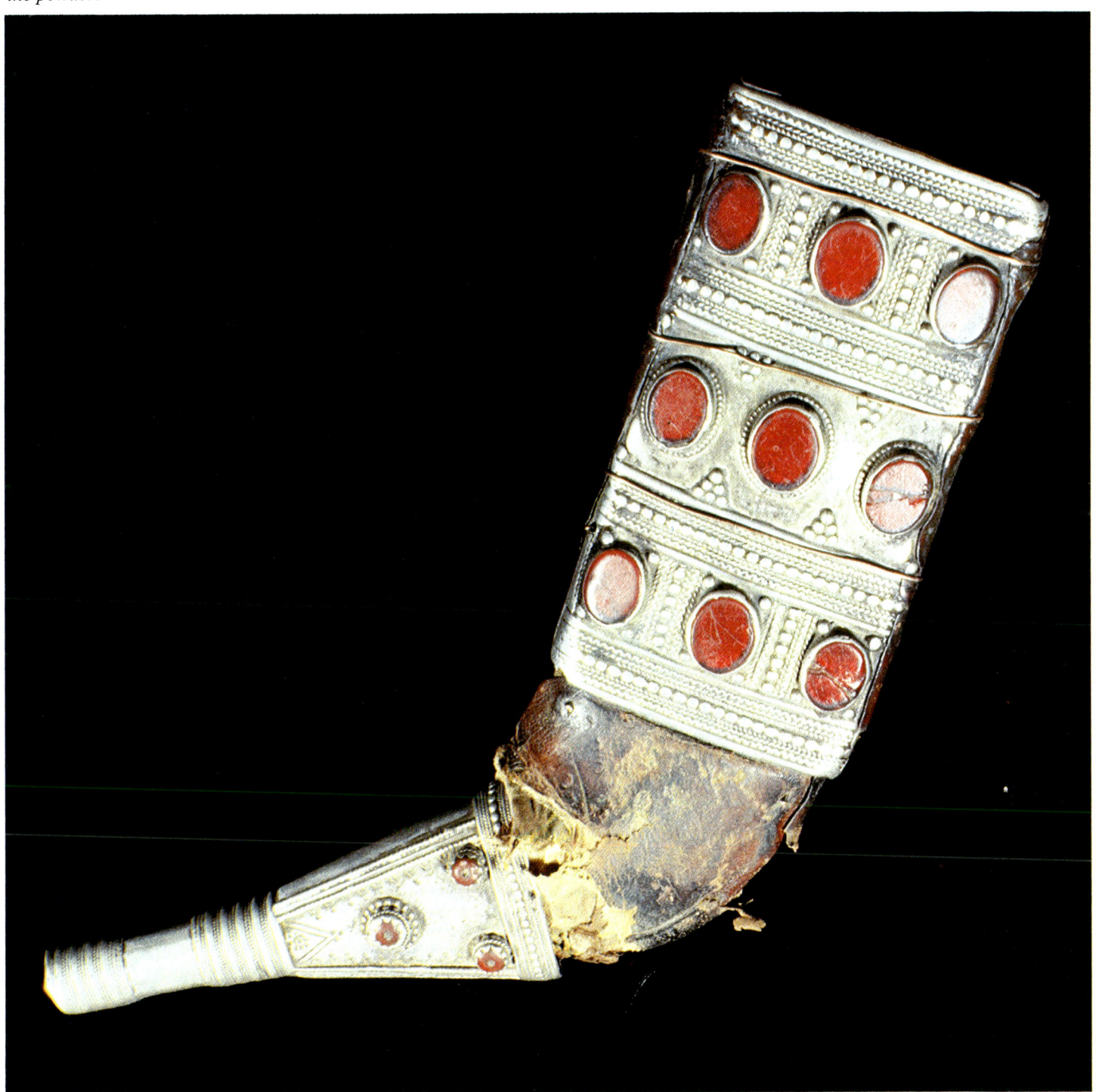

Opposite bottom: *Groups of pyramidical balls and wire edging are typical of both Yemeni and Omani silverwork. This Yemeni dagger sheath (above) is inlaid with agate and granulated.*

ARAB AND ISLAMIC SILVER

These Yemeni bracelets for children (above) *are simply embossed: one is inlaid with an Ottoman coin and the other has a large recessed agate. Some of these hollow Yemeni bracelets* (bottom) *have small stones or beads inserted inside them so that when a woman wears them they make a musical sound. Two large Omani bracelets* (below) *display repoussé work and floral designs.*

Above: *These Yemeni rings of agate, silver and copper display various shapes and decorative designs.* Below: *Three patterns of Omani bracelets, two of which have repoussé and thin wire ornamentation. The middle one is hollow with jagged edges.*

ARAB AND ISLAMIC SILVER

THE ARABIAN PENINSULA

Some Omanis wear as many as ten of these bracelets (left) *which give a remarkable decorative effect, and some of these have now been covered in gold. Some African influence is evident in the design of these two hollow Yemeni bracelets* (above) *which are granulated and decorated with coins found in the locality.*

ARAB AND ISLAMIC SILVER

Yemeni silver anklets (top) *display typical dome shapes.* Above: *The applicators form part of these Omani* kohl *containers. Silversmiths in the United Arab Emirates are normally expatriates from India and Pakistan who create such modern silver sculptures of ancient ships* (opposite) *and other objects and sell them in* suqs.

124

THE ARABIAN PENINSULA

ARAB AND ISLAMIC SILVER

Levant, Mesopotamia, Persia, Turkey and Caucasia

THE LEVANT, MESOPOTAMIA, PERSIA, TURKEY AND CAUCASIA

ARAB AND ISLAMIC SILVER

Jordan was only defined as an independent state in the twentieth century, but Trans-Jordan, the area that runs on both sides of the Jordan River, was the site of many small city states, such as Gilead, Ammon, Moab and Edom, in the distant past. It was variously ruled by the larger kingdoms of Mesopotamia which, as their influence expanded, consolidated the first recorded empires. The Assyrians, the Chaldeans and the Persians were in turn dominant until the Seleucids established a firm hold in the third century BC. They succeeded Alexander the Great, who had made the city of Ammon one of the Decapolis, the league of ten Greek cities. The southern part of the area was ruled by the Ptolemies of Egypt.

By the first century AD Trans-Jordan had become an Arab area, and the Nabataeans, who had established their capital at Petra some two hundred years before, extended their control north to Damascus, east to the Euphrates and west into Sinai. This was a strictly Arab empire. Roman armies forced the Nabataeans to recede, and in 105–106 AD Petra was incorporated into the Roman empire. The road to the East was thus opened, and the Romans marched on to the battlefields of Parthia.

While the Roman and Persian empires confronted each other, Arab traders began to make regular commercial expeditions from the Peninsula northward to Syria and Trans-Jordan, establishing camel trails, which are still mostly in existence and followed by the Bedouin today.

The holy city of Jerusalem, to which early followers of Mohammed turned to pray, was in Trans-Jordan, and was the original sacred city of Islam. The city remains as precious to Muslims as it does to Christians and Jews.

Jordan was absorbed into the early Caliphate of the Ummayads and stayed within the orbit of the Islamic empire. Its essentially Arab population displays the three fundamental divisions typical of Arab societies – the Bedouin, the villagers and the town-dwellers. The life of the villagers revolves around the oases; they are the suppliers of agricultural produce to Bedouin and city folk. Some of them are semi-nomads, whose attitudes are still linked closely with those of the Bedouin or tent dwellers. The city dweller has learned a more complex way of life, with higher cultural expectations and wider artistic interests.

Metalworking is prolific on the east

Decorated with mother of pearl, this Palestinian brooch (above) is also filigreed and engraved.

side of the Jordan River, where village craftsmen produce vases, coffee pots, pans, trays, pitchers, knives and all the accoutrements demanded by both the desert and the city dweller. Even the most basic objects are worked to a skilled decorative level with the use of calligraphic and arabesque patterns. One of the features of Jordanian jewellery is the inlaying of stones in earrings, bracelets, anklets, rings and necklaces.

Silversmiths are concentrated in cities like Amman, where workshops are established. The use of symbolism is common, but traditional Islamic features are also incorporated. Sea shells and mother of pearl are often combined with religious and floral motifs to create an original geometric design. These appear in craft objects made of wood as well as silver. Occasionally Christian patterns blend unobtrusively with these Islamic themes, and in music and art, no less than handicrafts, the richness of the Jordanian cultural heritage is evident.

In Palestine there is a very mixed population, including various religious and ethnic groups established there over centuries. The Canaanites, who were the earliest inhabitants of the area, also settled in Syria, Lebanon and Jordan, forming part of the Semitic migration from the Arabian Peninsula in the fourth millennium BC. Many different invaders followed: Jews, Assyrians, Babylonians, Greeks, Romans and Christian crusaders. Islam reached Palestine in the seventh century, and the region has maintained its Arab-Islamic flavour ever since.

Palestine reflects Arab tradition in many of her cultural features, but individual characteristics are apparent in her literature, her music, her plastic and applied art, as well as in her handicrafts. Palestinian towns are renowned for particular crafts: Al-Nassira, Nabuls and Gaza are famous for their textiles, Al-Khalil for its glassworks, Bethlehem for its mother of pearl and Jerusalem for its pottery and olive wood.

Metalworking occurs in most major towns and villages. Ya'afa, Akka and Al-Nassira are famous centres for copperworking, and Al-Ramla, Al-Khalil, Gaza and Nabuls for earthenware. Palestinian jewellery made of precious metals shares many common features with that of Syria, Lebanon and Jordan, in form, function and often in name as well. The best known silverwork centres are in Jerusalem, Nabuls, Bir al-Saba'a and Al-Khalil. Variations in techniques and design are difficult to detect. Palestine is famed for its weaponry; daggers, swords and belts are inlaid and decorated with Arab and Islamic patterns and with semi-precious stones. Mother of pearl and ivory are also incorporated, resulting in impressive and intricate compositions.

Many pilgrims and tourists visit Palestine, which is the Holy Land for three major religions: Islam, Judaism and Christianity. They demand souvenirs from such places as Bethlehem and

Jerusalem. These are often silverwork with architectural images on them. The craftsmen compete to attract customers; a rivalry which has stimulated the workshops, making Palestinian handicrafts one of the country's main sources of revenue.

The first inhabitants of Lebanon, the Canaanites, settled between the White Mountain and the sea in 3,500 BC. They established fishing and agricultural communities, which later developed into advanced city states with laws, traders and craftsmen. The Canaanites came from Arabia, but probably originated in Magan, today's Oman.

The Princes of the Canaanite states styled themselves "Sons of Ra." Their subjects excelled at weaving silk and dyeing cloth. The Greeks called them "Phoenicians," the men of the purple cloth. The Phoenicians sailed as far north as the English Channel, and the city states were established all round the Mediterranean littoral. The most famous were Berytus (Beirut), Sidon, Tyre and Tripoli.

Phoenicia emerges from the region of legend into the light of history in the early third millennium BC, when Egyptian kings established commercial relations for the sake of the cedar wood of Lebanon, which they wanted for shipbuilding. The Phoenicians also exported grain, fruit and fish to Egypt. In addition to the distributing trades, they engaged busily in all kinds of industries – purple-dyeing, textile weaving, metalwork, glasswork, ivory carving, building and mining. They were not inventors and did not originate these arts and industries, but they developed them with a high degree of skill and spread knowledge of them around the world. Phoenician artists similarly did not invent any new style of their own but were extraordinarily adept at borrowing subjects and designs from neighbouring countries, such as Egypt and Syria. Engraved vessels of bronze, gold and silver, adorned with gems, are amongst their most common surviving products; Egyptian decorative elements are frequently conspicuous.

Objects found in the tombs of the Pharaohs reflect this energetic interaction. Greek culture too is steeped in Phoenician influence, and Homer's *Iliad* is full of praise for Phoenician weaving and metallurgy. Only after Rome destroyed Carthage did the Phoenicians' power decline; their skills and love of adventure remain recognisable in the Lebanese of today. The country has always welcomed new challenges, ideas and peoples. Islamic rule was never as powerful there as in other Middle Eastern regions, but Arabic and Islamic culture was, and is, strongly influential and evidence of Islamic traditions can be seen in most cities. Because it has been urbanised for so long, Lebanon has no tribal history and no Bedouin population.

Before 1918 the term 'Syria' was rather loosely applied to the whole of the territory forming the modern states of Syria, Lebanon, Palestine and Jordan. To the Ottomans as to the Romans, Syria stretched from the Euphrates to the Mediterranean, and from Sinai to the hills of southern Turkey, with Palestine as a smaller province within this wide territory. From early times until the end of the Middle Ages, there was a flow of traffic east and west which raised a number of Syrian cities and ports to the rank of international markets.

Syria has experienced successive waves of Semitic immigration – the Canaanites and Phoenicians in the third millennium BC, the Hebrews and Aramaeans in the second and a constant flow of tribes coming from the Arabian Peninsula. Before Rome assumed control of Syria in the first century BC, the Egyptians, the Assyrians, the Hittites and the Persians and the Macedonian Greeks all left their mark. Damascus is claimed to be the oldest capital city in the world, having been continuously inhabited since about 2000 BC; but Aleppo may be even older.

Immediately prior to the coming of Islam, Syria was predominantly Arab with a few Greek and Christian settlements in Damascus, Antioch and Hama. When the first followers of Mohammed emerged from the Arabian Peninsula, they naturally chose to establish their first centre in Syria, which was inhabited by their kinsmen. The new faith was quickly accepted and the Ummayad Caliphs made their capital in the securely Arab city of Damascus. Within a few years they ruled Iraq, and thus encountered Persian Art and a culture which was to provide an inspiration and foundation for their own.

The Ummayad style was the first Islamic school of art which developed when the Caliphs moved their capital from Kufa. New towns were built, containing vast palaces and mosques, numerous examples of which are still in existence – the Dome of the Rock in Jerusalem, the splendid Ummayad mosque in Damascus, the Sidi Okba at Kairouan in Tunisia, the Jama Zeituna in Tunis itself, Mshattah and Kharbat al-Mafjar in Syria and many others.

A feature of the Ummayad style is the use of frescoes, mosaics and plaster decoration. Another art form which quickly became popular under the Caliphs was the illumination of manuscripts. Very little is known of the minor arts of this period, although there is evidence of engraving on wood and of metal vessels with animal and floral motifs.

Syria's lasting contribution to Islamic Art was made in the field of metalwork and was known as Damascene. This is an intricate inlaying of gold and silver on to baser metal in a complicated interwoven design which covers the entire piece. This style was widely adopted in many Islamic countries and the unique combination of design, patterns and calligraphy is still regarded as the epitome of Islamic craftsmanship.

The cultural heritage of Iraq is strongly Islamic, and its craftsmen are among the finest. Mosul became one of the main centres for metalwork in Islam, and the rule of the Abbasid Caliphate heralded one of the richest periods of Islamic culture. Iraq has remained a seat of learning in the Arab world; her intellectual and creative activities continue to flourish. The first educational academy was established at Tell Harmal in Ur, where literature, mathematics and law were studied. The Assyrian King Ashur-nasir-pal's library was one of the largest in antiquity.

Iraq adopted Islam within a decade, a remarkably swift conversion in a country which for centuries had remained culturally aloof from the other great powers of the ancient world, despite constant invasions and infiltration. Before 3000 BC, the Sumerians had established a complex civilisation at the head of the Arabian Gulf, where a number of city states developed. Cities like Eridu, Uruk, Ur, Kish and Lagash were founded. The Akkadians, the Amorites, the Hittites, and the Assyrians ruled the area. Under Nebuchadnezzar (604–562 BC) Iraq included much of the Fertile Crescent, until it was conquered by the Persians, who seized Babylon in 539–538 BC. The Greeks, Romans and Sassanians all held sway there at different periods.

Under the rule of the Sassanian Persians, Ctesiphon became the capital and great architecture emerged, which was later to be one of the models for the

ARAB AND ISLAMIC SILVER

Islamic style. Today, only the arch of Ctesiphon remains. The Sassanians, who excelled in metalwork, ruled until the coming of Islam. With the rise of the Abbasids, Iraqi culture flourished, using knowledge acquired from the Sassanians and Ummayads to create high standards of craftmanship, which rivalled the art forms of Byzantium, Rome and Greece.

As part of that tradition, the first Islamic University *Dar-Al-Hikma*, the House of Wisdom, was founded, where the classics were translated into Arabic and mathematics and the arts were taught and studied. Baghdad became the cultural centre of the Islamic world. The Caliph attracted the services of craftsmen and builders from many countries, and a period of unparalleled enlightenment began.

Baghdad soon developed into a great emporium of trade and a political centre of vast importance too. The Abbasid Caliphate brought to Iraq a splendid prosperity, derived from thriving agriculture and industry and from the lucrative trade between India and the Mediterranean.

Between the eighth and ninth centuries, towards the end of the reign of Ma'mun, beautiful palaces, gardens and mosques were built, especially in Baghdad and Samara'a. The famous mosque of Samara'a with its spiral minarets, and the Al Mansur mosque in Baghdad, are obvious examples. Another fine architectural achievement was the Palace of Jawsaq in Samara'a. Frescoes and calligraphic decorative motifs abounded, and these features were copied in Syria, Iran, North Africa and Andalusia. Pottery with a fine lustre finish, which made it shine like precious metal, was popular. The arts of book binding and the illumination of manuscripts flourished; the Caliphs possessed beautiful editions of the Quran and other religious texts.

Even Mediaeval Europe was influenced by these endeavours. Exchanges between El-Raschid and the Christian emperor Charlemagne were important culturally, for his Carolingian School drew heavily on Abbasid themes.

The decline of the Abbasids brought strife again and internal conflict, and the Seljuk Turks succeeded as the caretakers of Islam. Their influence on the city of Baghdad was to be lasting. Under a further brief spell of Abbasid rule Iraq enjoyed a short-lived renaissance, and at the beginning of the thirteenth century, under the Beni-Zenki dynasty, Mosul became the main centre of metalwork. The special technique of inlaying gold and silver developed there. Master craftsmen who emigrated to Aleppo, Cairo and Damascus before the Mongol hordes set up new centres of metalwork in those cities. When Ghenghis Khan's grandson Hulaku captured Baghdad in 1258 with huge Mongol forces, Iraq became a frontier province, bereft of all its former wealth and splendour and much neglected by its rulers. Artists and craftsmen fled to Egypt and it was not until the arrival of the Ottomans that

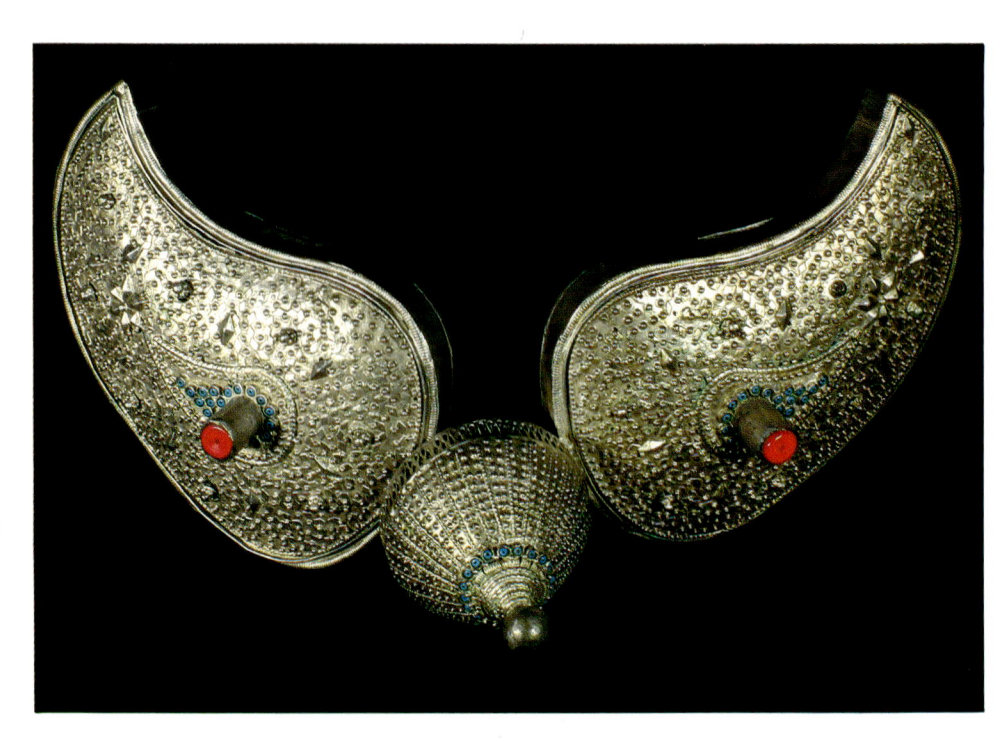

Above: *A buckle from northern Iraq consists of two symmetrical pieces. An Iraqi coffee pot* (below) *demonstrates niello work on the body and lid.*

Iraq regained internal stability.

Iraq is famous for its niello on silverwork, fine filigree and granulation. Its rich historical heritage and varied population are reflected in all its arts and crafts. Vestiges of Caucasian, Turkomanian, Persian and other styles are all still in evidence. Some of the more traditional Bedouin patterns may have originated in the ancient kingdom of Ur, for silver and gold mines existed in the Kurdistan hills and the craftsmen there developed smithing skills in very early times.

Ethnically the Kurds are of mixed race and have affiliations with the Aryans, Iberians, Georgians and Armenians. They speak an Indo-European language with three dialects. The tribes spread across five modern boundaries – those of Syria, Turkey, Iran, Iraq and the U.S.S.R. – but have a strong sense of national self-awareness and cultural and linguistic unity.

Their history has been one of constant conquest and subjugation by others; by local tribes in the seventh century, by the Mongols and Seljuks in the eleventh century and by the Turks until the collapse of the Ottoman empire. The Kurds were among the first people to be ruled by the early Caliphate, and they adopted and assimilated the Islamic creed into their own culture. They were always famous for their fighting skills. One of the legendary warriors in the days of the Crusades was the Kurdish Salah El-Din (Saladin) whose name is as renowned as that of Haroun El-Raschid.

Then after World War I their lands were divided between Syria, Turkey, Iran and Iraq. Ever since the Kurds' harsh mountainous territory was first called Kurdistan in the twelfth century, they have persistently struggled for self-determination. They are a proud, hardy people whose links with the past are evident in their art and splendid metalwork. Their weaponry, belts and buckles are particularly remarkable. Their jewellery is tribal and traditionally associated with the idea of transportable wealth. The Kurds in northern Iraq have developed a rich diversity of patterns and designs, which make this area an important centre for silverwork.

Iran or Persia is a country whose past glories are a source of pride to its inhabitants, for although ethnically modern Iranians have few links with their early ancestors, a conscious affinity with the ancient cultures of the Achaemenids and Sassanians persists.

Already by the fifth millennium BC, the earliest unpainted pottery gave way to pottery decorated with geometric motifs. Throughout the country there was a wide assortment of painted pottery, varying in material from district to district and as distinctive in texture, colour and design as the relatively modern Persian carpets from both tribal areas and the cities. Copper was worked at a very early date in Iran, as revealed in the lowest levels of Sialk near Kashan. Probably as early as 3000 BC it was being cast in open moulds. With the dawning

Niello

Above: *Nielloed well-known Iraqi subjects and landscapes appear on this Iraqi buckle.*

The niello technique has been used for centuries in many parts of the world. The word "niello" is derived from the Latin "nigellus" or "niger", meaning black. The effect is achieved by engraving a design on to a piece of precious metal and filling the grooves with a finely pound mixture of silver, copper, lead and sulphur. The mixture is then fired and the end product polished to a smooth surface.

It was an early form of enamelling and is one of the oldest decorative methods. The ancient Egyptians and Byzantine artists practised it, and the method was used in very old Yemeni weaponry and jewellery. For a while the technique was lost in Europe, until the Italian goldsmith Maso Finiguerra revived it and gave it its name.

It was common from the Middle Ages until the period of Art Nouveau, and although it has virtually disappeared from modern European silverwork, it is still prominent in Asia and the Far East. It is particularly popular in Iraq and Persia, where it was introduced by the Sassanians. They used niello to accentuate silver decoration, and in the British Museum there are belt trappings dating from the eleventh and twelfth centuries which display the high standards of Nihavand in western Persia.

After the Mughal invasions, the migration of Persian silversmiths to Anatolia (Turkey) and to Transoxiana (Uzbekistan, Turkomania, Tadjikistan and part of the Caucasus in the U.S.S.R.) probably led to the extended use of niello in these areas, where it is still prevalent.

From the thirteenth to the fifteenth centuries, the Caucasus became one of the most important metalworking centres. As friendly relations were established between Persia and Iraq, Iraqi masters copied and adapted Persian techniques. It is therefore common to find similar shapes in silver pieces from Turkey, the Caucasus, Iraq and Iran.

The place of origin can be identified by the subject matter inlaid on to the surface. Palm trees, camels, mosques, views of Ctesiphon, the Lion of Babylon and, most frequently, boats floating on rivers are typical Iraqi patterns. Calligraphic designs are also featured in niello inlay. These pieces have sparkling flat surfaces with the subject picked out in niello against a light plain silver background. Occasionally too one can see a mixture of flower and niello patterns, characteristic of the Caucasus, combined with Iraqi subjects.

Deep-set engravings in niello distinguish Caucasian work from that of other Islamic countries, and these are particularly evident in vases, trays, jugs and daggers. While the silversmiths of the Caucasus region increasingly used the niello technique during the eighteenth and nineteenth centuries, it was only between the two World Wars that niello flourished in Iraq among the craftsmen of the Sabi'ite sect. A modern movement in Iraq is producing new niello work, but the quality is not comparable with that of former times. High grade silver is generally used for niello because lead lasts longer when applied to good quality metal.

ARAB AND ISLAMIC SILVER

of the copper age, pottery was decorated with naturalistic motifs, such as ibexes, birds, leopards and trees, as well as geometric designs; the two styles often being combined in a pleasing harmony. As metallurgy progressed, seals and weapons and other objects appeared which were similar to those of early dynastic Sumer. Hoards of silver and gold objects, including weapons, vessels and jewellery, were discovered at Hissar, dating from 2000 BC, and bearing a close resemblance to Mesopotamian objects of the Sargonid and third dynasty Ur periods.

In about 840 BC the Assyrians first came into contact with the Medes and Persians, who, two centuries later, were to destroy Nineveh. When the Persian kings and nobles acquired a taste for luxury from their foreign conquests, they had to introduce artisans to gratify it, with the result that much of their art is an amalgam of that of their subject peoples. The Achaemenid empire was founded by Cyrus, who revolted against the Medean empire in 533 BC. The famous wars between the Greeks and Persians followed, during which Darius I began the construction of the magnificent palaces of Persepolis, which were completed and embellished by Xerxes and his successors.

The Persian empire was conquered by Alexander the Great. After his death, Seleucus, the ablest of his generals, finally emerged triumphant in Asia. It was not until 224 AD that Persia once more became independent under native rulers. The Sassanian dynasty was founded, and a period began which was perhaps the greatest in Persian history. The Shahanshah seated on his throne at Ctesiphon was at the centre of a national revival. Architecture achieved a splendour hitherto unknown and art flourished.

Iran has its own silver mines in various inland regions of the country, such as Isfahan and Yezd, and has therefore always had access to large reserves of precious metals, which encouraged the early craftsmen of the Achaemenid and Sassanian empires to develop their skills and artistic imagination. The most intricate and delicate embossing, engraving, filigree and carving were routine to the smiths of this period, but they are still admired as some of the finest examples achieved in the history of metalwork.

After the fall of the Sassanian dynasty in the seventh century, Persia became part of the Islamic empire. There is no doubt that Persian ideas, skills and techniques strongly influenced Islamic Art from the very earliest times. When the Arabs made their capital in Damascus and subsequently in Baghdad, they were in close proximity to Ctesiphon, which is in modern Iraq; but there had always been links between Persia and the northern part of Arabia. Many Arabs settled in the southern part of what is now Iran, in "Arabstan."

Iran's art has always been decorative and symbolic rather than representative, reflecting traditional Iranian philosophy and its search for the purpose of life. A concept of monotheism which was in some ways similar to the Muslim faith developed early, although Mazdakism and Zoroastrianism were afterwards

Right: *It is very rare to see the bas relief of human subjects on an Islamic piece.*

submerged by Islam. The social system of old Iran was based on a feudal concept of kingship, so the coming of Islam brought conflict between deep-rooted allegiance to the Shahanshah and the new ideas of freedom and equality which the Muslim faith engendered. Persia adopted Islam. Many of her craftsmen went to the courts of Damascus and Baghdad, Turkey and Asia Minor. The Sassanian skills were revived and widened in scope; their old symbolic and decorative designs suited the Islamic ban on representing the human form.

The Buyids ruled in Iran in the tenth and eleventh centuries. Their influence spread to Iraq. Important metalwork from this period has survived as can be seen at the Freer Museum in Washington. Gold medals engraved with the heads of princes, table dishes in silver and vessels made of gold with winged patterns and human heads are among the collection there. Other minor objects have also survived, such as pottery with deep engraving similar to pieces found in Kurdistan.

The Mughal style reached Iran with the Al-Khan family, who established their capital at Tabriz and ruled in the thirteenth and fourteenth centuries. The new town of Sultaniya was built, as well as numerous mosques and domed mausoleums with decorations on marble and plastic tiles with glazed mosaics. Special attention was lavished on the making and decoration of swords, daggers and helmets.

When the Safavids ruled between the sixteenth and eighteenth centuries, their influence spread to Samarkand, Bukhara and Iraq. They established centres in Ardable, Tabriz, Qazvin and Isfahan. Marvellous architecture was commissioned by Shah Abbas in Isfahan, such as the Mosque of the Shah, the madrasah of Mader-shah and the Palace of Jahel Stan. In these and other monuments in Iraq, such as the mausoleums of Karbalah, Nejef and Kadimiya, glazed mosaics of gold tiles covered the walls and domes. Arabesque designs, honeycombs and decorated wooden panels are also frequent features. The crafts of porcelain and pottery flourished in

THE LEVANT, MESOPOTAMIA, PERSIA, TURKEY AND CAUCASIA

Kerman and Meshed, exhibiting a Chinese influence much admired by Shah Abbas himself.

The silk industry also thrived at this time, and the interlacing of gold and silver threads was particularly popular. Carpet centres at Kashan and Tabriz produced high quality work. The art of miniature painting was cultivated under Shah Thamasp; many examples were signed by the artists. Under the Safavid dynasty, book binding and illuminated manuscripts were produced in Tabriz and Qazvin. Cigarette boxes are still enamelled in a way which is reminiscent

The fine enamel picture on this Persian silver box (left) *was created separately on a panel of copper or silver and added later to the lid. This fourteen-piece Persian tea-set* (below left) *includes a sugar bowl, a tray and holders for glasses which are all decorated with the same floral design.*

133

ARAB AND ISLAMIC SILVER

The cast handle of this Turkish bowl (left) *has a flying bird as a thumb piece. The body of the bowl is embossed with arabesque decoration.*

of miniature painting.

Iranian silverwork with the same fine technique can still be found in bazaars and market places today. Caskets, trinkets, vases, bowls, plates, trays, tea services and countless other objects are worked in relief with delicate lacework, embossing and chasing. The overall effect is no longer Sassanian or Achaemenid, but truly Islamic in its general style. Different cities are renowned for particular patterns and designs: Shiraz in the south for bird motifs; Tabriz, in the north-east, for strawberries and thistles; and Isfahan for its flowers and cherries. Tehran and Kermanshah are also considerable centres of silverwork. Islamic mysticism finds its highest expression in Iranian Art.

After the break-up of the Hittite empire in 1200 BC, Asia Minor was split among a number of dynasties and peoples, and the Greeks began to invade the Aegean coast. Greek culture spread into western Arabia, which was gradually becoming part of the Hellenic world. A series of political changes, of which the most important are the Persian conquest in 546, the conquest of Alexander in 334, and the constitution of the Roman province of Asia in 133 BC, did not impede the steady spread of Greek language and culture in the cities. In 330 AD the Emperor Constantine inaugurated the new city of Constantinople on the site of the old Greek trading settlement of Byzantium. This city at once became the capital of the Eastern Roman, and then of the Christian Byzantine, Empire. As the metropolitan province of a great empire, Asia Minor grew in wealth, prosperity and importance.

At the beginning of the eleventh century a new conquest of Anatolia began – that of the Turks. A steppe people called Tiu-Kiu who originated in Central Asia, the Turks came into ever closer contact with the Islamic peoples of the Near East, from whom they adopted the Islamic faith and the Arabic script and much of the complex civilisation of Islam. From the ninth century, Turks entered the service of the Caliphate in increasing numbers and soon came to provide the bulk of its armies, its generals and eventually its rulers.

The decline of Byzantium facilitated the establishment of their rule, and, with the decline also of the Abbasids, the Seljuk Turks became masters of an empire which, between 1037 and 1300, stretched from Afghanistan to the Mediterranean. The Seljuks influenced Islamic Art, particularly between the eleventh and thirteenth centuries when they ruled Iran and Iraq too. A style of mosque developed of which the best examples are the Jama'a mosque in Isfahan and the Al-Adin Jami in Qunya. Mausoleums, palaces and madrasahs were also constructed. Turkish architecture was influenced by Byzantine and Armenian ideas, and in Khurosan metalwork flourished. The main technique used was surface chasing, but the inlaying of silver on copper was common too. Examples of Seljuk metalwork can be seen in various museums, and there is one particularly rare piece in the Boston Museum. It is a silver plate engraved with calligraphy, floral designs and winged animals, which was crafted for the Sultan Alb-Arsalan in 1066 and is signed by its maker, Hassan Kashani. This is probably the oldest known signed piece of Islamic silverwork.

In the Freer Museum in Washington is a silver gilt water sprinkler from the twelfth century, decorated in bas-relief with animal, floral and calligraphic designs. Some metal vessels from the Caucasus and Central Asia are in the Hermitage Museum in Leningrad and display hunting scenes with animal, human and calligraphic motifs. While metalwork flourished in Iran under the Seljuks, comparably high standards were not achieved in Turkey itself.

Ghenghis Khan and his hordes diminished the Turkish empire and the Turks retreated into a small area of Asia Minor. The leader of one of the resulting principalities of frontier warriors was a certain Othman, from whom the name Ottoman is derived. He united Asia Minor under his rule and thus founded the second great Turkish empire, which was to be dominant until the twentieth century – the House of Ottoman. The Ottomans made their capital at Constantinople in 1453 and acquired the treasures of Byzantium.

Many craftsmen were imported to create an Islamic city, and a new coinage was introduced. Ottoman architecture borrowed from Byzantine styles. These are evident in many examples, such as the Aga Sophia mosque and Jeenely palace in Istanbul, the Mohammed Ali mosque in Cairo and the Salimiya mosque in Adana. Glazed mosaics and star-shaped tiles, as well as plaster decoration, are characteristic of the Ottomans. Iznik became an important centre for pottery, Borsa for textiles. The Turkoman tribes were famous for their carpets, into which Arabesque designs were incorporated.

Turkish silver appears to have reached its zenith in the Ottoman period, derived both from Islamic and from other smithing patterns, as exemplified by the

134

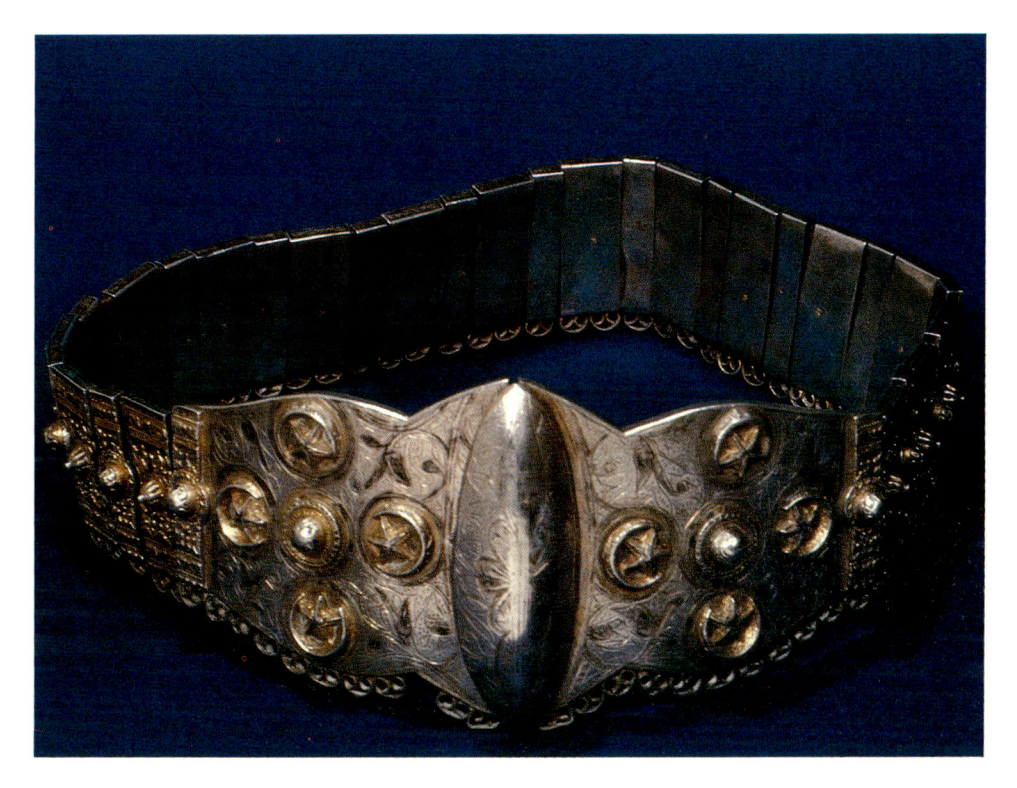

Engraved, nielloed and gilded, this Caucasian heavy belt (left) *has a big buckle and different types of panels.*

enormous variety of shapes and techniques used in vessels, bowls, trays, weaponry and jewellery. Trinkets worn by women retained amuletic qualities, and horn-shaped talismans were commonly worn with Quranic verses inscribed on coin pendants – a blend of traditional and Islamic beliefs. Ordinary men wore very little jewellery, in sharp contrast to courtiers and the Sultans themselves, but rings were, and remain, generally popular. Belts, swords and other weapons created the largest demand for silverwork.

Turkish women love to adorn themselves with rings, bracelets, jewels and strings of pearls. The poorer women sew silver coins on to headscarves and these sometimes represent the wealth of a whole family. The rituals attached to marriage, and particularly the exchange of gifts between the bride and groom, are especially important customs in Turkey. The groom presents his bride with gifts of silver, jewels and toilet articles; she presents him with tobacco boxes or a mouthpiece for his *nergileh*, the Turkish and Iranian *hookah*.

The Turkish custom of the groom asking his bride to jump over a ceremonial sword is another relic of tribal days. The sword is specially designed and made by the best available craftsmen, and the performance of this ritual is supposed to bring luck, happiness and children.

Part of the ceremony involves a procession to the *hammam*, or Turkish bath as it is known in the West. Musicians, men on horseback and water-carriers file through the streets, displaying the finest craftsmanship in the decorative pieces made for their steeds and in the ceremonial belts, swords and jewels worn by the wedding party. The tradition of the *hammam* dates from Roman times. Washing and hygiene are ritualised in Islam, and the Seljuk Muslims inherited splendid Roman baths when they took control of Byzantium. The continuance of this tradition is to be seen from Cordoba to Baghdad, and smaller versions of the *hammam* can be found all over the Islamic world, particularly in Algerian and Moroccan cities. The *hammam* is a meeting place for friends, and a focus for various festivities, especially weddings. Many of the ewers and other vessels are made of silver with particular care because of their ceremonial function.

Formality is a feature of evening meals in Turkey. Every prosperous household had dishes, bowls and servers made of silver. Tray tables were also silver and finely decorated. Hunting parties were common in Turkey, and craftsmen turned their skills to producing the necessary accoutrements for the sport. Smoking was another custom enriched by Turkish craftsmen; many extremely fine mouthpieces were made in silver and encrusted with semi-precious stones.

The standard of Turkish work in precious metals has remained high and so has the quality of the silver itself. In Wan, a lake settlement near Iran, the silver is stamped not with the smith's name but with the place name instead; which is very rare in Islamic silverwork, but also occurs in Amara in Iraq and in Brunei in Indonesia. The pieces which come from modern workshops still characteristically reflect various stages of development in Turkish history.

The crafts of Dhagestan are its history, its language, its literature, its music, its traditions and its aspirations, for the whole of an ancient culture is portrayed in its pottery, its weaving and particularly in its metalwork.

The variety of shapes and designs is extraordinary. The earliest work was in bronze casting, of which some fine examples still exist. These people have translated their environment into metal and created a "language of craftmanship." It is a language which the people well understand, but it has its own distinctive dialects. Each village is a silverwork centre, although places like Kubachi have achieved international fame. Each village is also characterised by its techniques and methods of decoration, so much so that an expert can enter a house and know immediately from the metalwork exhibited there how long that family has lived in the village and who are its kinsmen.

Dhagestan's history is tribal. Small village communities grew up and provided agricultural produce for the separate tribal units. The customs and traditions of this culture are evident in such silver pieces as the bucket used ritualistically at weddings. Traditionally it was filled with flour, cereal and sugar, the staples of an agricultural community. Spoons were placed upside down in the bucket and presented with the dowry to the prospective bride.

Enamelling has recently been introduced and has been perfected by Kubachi masters. Other centres are famous – Amouzgui, Kharbuk, Kumukh, Kazanistchi – but none has surpassed the brilliance of the Kubachi. Modern pieces such as jugs and buckets are decorated with abstract human forms, and covered in gold enamelling, granulation and filigree. These excellent craftsmen continue to experiment and perfect their skills, which must surely advance Dhagestan into the forefront of international craftsmanship.

An Iraqi iklil *or hairdress* (below) *consists of a silver-plated band with pendants of modern chains and ancient semi-precious stones.*

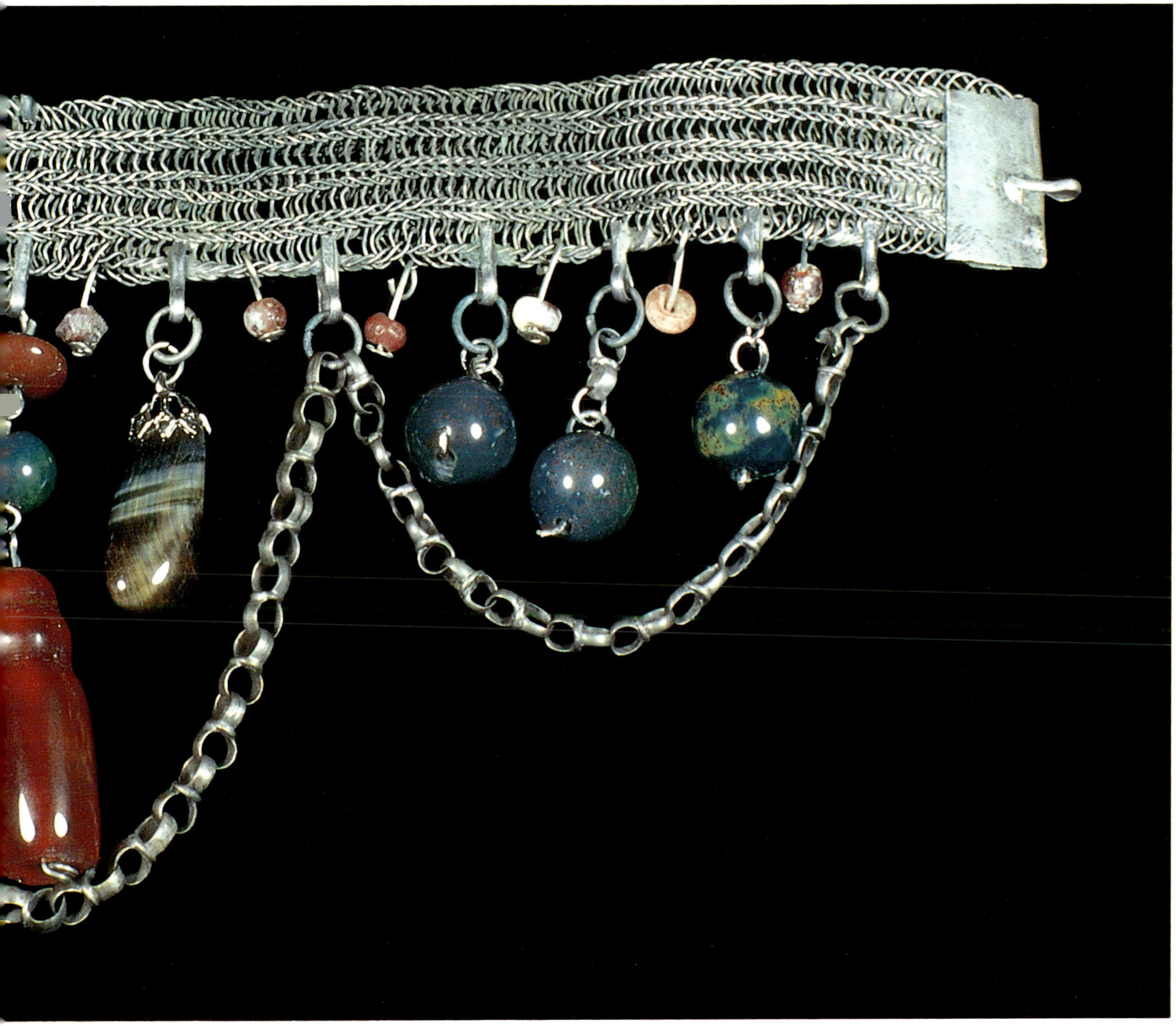

ARAB AND ISLAMIC SILVER

Left: *A Kurdish headdress which is worn encircling the face. The small filigree leaf patterns are also known in Greek jewellery designs. This fascinating old Iraqi headdress* (above) *has various kinds of beads and stones: agate, pottery, tiger-eye and turquoise.*

THE LEVANT, MESOPOTAMIA, PERSIA, TURKEY AND CAUCASIA

Above: *An Iraqi hairdress which is worn as a pair symmetrically on each side of the head to secure the hair.*

ARAB AND ISLAMIC SILVER

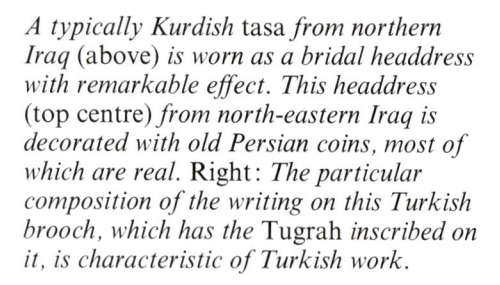

A typically Kurdish tasa *from northern Iraq (above) is worn as a bridal headdress with remarkable effect. This headdress (top centre) from north-eastern Iraq is decorated with old Persian coins, most of which are real.* Right: *The particular composition of the writing on this Turkish brooch, which has the* Tugrah *inscribed on it, is characteristic of Turkish work.*

THE LEVANT, MESOPOTAMIA, PERSIA, TURKEY AND CAUCASIA

Above: *Four rows of agate and silver pendants have been recently added to this old Iraqi torque.* Left: *Two Safavid coins serve as the bases for two brooches. The right-hand one is dated 1172 AH and is about 230 years old.*

141

ARAB AND ISLAMIC SILVER

This Turkish necklace (left) has a main medallion which is inlaid with turquoise and ended with old Ottoman coins. This icon (below) from the Mosul region in northern Iraq demonstrates Christian silversmithing. The chain of the icon is of the typical Iraqi flower-shaped type and there are Cyrillic inscriptions on the back of the icon box. A Kurdish necklace (bottom left) with a main hollow filigree silver ball, bell-shaped pendants and some coral decoration.

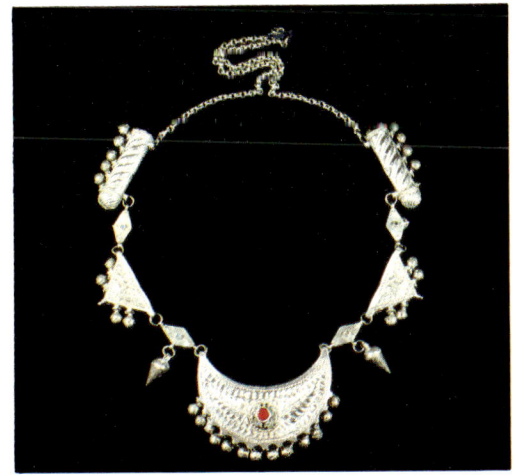

THE LEVANT, MESOPOTAMIA, PERSIA, TURKEY AND CAUCASIA

Above left: *An Iraqi* silah *uses some Ottoman and other old coins as pendants. The main ornament of this northern Iraqi necklace* (above right) *is inlaid with red and small turquoise stones.* Top: *A Syrian* silah *(weapon) is worn over the shoulder and under one arm and is reminiscent of the* manjad *style of necklace in Oman.*

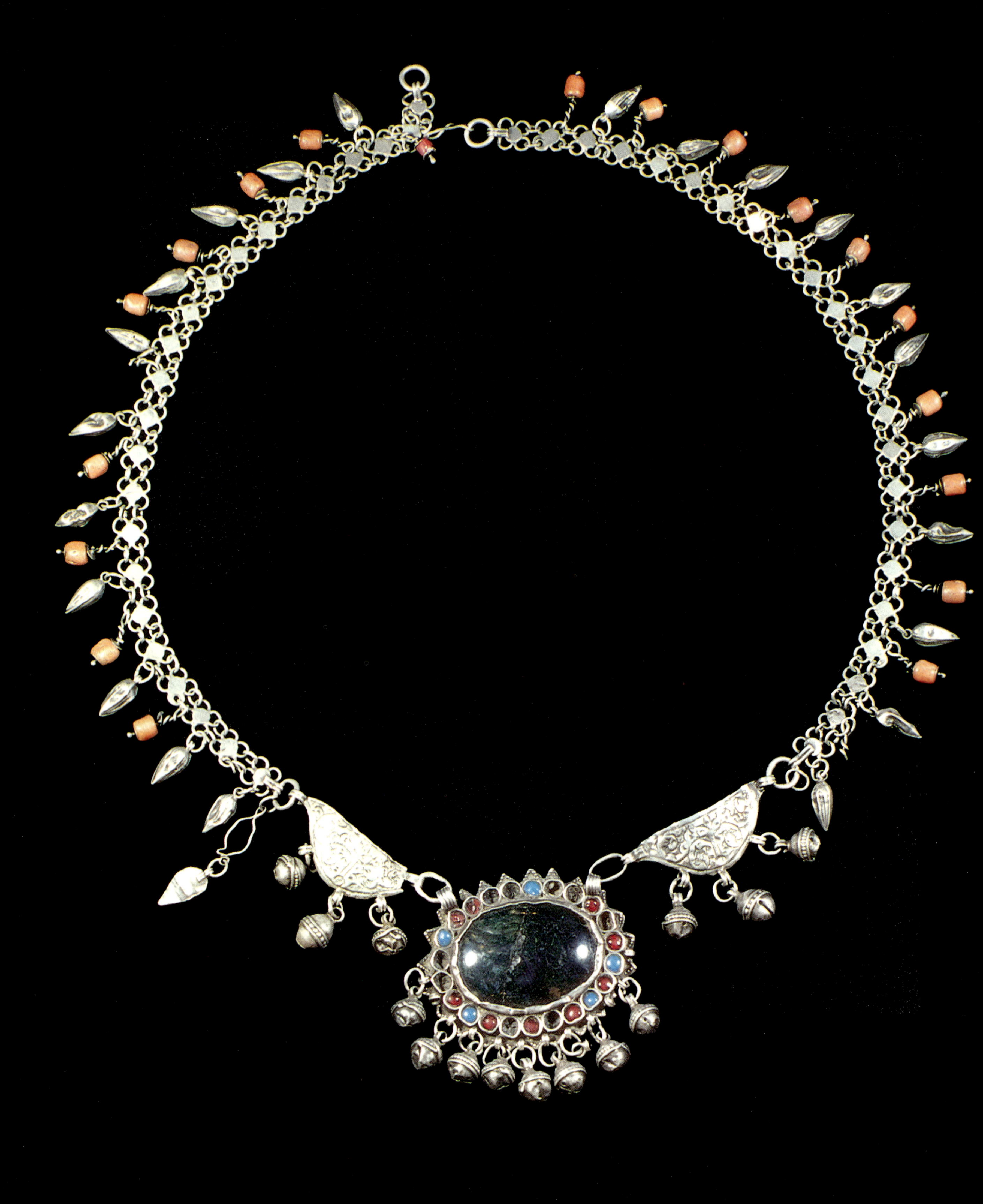

THE LEVANT, MESOPOTAMIA, PERSIA, TURKEY AND CAUCASIA

In the Iraqi necklace (opposite) *the main pendant is heavily inlaid with colourful beads and a central square stone ended in bell-shaped pendants.* Top left: *Old coins and engraved hollow silver balls decorate the main piece in this Iraqi necklace.* Left: *Circular shaped pendants and various coloured beads and pottery ornament this Iraqi necklace.* Below left: *Filigree work and nielloed Iraqi subjects appear on this bracelet and necklace.*

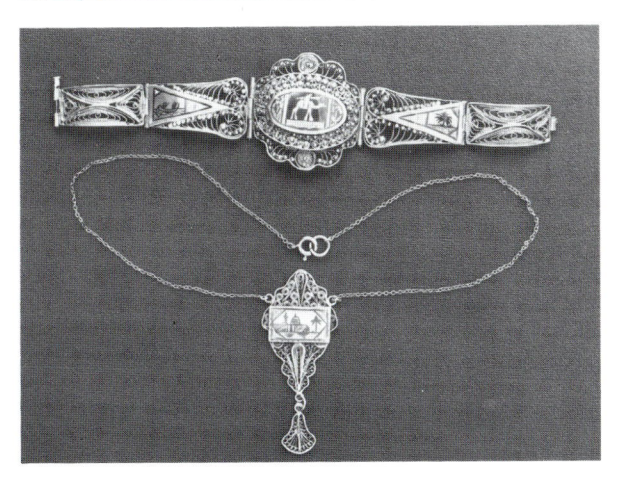

145

ARAB AND ISLAMIC SILVER

146

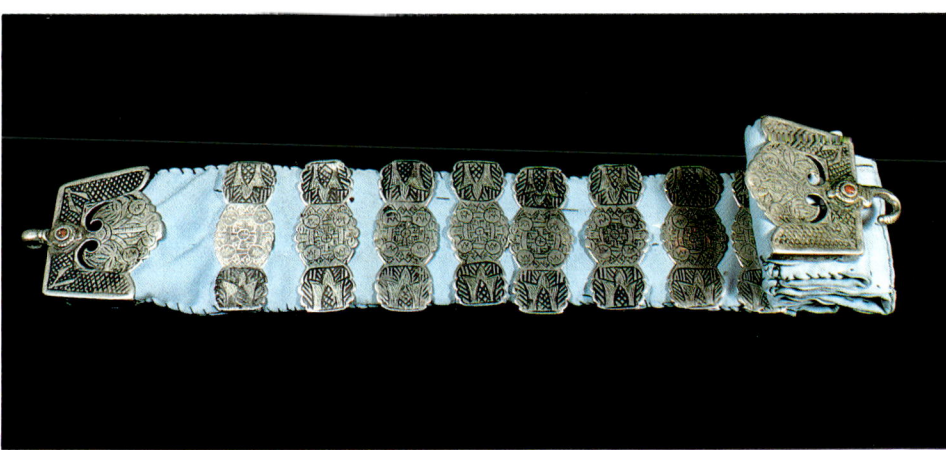

THE LEVANT, MESOPOTAMIA, PERSIA, TURKEY AND CAUCASIA

Opposite left: *Niello work and floral decoration are seen on the various silver pieces which make up this Caucasian belt. An ornate filigree and granulated northern Iraqi belt* (top) *is backed by red material. Studded with coral and turquoise, decorated with granulated balls and gilded, this delicate Turkish belt* (top right) *displays granulation and plaiting. Niello and filigree ornamentation alternate on the panels of this Iraqi belt* (above right). *The Kurdish belt* (above left) *consists of heavy silver panels which, although fixed on material, are flexible to permit movement.*

147

ARAB AND ISLAMIC SILVER

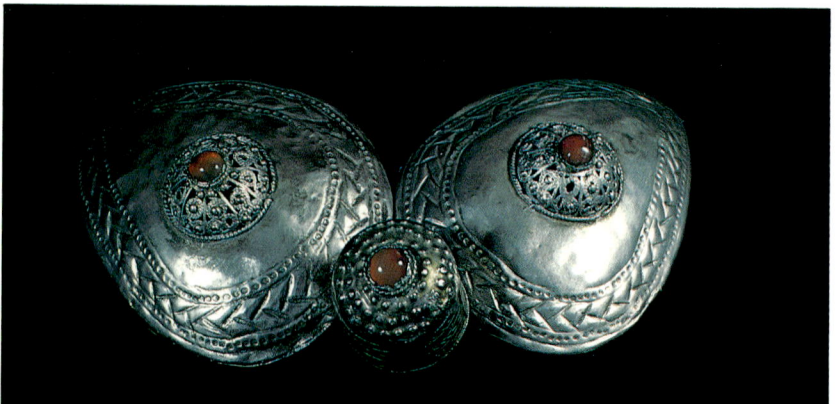

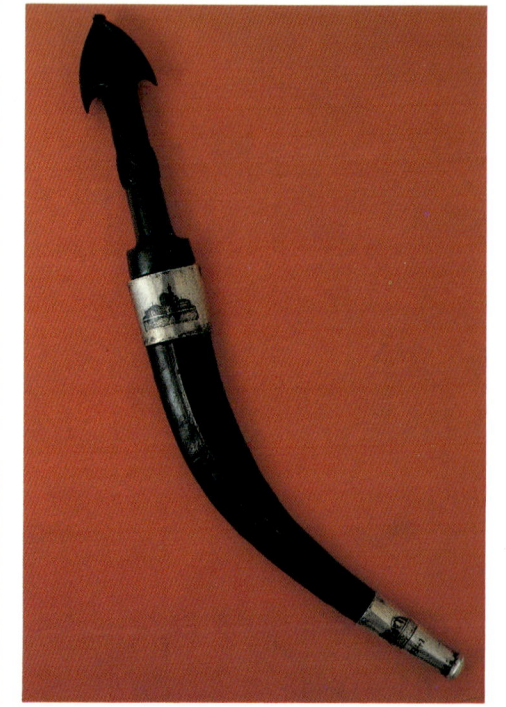

The Persian buckle (top left) *is inlaid with turquoise. These northern Iraqi buckles* (top right and above right) *display different techniques – ornate repoussé, engraving, granulation and chasing. This Iraqi dagger* (far right) *displays nielloed work and is signed 1941. A guffa boat is depicted here amongst other Iraqi subjects on this paper knife* (right). *It is a circular vessel with asphalted sides, which has been used since Mesopotamian times in local swamps and rivers. This Iraqi clasp* (below far right) *is for a children's belt and displays the much favoured design of an eight-pointed star. The partly-gilded and partly-nielloed belt buckle* (below right) *is inlaid with a silver rose design and probably from Turkey.*

148

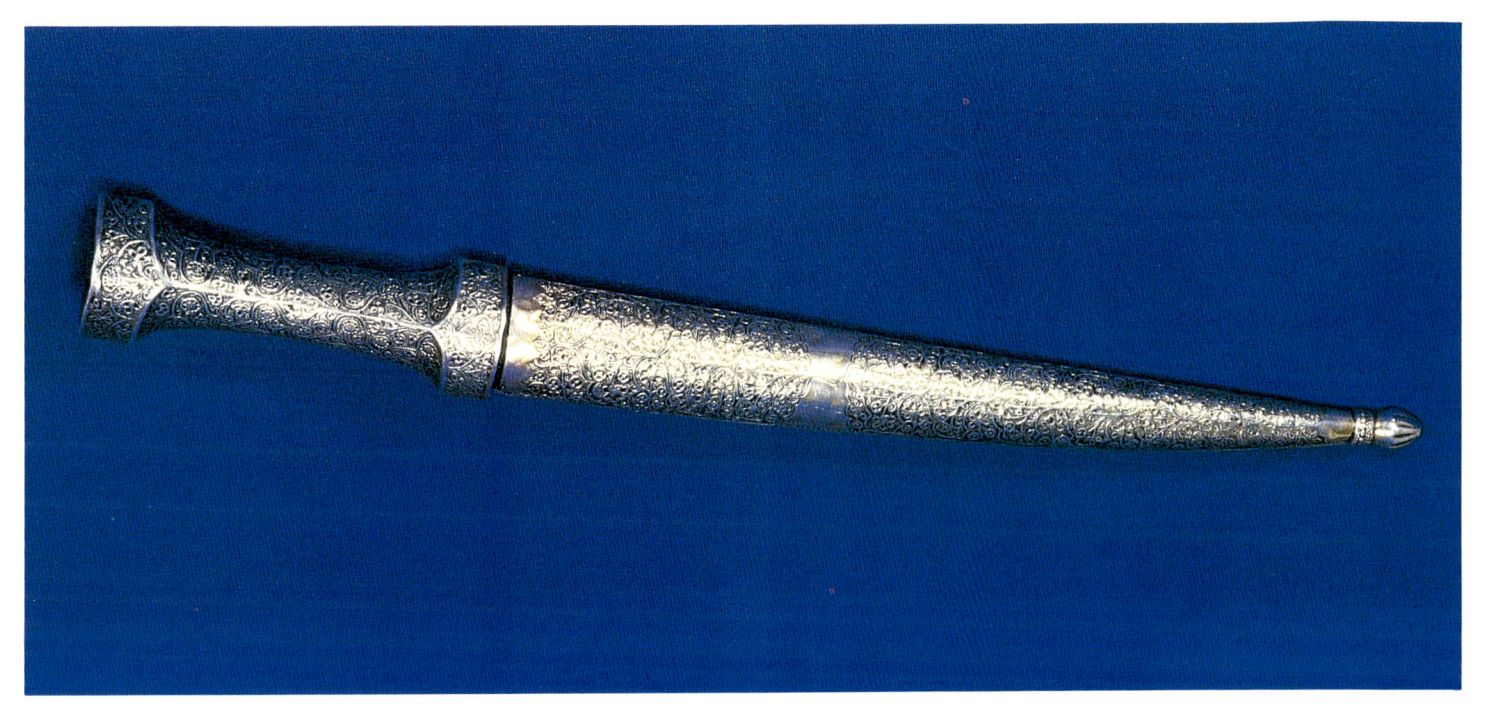

THE LEVANT, MESOPOTAMIA, PERSIA, TURKEY AND CAUCASIA

This Persian dagger (top) *is gilded and has floral decoration. Deeply engraved and florally ornamented, this Turkish sword* (middle left) *is also signed and dated in Arabic (Wazoon Mustapha 1211 AH). Inlaid with gold and green stones, this Iraqi dagger* (middle right) *is about 60 cms long. The dagger's hilt and sheath were created at different times, which is evident from the dissimilar smithing patterns. Above: A Caucasian dagger or* kinjal *is nielloed and signed with the Arab silversmith's name. The reverse displays deep engraving of realistic floral design.*

ARAB AND ISLAMIC SILVER

The links of this Iraqi bracelet (right) *were originally round. They were crushed simultaneously by the craftsman to attain oval shapes and very close linkage to create a distinctly Iraqi style.*

An Iraqi jinjil *or baby's anklet* (above) *is often finished off with bells so that it jingles when the child walks, and in this example agate has been added for decoration. These heavy Iraqi anklets* (below) *with snake-shaped terminals are granulated and inlaid with blue stones.*

150

THE LEVANT, MESOPOTAMIA, PERSIA, TURKEY AND CAUCASIA

This Iraqi nielloed box (below) *was made to hold a pumice stone.*

Above left: *The clasps are the main decorative focus of these three designs of Iraqi anklet. In these rare and old Iraqi anklets* (above right) *one can see where the metal has been eroded by long contact with a leg.*

151

ARAB AND ISLAMIC SILVER

The figures in the courtly scenes depicted on this set of six Persian plates (on this page, opposite and overleaf) *are recognisable characters from Islamic stories. Each plate is signed by Laiichi, who was one of the most famous Persian silversmiths.*

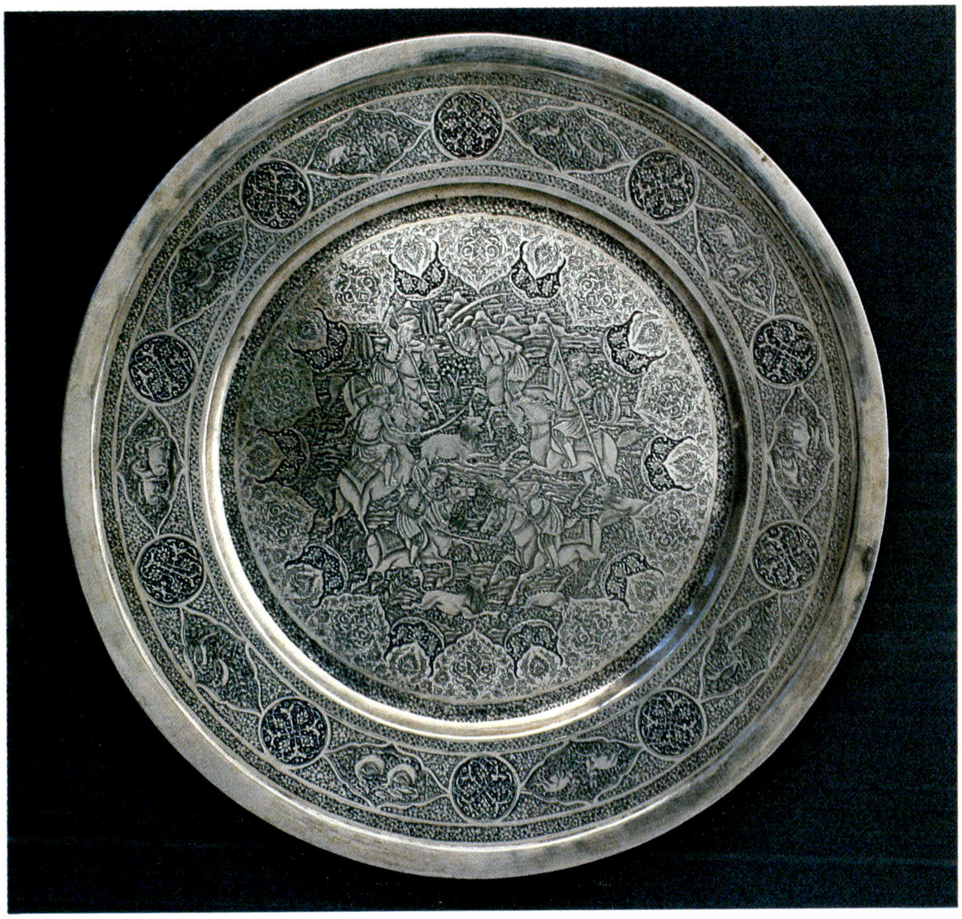

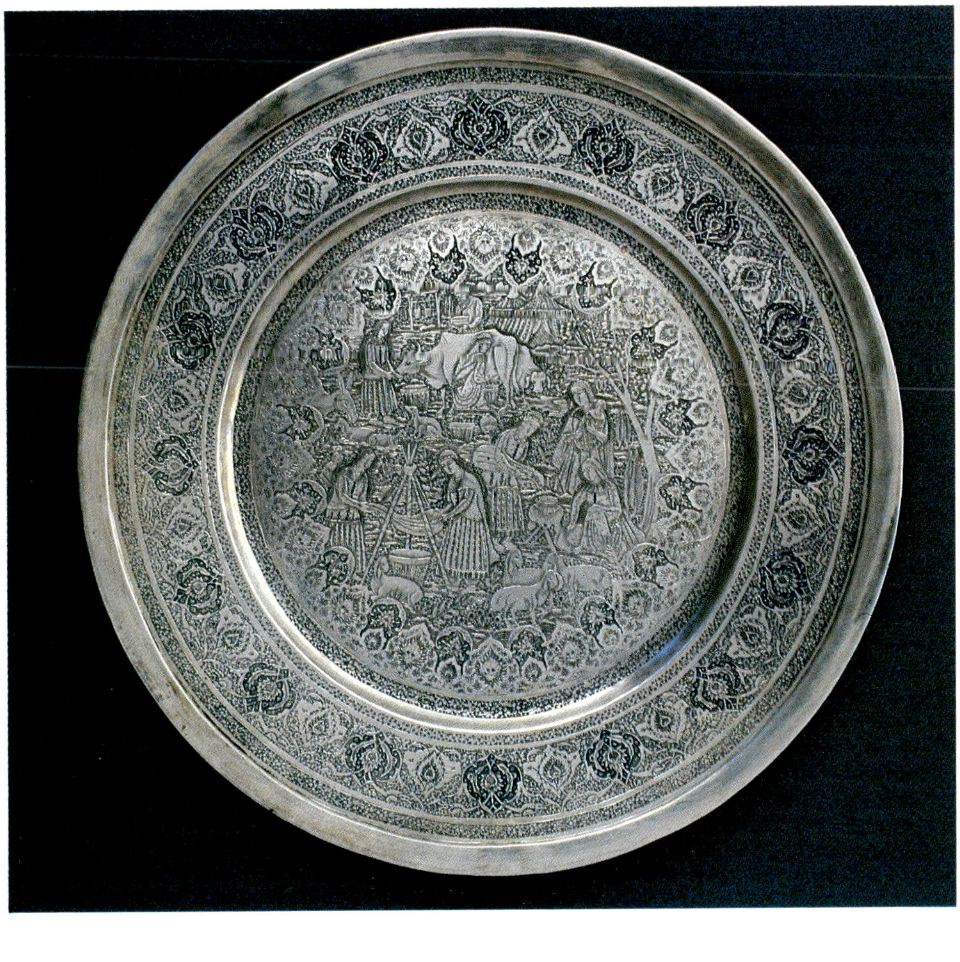

ARAB AND ISLAMIC SILVER

154

A fine Persian dish (above) is decorated with embossed flower shapes and enamelling.

ARAB AND ISLAMIC SILVER

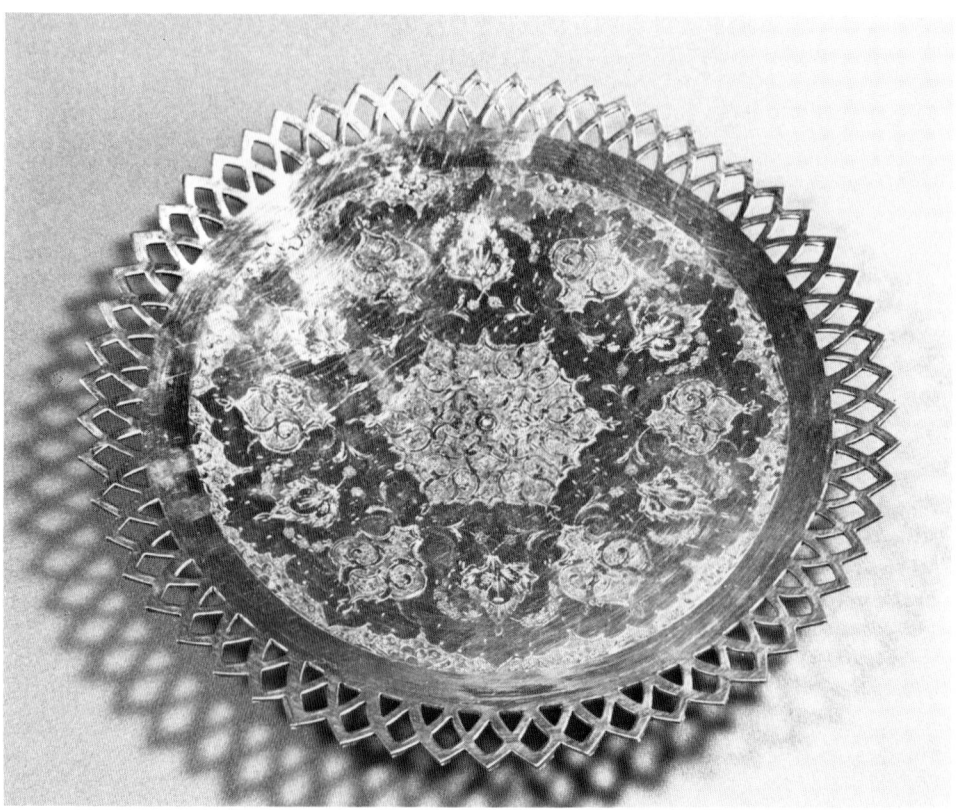

Above left: European influence is visible in the shape of this fine Persian dish, although the pattern is typical of Persian work. Below left: The beautiful engraving of human, animal and floral decorations is excellently executed on this fine Persian oval-shaped tray. Above right: This entire Persian dish is fashioned from a single piece of silver. Below right: The edge of this Iraqi circular dish is strikingly decorated with a repeating openwork pattern. Opposite: This Persian decorative basket shows scenic and floral decoration, openwork, engraving and repoussé.

THE LEVANT, MESOPOTAMIA, PERSIA, TURKEY AND CAUCASIA

ARAB AND ISLAMIC SILVER

This set of coffee cups, pot and tray (top) *exemplifies modern Iraqi niello work. Typical Iraqi motifs appear on this flask* (right) *which is also signed. Iraqi coffee or tea-glass holders* (opposite top) *display engraved openwork.*

THE LEVANT, MESOPOTAMIA, PERSIA, TURKEY AND CAUCASIA

This partly gilded and nielloed Turkish cup (left) may date from the early Ottoman period. Some Turkish tea or coffee cup holders (above) are tulip-shaped with interlocking twisted leaf panels.

ARAB AND ISLAMIC SILVER

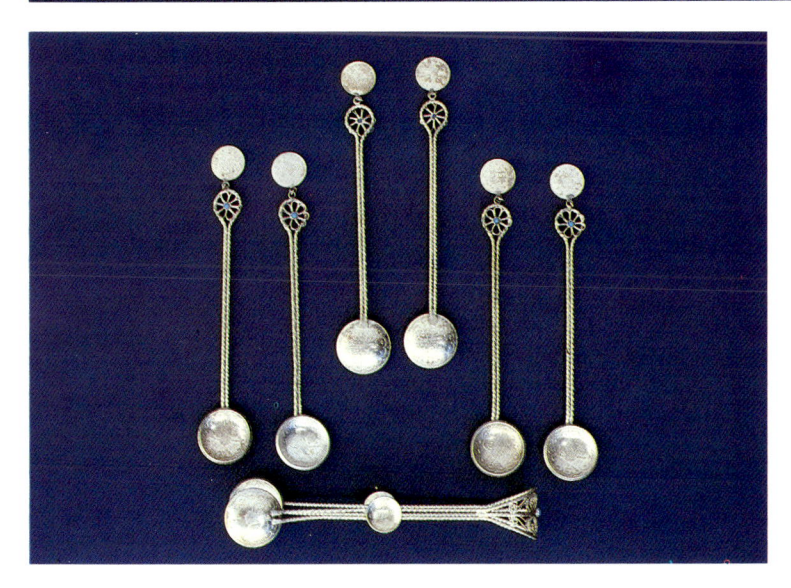

THE LEVANT, MESOPOTAMIA, PERSIA, TURKEY AND CAUCASIA

The bowls of these small Turkish teaspoons (left) *are fashioned from old coins and the tongs display filigreed decoration. This partly gilded Turkish spoon* (above) *is decorated with flower and bird images. A hookah ornament* (top right) *displays typical Persian embossing. Second from top left:* Nielloed Iraqi subjects appear on this set of salt, pepper and mustard containers. Various Iraqi nielloed pieces (top), *many of which are signed.* Opposite: *The pipe is missing from this fine Turkish hookah which has excellent enamelling and a characteristically Turkish chain.* Overleaf: *This Turkish pen case and inkwell are engraved with Arabic calligraphy and human figures.*

161

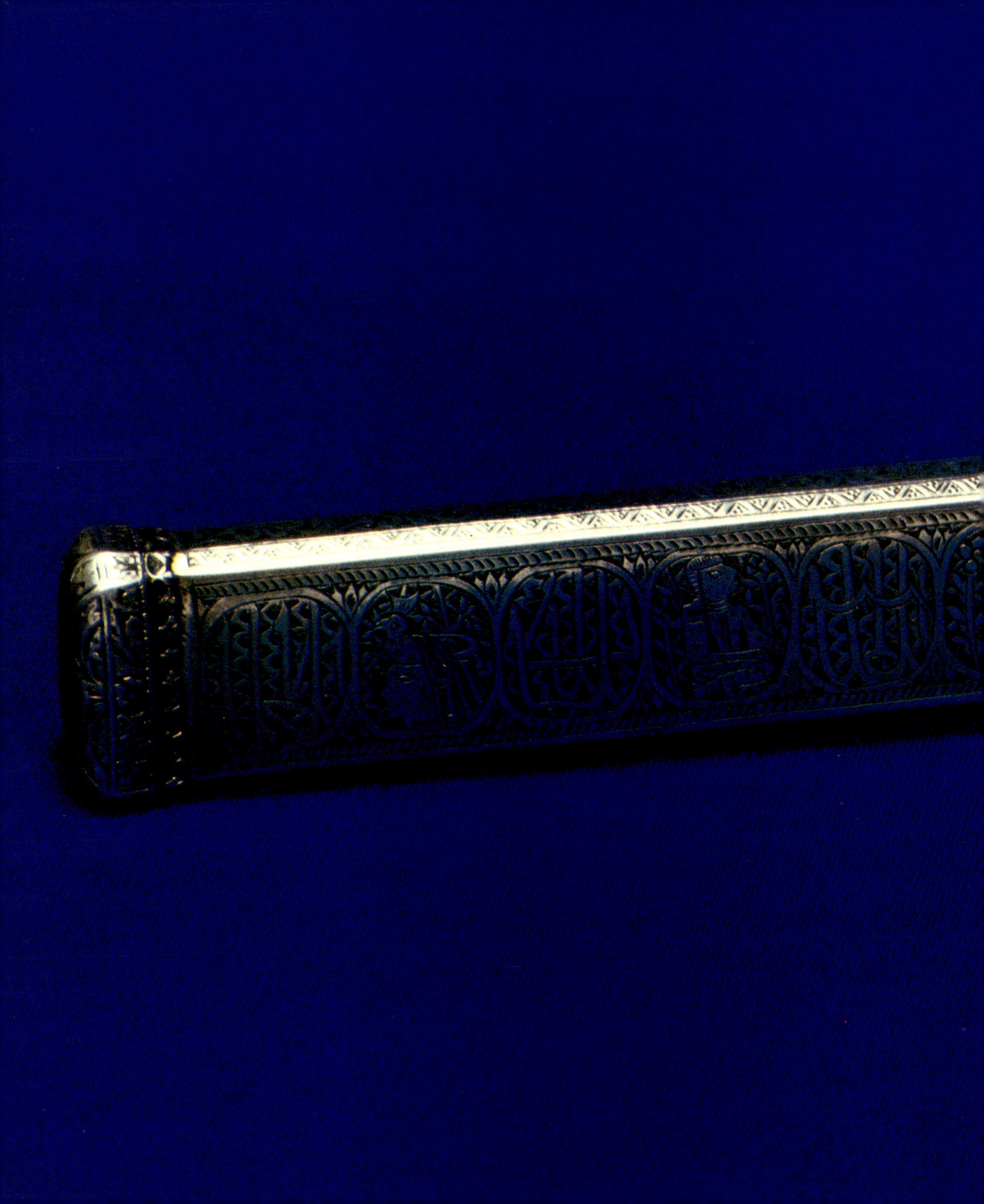

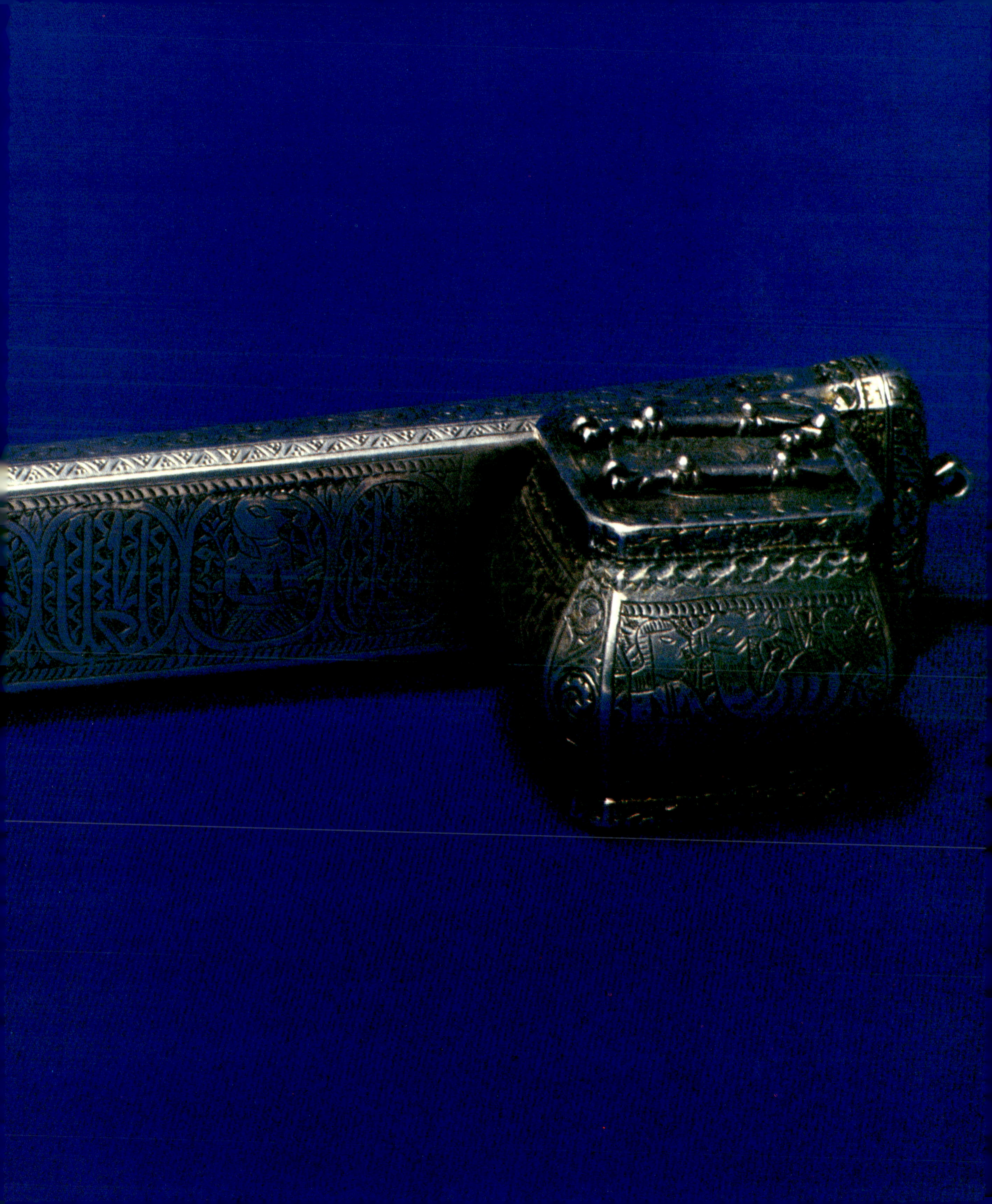

ARAB AND ISLAMIC SILVER

Top: *Square and circular patterns are repeated in a geometrical composition on this round Persian box.* Above centre: *A gold central ornament provides the focus of this Persian cigarette box. Iraqi square and hexagonal powder compacts* (above) *display geometrical, floral and animal designs and also a six-pointed star with a river view.*

THE LEVANT, MESOPOTAMIA, PERSIA, TURKEY AND CAUCASIA

These fine Persian silver cigarette boxes (top, above centre and above right) *display social scenes and floral designs.* Above left: *An image of a Bedouin mounted on a camel is depicted in fine Iraqi niello on this free-standing decorative panel.* Far left: *Turquoise of various shades and agates are lavishly inlaid in this Persian circular box.*

165

ARAB AND ISLAMIC SILVER

This delicate Turkish vase (top left) *has an interesting and ornate shape. Domestic scenes are engraved on this Persian vase* (above left) *in various depths. The bowl of another fine Persian vase* (above right) *is interestingly shaped with animal and floral designs. The holes in this Persian rose-bowl* (right) *are for positioning the flowers through its lid. Opposite: Arabic calligraphy appears around the top, and Kufic script underneath, this tumbler, which was probably made in Persia.*

166

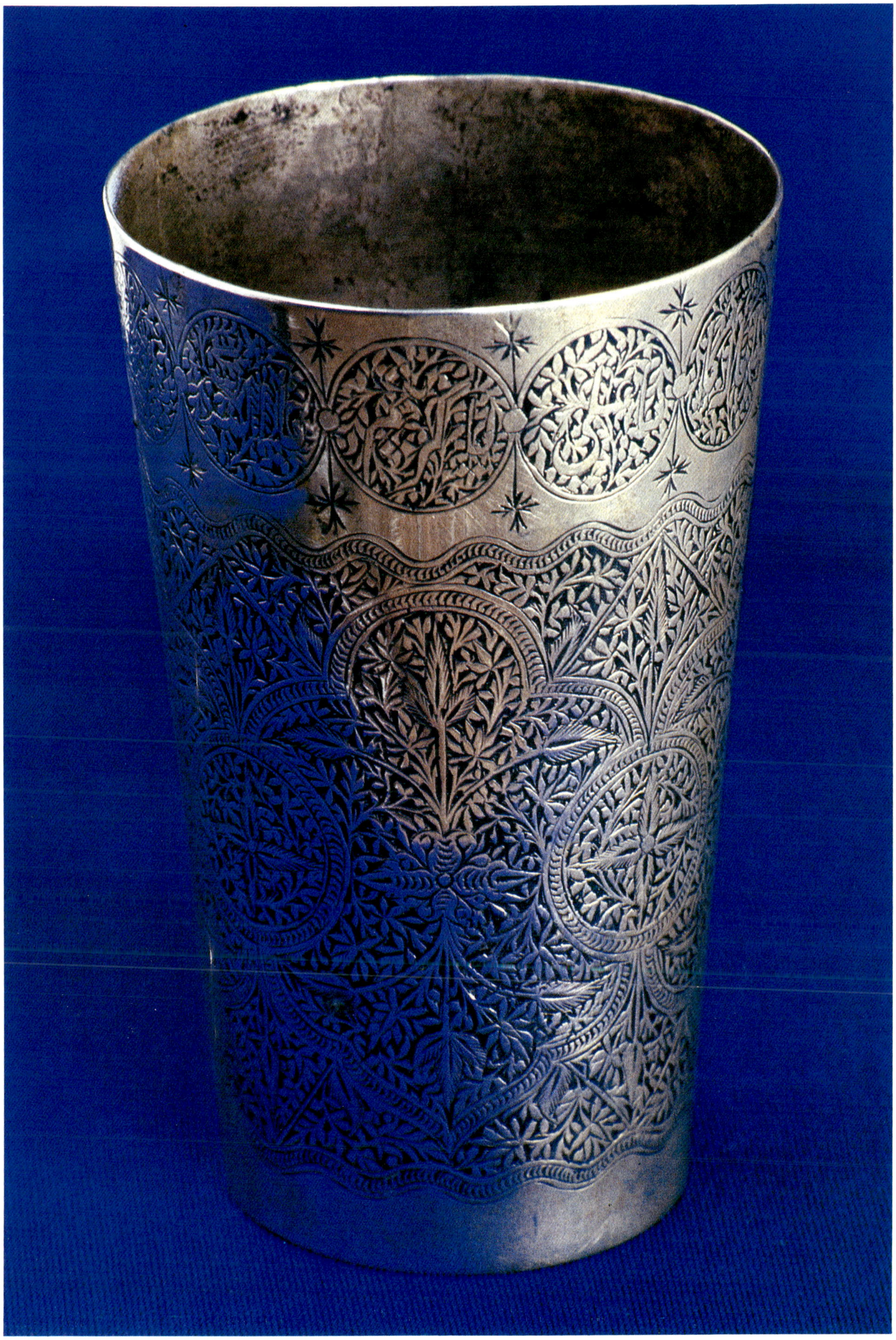

ARAB AND ISLAMIC SILVER

These decorative stirrups (top) *are signed and nielloed with typical Iraqi subjects.*
Above: *An Iraqi sweetmeat dish.*

THE LEVANT, MESOPOTAMIA, PERSIA, TURKEY AND CAUCASIA

These three patterns of Persian candlesticks (top) *show different styles of embossing. Above left: Chinese influence is to be seen in the dividing arches and patterns on this octagonal Persian tea caddy. Above right: Iraqi subjects are presented in a modern ornamental sculpture in niello.*

169

ARAB AND ISLAMIC SILVER

Central and South-east Asia

AKHSTAN
Tashkent
KIRGIZIA
AJIKISTAN
Peshawar
Rawalpindi
ABAD
Srinagar
KASHMIR
ore
0 Kilometres 500 1,000
N
Meerut
DELHI
Agra
NEPAL
SIKKIM
BHUTAN
Lucknow
Gwalior
Jaunpur
Bhopal
R. Ganges
BANGLADESH
DACCA
Calcutta
INDIA
CHINA
Hyderabad
BAY OF BENGAL
BURMA
RANGOON
THAILAND
ANKA
OLOMBO
MANILA
INDIAN OCEAN
PHILIPPINES
Medan
MALAYSIA
KUALA LUMPUR
SINGAPORE
Kota Kinabalu
SABAH
BRUNEI
SARAWAK
Kuching
SUMATRA
BORNEO
Palembang
INDONESIA
CELEBES
NEW GUINEA
DJAKARTA
Bandung
JAVA
Surabaya
Macassar
WEST IRIAN
BALI

ARAB AND ISLAMIC SILVER

The majority of the Turkomans live in the area surrounding the Kara Kum (Black Sand) desert, which is east of the Caspian Sea, bordering the northern edge of the Iranian plateau. The Kara Kum itself is too arid to support a human population of any significant size, but the semi-arid fringe is inhabited by agriculturalists. This home of the Turkomans extends into Afghanistan and Iran, although most of them live in the U.S.S.R.

Much like the Bedouin of Arabia, the Turkomans are divided into nomadic tribes with common traditions; but unlike Arabia, Turkomania's geographical position made her vulnerable to invasion throughout her history and those foreign influences are reflected in much of her art. Typically of a nomadic people, their wealth is transportable, consisting of livestock, rugs, silks and silverwork. Their jewellery conveys a feeling of vastness. Silver is decorated with cornelians, and sometimes with blue and red glass. Heart shapes in double or even triple forms, intricately interwoven, are characteristic of Turkomanian jewellery. Early pieces display the distinctive lozenge shape. Later, metalwork developed under the Greeks who settled in the region and taught their techniques to the Turkomans. Vestiges of Hellenic influence, including a few mythological Greek figures, are still evident.

Turkomania was the land of Zoroastrianism, a religion which preached great tolerance, which led the Turkomans to accept and assimilate alien influences with relative ease. The Greeks had numerous gods, whereas Zoroastrianism was one of the first monotheistic religions. Islamic influences further modified Turkomanian customs and art forms.

Turkomanian women wear quantities of jewellery with different names and functions, from large headdress pieces to hair ornaments, necklaces, amulets, rings, bracelets, breast pieces, earrings and the Quran boxes which women sling across their backs. They generally cover their heads with a scarf or shawl, interwoven with ornaments. It is given to the bride by the groom's sisters, who come the day after the wedding to rearrange the bride's hair. Two plaits are brought forward to hang down to her shoulders: the headdress or *aldoni* is placed on her head and additional decoration of coins and other ornaments made visible under her headdress.

Each tribe has distinctive features in its jewellery. That of the Tekke is heavy,

The necklace (above) *is typical of the Turkomanian regions in U.S.S.R., Afghanistan and Iran. It is a heavy colourful piece inlaid with small gilded silver circles and four agates and finished with bell-shaped pendants. Each silver panel is decorated with a thin gilded diamond-shaped leaf, set on a three-stranded chain.*

with gold arabesque chasing, while that of the Yamud is lighter, with lozenge or crescent shapes and gold embossing. Both use flat cornelians for embellishment. In times gone by, such pieces were worn by women constantly, even when they were working, but modern life has changed this. The old nomadic ways are disappearing and, as the Turkomans became city dwellers, their needs and values altered. In nomadic life silver represented a family's wealth and investment, but now cash is necessary. Unfortunately, at the end of World War II, the Turkomans were told by unscrupulous dealers that their jewellery was almost valueless. They sold it at absurdly low prices, which is why there is now so much Turkomanian silver on the market.

The Persians have always regarded

tribal pieces with contempt, and the new city-dwellers among the Turkomans have been affected by this attitude and now prefer to wear gold. However, although their women have abandoned heavy ornamental pieces for everyday wear, some are still displayed in their homes, as decorative reminders of their heritage.

Modern smiths are meeting a new demand for gold and smaller pieces, but they strive to keep the age-old customs and traditions alive. Many fine pieces of modern Turkomanian silver jewellery continue to be produced in the workshops of Ashkhabad.

Islamic influence remains evident in the other Soviet Central Asian republics – Tajikistan, Uzbekistan and Kirgizia. Although many of the antiquities of Samarkand, Bukhara and Khiva date from the later Timurid and Samanid periods, Islam reached Central Asia as early as the seventh century. At that time a stable Muslim community was established with its centre at Bukhara. Qasim Ibn Abbas, reputedly a cousin of the Prophet, is buried in the Shah-i-Zinda in Samarkand. The city became a place of pilgrimage for early Muslims, perhaps those too poor to undertake the journey to Mecca.

Central Asia suffered turbulence and destruction at the hands of empire builders who successively invaded in great numbers, attempting to consolidate their power both to the east and to the west of the area. The history of the city of Samarkand exemplifies this. After Alexander defeated the Soghidians, he established on the river banks a Greek city which he called "Marakands." It was twice razed to the ground and twice rebuilt. Then the hordes of Attila used Samarkand as a resting place for their armies. The Arabs arrived, and wars started between them and the Turkic tribes, followed by a period of Chinese infiltration. The continuance of Islam was assured when the Muslims defeated the Chinese at Ferghana in the eighth century.

Ghenghis Khan and his terrible Mongol warriors swept through the area, but finally, the rule of Timur, who was descended from Ghenghis Khan, turned Central Asia into a resplendent example of Muslim cultural achievement. Timur was both a destroyer and a creator. He could not rest from his civilising ambition until he turned his residence at Samarkand into the most glittering and grandiose metropolis of the Orient. Magnificent mosques, mausoleums, palaces and madrasahs bore witness to the quality of Islamic architecture. Timur revived the ancient traditions of public service when he assembled craftsmen from all his lands to work together on his buildings. He gave new stimulus to the arts without estranging them from their national individuality.

With the conquerors a stream of Far Eastern motifs flooded over Persia and the neighbouring lands. Chinese patterns of fabulous animals very soon became stylised in the Islamic manner, fitting so easily into the native repertoire that the revolution in content paled before the continuity in form.

Samarkand was bequeathed one of the world's most curious necropolises in the street tombs of Shah Zinde, which are reckoned to be among the most impressive monuments of Islamic architecture. Although the most striking buildings were erected in Samarkand, the most varied and picturesque were in the cities of Bukhara and Khiva.

A great advance was made in various techniques, and the progress even of decoration in unglazed brick can be seen in the Kalyan minaret at Bukhara. It has large scale richly varied horizontal patterning and the surfaces are animated by varied courses of glazed bricks.

Inlay on steel and iron raised weapon-making to a fine art, and the methods of incrustation underwent many changes. The ribbed bell shape of helmet emerged, to be worn over the turban with eye slits, the body of it decorated with inscriptions and floral scrolls drawn in close lines of fine hammered-in wire.

While metalwork flourished during this period in Egypt and Syria under the Mamelukes, less attention was paid them by the Timurids. A few vessels carry Timur's name; they date from the fourteenth century and have some decorative work. Jewels were set in precious metals surrounded by engraved floral and calligraphic designs combined with jade. Pottery did not really attain a high artistic level, but carpet weaving was stimulated by the introduction of Chinese themes. Great progress was also made in painting and book illustrating. In many manuscripts one can see a Far Eastern element both in landscape and in the figure compositions. In Samarkand and Bukhara fine brush drawing, touched with gold, became fashionable and later spread into the Persian and Indian schools of painting.

Khiva is a major city in Uzbekistan, containing many well-preserved monuments. Its isolation from other centres created a purity in its Islamic craftsmanship. In this market town, with a large bazaar which still exists, the people were allowed full freedom for their artistic activities once the autocratic rule of the local Khan had been relaxed. The mausoleum of one of their heroes, the poet-wrestler Pahlovan Mahmoud, is a good example of fine Uzbeki craftsmanship, in which elaborate designs of interwoven leaves, stems, flowers and gazelles are interlaced with Quranic calligraphy. The blue and white mosaics covered with these patterns, stretch up into the dome. A similar style can be seen in many other Khiva monuments, such as the palaces of Kunya Arg and the Tash Hauli. The Kok Minar and Kalta Minar are perhaps the most striking examples of Khiva architecture. Motifs ranging from the traditional star shape figures made of pentagons to intricate floral and calligraphic patterns demonstrate Uzbek skill.

The Ichan Khala, or inner city, was the site of the Khiva bazaar, where the tradition of fine mosaic could be seen reflected in its metalwork. Silver necklaces, pendants, bracelets and hairpieces were all produced in the Ichan Khala workshops.

Afghanistan links the West with India and China and offers a back-door to the U.S.S.R. Countless merchants and armies have crossed Afghanistan throughout history, either by way of the Amu-Darya or Oxus River or going through the narrow passes and defiles of the Hindu Kush. Caravans laden with ivories, silks, spices, jewels, gold and silver used the fabled "Silk Route" between Rome and China, which wound its way through the mountains of Afghanistan. Alexander the Great followed the same trail, as did merchants with indigo and Chinese silk, nomads from the Steppes, Buddhist monks and the often hard-pressed armies of the British Raj.

Such great waves of human history have flowed over what is known today as Afghanistan, that it is surprising they left so little permanent trace. Persians, Greeks, Indians, Chinese, Huns, Mongols, Mughals and others all swept in and conquered but finally fell to local tribes who were themselves migrants. No invader could destroy the traditions of these people, whose mountain heritage gave them a strength, stability and love of freedom which have always been characteristic of the Afghans.

The brotherhood of Islam is perhaps

ARAB AND ISLAMIC SILVER

best seen in Afghanistan, where, in the Pul-i-Khisti mosque in Kabul, Pushtuns, Tajiks, Turkomans and Uzbeks with their differing tribal histories and traditions meet to turn toward Mecca in prayer. They kneel at the place where the first Arabs are believed to have made their thanksgiving prayer after entering Kabul in the seventh century. A stone marks the spot and remains a symbol of unity for thousands of Afghani Muslims.

Although the Arabs also came as conquerors and encountered great resistance to their rule, the impact of their faith gradually permeated the life of the people. There followed a succession of dynasties as the Caliphate weakened – the Tahirids, Safavids and Samanids, under whom the magnificent mosques as the Masjid-i-Haji and the Haji-Payada were built. Muslim culture reached its peak under the Ghaznavids, whose centre, Ghazni, was a little to the south of Kabul.

Mahmoud of Ghazni came to power in AD 998, brought all Afghanistan under his rule and conquered the Punjab as far as Multan. The wealth drawn from this Indian province provided him and his successors with vast treasure. His dynasty was responsible for much of the conversion to Islam in the Indian subcontinent.

The glorious court of Mahmoud of Ghazni attracted celebrated scholars, scientists, artists, craftsmen and poets to this new cultural centre. Here they were able to express themselves freely, to the lasting enrichment of Afghanistan. Persia's most eminent poet, Firdausi, came to Ghazni where he wrote the *Shahnamah*, the Book of Kings, which became one of the Muslim classics. The great scholar Al-Biruni also worked there.

During the Ghaznavid period smiths produced some fine metalwork. Many of them came from India, where this art was ancient and had achieved high standards of craftsmanship. Ewers, vases, sprinklers, bowls, incense burners and all the traditional artefacts of Islamic life were created and now fill the museums of Afghanistan, Persia and India. Ornate designs with floral, animal and Arabic calligraphic patterns were engraved or inlaid with delicacy and skill.

The Ghaznavid empire fell to the Seljuks in the eleventh century. One hundred years later all traces of Ghaznavid rule were literally burned out of Afghanistan by the Ghorids, who sacked and put to the torch Ghazni itself in 1152. Thus a long period of turmoil and

This ornate Afghani rosewater sprinkler (above) is embossed, studded with glass and has coin-shaped pendants.

destruction began. The Ghorids were defeated by the Turk, Kharezm Shah, but then the Mongol hordes under Ghenghis advanced from the Steppes and the Gobi desert. To punish the country for its resistance, Ghenghis Khan slaughtered the people and laid waste their cities. The historic Buddhist city of Bamiyan was besieged and desolated, as were many thriving centres of Muslim culture.

Ghenghis Khan's empire proved to be a personal one which did not survive his death in 1227 but fell quickly into a series of petty kingdoms. Timur the Lame (Tamburlaine) reunited the country and its armies in the fourteenth century, and continued repressive and violent rule. He forced craftsmen and artists to his capital at Samarkand where he built his "City of Splendour." However, his successors, the Timurids, brought an era of peace and stability and patronage of learning and the arts.

Timur's son, Shah Rukh, and his remarkable Queen, Gawhar Shad, founded this new golden age of Islamic

174

culture. His empire spread through Iran, Afghanistan and Khurosan. It was essentially Persian in its inception and ideas, but its capital was Herat in Afghanistan. As in previous ages of Islamic enlightenment, the most brilliant minds and skills were drawn from every part of the Islamic world.

The achievements in arts and crafts during Timurid rule set new standards of excellence which were to be models for later periods. The School of Herat founded by Shah Rukh's poet son, Baisungar, promoted art in books; an enthusiasm which was to be emulated by subsequent schools in Iran, Turkey, Transoxiana and India. Their Arabic calligraphy, miniature painting, illumination and binding were the finest ever produced during the history of Islam.

Queen Gawhar Shad is believed to have sold her own jewellery to finance the construction of a magnificent *madrasah*. Sadly almost nothing remains of the splendid Timurid achievements except a few minarets and the Queen's mausoleum.

In 1504 Babur, a Barlash Turk and founder of the Mughal empire, made Kabul his capital before conquering India in 1525. Afghanistan then became part of his empire until between 1739 and 1741, when it was once more overrun by the Persians under Nadir Shah. On his assassination in 1747, the commander of his bodyguard, Ahmad Shah Abdali or Durrani, was proclaimed first King of the Afghans with his capital at Kandahar.

Traditional Afghan jewellery is similar to that of northern Pakistan. Both are characterised by relatively crude work, and this roughness gives Afghan work a primitive flavour. Amuletic pieces exist in an infinite variety of shapes and sizes. Heavy pieces are common, and the dominant techniques used are granulation and engraving. Panels of ornamented silver are often linked with chains or fixed to fabric backings. Silver shots, bells and twisted wire are favourite decorations.

Women's clothing may be ornamented with a series of pins, positioned from the waist up to the neck, forming a mosaic of metal designs. These pins are light and pretty and inset with small stones and delicate gilding. Some pieces exist which are finely chiselled and worked with floral motifs, others are inset with semi-precious stones and have coins hanging from them. Turkomanian features can be seen in much Afghani jewellery.

As in other Islamic countries where tribal traditions persist, the main differences between urban and rural jewellery are that the urban pieces are smaller and generally lighter. They are also more likely to incorporate precious and semi-precious stones rather than the coloured glass which is typical of rural work. The skill and versatility of Afghan smiths is evident in both types.

A very advanced civilisation is known to have existed around 2500 BC in the land which is now Pakistan. Its two important cities were sited along the course of the Indus, at Mohenjodaro in Sind and at Harappa in the Punjab. The antiquities found there resemble those found on Sumerian sites at Kish and Susa in Mesopotamia. The Indus Valley folk were highly cultured and are chiefly known to us by finely carved seals in white steatite bearing the figures of bulls, antelopes, elephants and other animals, and by pictographic inscriptions which

Partly gilded and enamelled, this extremely ornate Pakistani anklet (above) *is heavy, old, big and inlaid with glass.*

have so far baffled all attempts at interpretation. The city of Mohenjodaro is well laid out, with a great public bath and broad streets. Historians have yet to discover why these early peoples abandoned their cities.

Since then numerous peoples have settled, invaded, destroyed, rebuilt or in some way made an impression on the region: the Persians, the Greeks, the Scythians, the Kushans, the Huns, the Buyids, the Turks, the Ghaznavids, the Ghoris, the Khaljis, the Tughlaqs, the Sayyeds, the Lodhi Afghans, the Mughals, the Portuguese and the British. They introduced Buddhism, Hinduism, Sikhism, Christianity and Islam – which is now the declared faith of ninety-nine per cent of the country.

In its various ethnic groupings, traditions and religious affiliations, Pakistan of today reflects the influence of these diverse cultures. Craftsmen are adept at rug-making, silk-weaving, wood-carving and metalworking; their art reflects Greek, Persian, Arab, Indian and Chinese inspiration.

The silverwork is finely carved and chiselled in intricate floral designs, enriched with enamelling and lacquered inlay and decorated with precious stones, glass and ivory insets. Teapots, cigar boxes, mirror backs, hookah bases, bowls, vases and jewellery reveal the people's liking for delicate work in their homes or to adorn their bodies. Skills have been developed through centuries of expertise in casting, chasing, incising, repoussé and filigree.

In each of the four provinces of Pakistan one can find the mixed cultural strains typical of the country as a whole, while each area still preserves individual characteristics. Sindhi work is the richest in colour and variety, maintaining a true folk tradition. Hyderabad and Karachi are its chief smithing centres, the former excels in enamelling, the latter is renowned for its cut work, repoussé and delicate decoration. The Punjab is much more cosmopolitan and has produced some of the finest and purest of the country's silverwork in the Arab styles of damascene and arabesque. The most famous of Pakistan's metalworking centres is Multan, which lies in the heart of the Punjab. Sialkot and Lahore, the famous centres of damascene, are in the same province. *Koftgari*, as damascene is called in Urdu, is also made today at Peshawar in the North-West Frontier. In the latter region and in Baluchistan strong links have been maintained with the people's tribal origins. Silverwork from these areas is not as sophisticated as those in other areas; it has a heavier appearance and is roughly finished.

Modern workshops are attempting to reproduce and revive the past glories of Pakistan's arts and crafts, which flourished long ago under the unifying rule of the Mughals. Both Pakistan and Bangladesh were so recently part of India that not surprisingly their silverwork is still strongly influenced by Indian themes and techniques.

"*Atma sans kritir shilpam*" is an ancient Indian saying – "Handicrafts are the surest means to salvation of our souls." Indian Art generally appears highly ornate and complex, full of mythological symbols which may be confusing at first. But it is immediately impressive and is pervaded by a certain spiritual quality reflecting the bond between the craftsman and his work.

From the earliest civilisations of the Indus Valley, Indian craftsmen have seen their role as that of artist creators. Their art demonstrates the conscious efforts of man to perfect himself, his appreciation of beauty and his attempts to emulate Visvakarman, the Lord of Arts. In Indian mythology Visvakarman was master of a thousand crafts, carpenter of the gods, builder of their palaces and fashioner of their jewels. This myth may sound whimsical to an outsider, but it has been the inspiration for some of the most beautiful and powerful creative work ever achieved.

In discussing the arts and crafts of India, one can safely generalise by saying that its artists have retained a spiritual unity inspired by early philosophy, that art is not separate, but integral to life. Symbolism has played a large role in Indian Art and the interaction between Hinduism and Islam broadened its abstract language. Despite the conflicts between the two cultures, there is also an affinity which manifests itself in art.

Islam came to the subcontinent in the eighth century under the Ummayads. It was strengthened under the rule of the Abbasids, during the period of the Ghaznavids. Many craftsmen were drawn to the Sultan's capital in Delhi, where they built palaces and fashioned objects to the glory of the new faith. Hindu arts were given an impetus to compete for survival and to outshine these Muslim achievements.

Hindu craftsmen helped to build and decorate mosques and inter-marriage was not uncommon. The Delhi sultans welcomed learned men from Persia. Amir Khusrau, one of the most famous Indo-Persian poets, lived at the court of Ala-ud-Din. These Turkish sultans introduced the dome, the true arch and the minaret to India. Calligraphy was used for decorative purposes. Many Hindu characteristics are visible in the work of the period, especially in the combination of strength and grace. The result is known as the Indo-Saracenic style, which may also be seen in centres of Muslim culture throughout northern India.

As the central authority was weakened by dynastic disputes, the Viceroys who governed the provinces quickly became independent. A few of them lived magnificently and were considerable patrons of the arts. The rulers of Jaunpur in Bengal were cultured men and the fine buildings with which their city state was adorned earned Jaunpur the title of the "Shiraz of India." The capital of Gujarat was Ahmadabad, which was a beautiful and prosperous city situated in fertile country and famous for its weavers, who used silk, cotton and gold thread.

The city of Vijayanagar reached its zenith in 1509–25 under Khrishnadeva Raya, an enlightened monarch and a patron of the arts, who spent large sums on endowing religious institutions. Covered bazaars lined the streets and in them were displayed "all sorts of rubies, diamonds, emeralds, seed pearls and cloth," according to the Portuguese traveller Domingo Paes who was much impressed by the capital. The palace was exquisitely decorated with ivory, and the vessels, even the water jars, were of gold and silver.

But it was the coming of the Mughals much later in the sixteenth century, which gave Muslim Art in India its fullest expression. Metalworking was one of the oldest Indian crafts, and it reached its zenith under their rule, for the Mughals loved jewellery and *objets d'art*. They introduced new emblems and symbols into Indian crafts and demanded perfection in even the smallest details, so that the plainest gold piece was produced to very high standards.

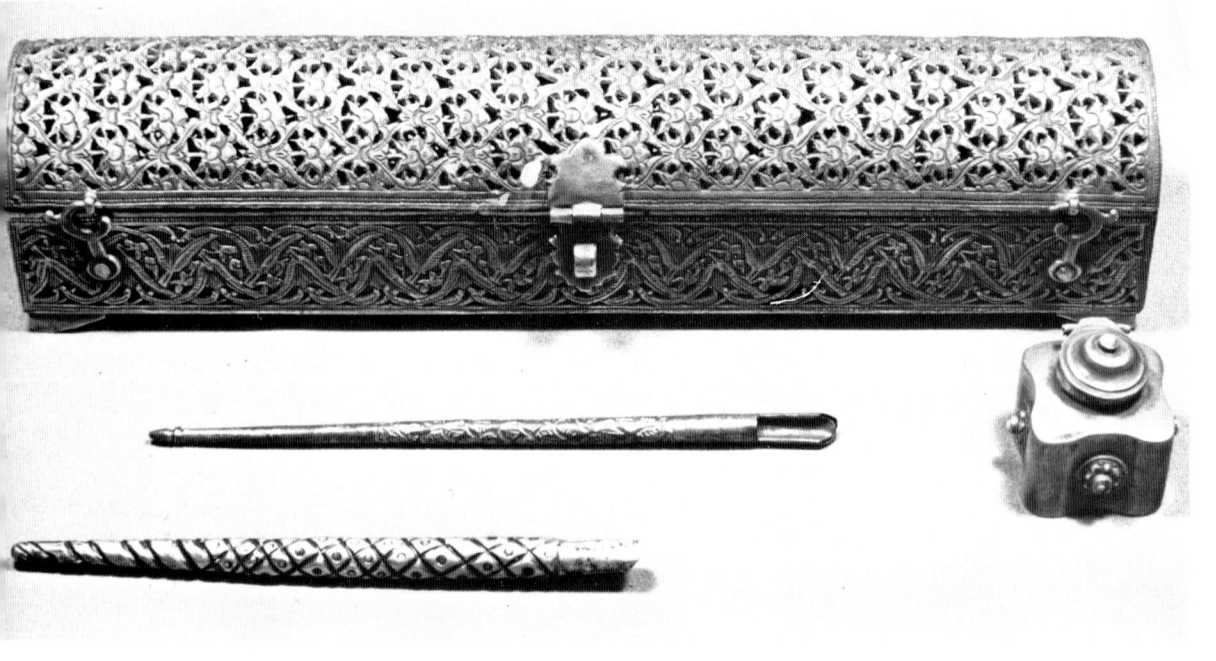

Above: *A Pakistani pen box, displaying openwork decoration of floral and geometrical design, two pen quills and an unusually-designed box for an ink bottle, which is flower-shaped and inlaid with silver balls.*

Enamelled and gilded, the Indian tumbler (left) is also engraved with floral decoration.

Mosques, madrasahs, mausoleums and palaces of all kinds were constructed. The emperor Shah Jehan built a sumptuous marble palace at Delhi, which he named Shahjehanabad. When his empress died, he built in her honour that incomparable mausoleum, the Taj Mahal, started in 1632 and not completed until 1647, although 20,000 workmen were employed. There are many other fine examples, such as the mausoleum of Mohammed Adil Shah in Bijapur, the Red Fort at Agra and the Palace of Hawar Mahal in Jaipur.

Among the minor arts, weaving flourished, especially silk decorated with realistic floral and animal designs. The carpet industry thrived, as did painting, especially miniatures.

Inspired by the rulers' interest, large metalworking centres sprang up throughout the empire: Gujarat, Sialkot, Jaipur, Alwar, Sirohi, Travancore and Bidar were famed for their damascene or *koftgari*. This characteristically Islamic style was imported to India from Damascus via Kabul and Persia. It was originally used to decorate weaponry. Swords, shields, daggers and belts were all worked by skilled smiths, and the individuality of the work was a source of pride to their warrior owners. Later, the same technique was used to decorate other, more domestic, objects.

Damascene work was at its best in the city of Bidar, where pieces were made entirely of silver and became known as *bidri*. The development of *bidri* was promoted by a marriage tradition current in Mysore and elsewhere, which survives to this day in Muslim parts of India. The bridegroom will present many articles of *bidri* to his wife as a dowry; they may include vases, bowls, water sprinklers and jewellery.

Colour contrast and an impression of depth give *bidri* work its special charm. Passages from the Quran, poetic verses and prayers are added. Today, such objects as book ends, cigarette boxes, tea services, ashtrays and decanters have all joined the *bidri* repertoire. Bidar is no longer the only centre for silver damascene work; Lucknow, Purniah and Murshidabad, among others, have adopted this successful technique.

Another famed and ancient method of decorating silver is the art of enamelling or *meenakari*. Traces of enamelling are to be found in the Buddhist centre of Taxila, but under the patronage of the Mughals craftsmen became so skilled that they could transcribe a complete miniature in enamelling onto a small piece of silver or gold. Beautiful birds, flowers, trees and leaves all appear in naturalistic colours set into the backs of ornaments. The detail was so fine that they looked like tiny paintings. The main centres for the craft were Delhi, Benares, Lucknow, Rampur, Alwar, Kashmir and Jaipur, where enamelling was done on gold, silver, copper and brass.

The art of enamelling declined with the power of the Mughals and although it still exists today, the standards which were routine under the great emperors have never been achieved again. The main centre now is Jaipur where the *champlévé* method is unequalled in India for its variety of design and purity of colour. Many articles, such as scent bottles, incense burners, ornaments, plates and boxes, are made in the typical colours of Jaipur craftsmen, which are red, creamy-white, green and yellow. Their main decorative designs include flowers and creepers.

Kashmiri enamelling follows the

ARAB AND ISLAMIC SILVER

strictly Muslim heritage even more closely, displaying the traditional arabesque style, rosettes and mosaic patterns. The Lucknow and Rampur styles are achieved by etching on silver. Then green-blue enamelling is added, with traces of brown, yellow and orange. The main motifs are of flowers and animals; the absence of human forms shows that the craftsmen's work has been influenced by Islam.

Different cities and areas in India are noted for particular techniques and skills. Kashmir has long been famous for its parcel-gilt silverware, of which a typical example is the *Surahi*, a goblet whose elegant form dates from Gupta times. Foliage scrolling is delicately and deeply engraved into the gilding until it reaches the silver beneath. Gold and silver tea sets, models of houseboats, bowls, vases, scent bottles and sprinklers bear minutely detailed floral designs, which demonstrate the excellence of Kashmiri craftsmanship.

Lucknow, Jaipur and other cities in Gujarat produce exceptional repoussé work displaying sprigs of leaves and flowers. A much more shallow form of repoussé distinguishes the work of the Rann of Kutch area. Every detail of a pattern is first carved into a piece of wood, then the piece to be decorated is placed over the wood and hammered with great care and precision. Many other forms of metalworking exist in different areas of the subcontinent. Objects made of brass or copper are as carefully created as those of more precious metals.

Jewellery is a vital part of India's heritage. Ancient statuettes and bronzes of gods and kings bedecked with jewels were found in the cities of Taxila and Ajanta among others. The fundamental principles laid down for the craftsmen of old are evident even in these pieces, for each piece had its place and was apt only for a particular occasion. Strict religious traditions dictated certain conventions in the wearing of jewellery. Even the poorest of women had to wear toe-rings and bangles. In the predominantly Muslim northern areas, the nose-ring was obligatory after marriage: in Bengal iron bangles were imperative, and in Punjab and Gujarat ivory ones were a religious necessity.

The Mughals introduced new forms and standards to this long tradition of jewellery. Hair pieces, tiaras, necklaces and pendants were fashioned with the new Islamic motifs and studded with precious and semi-precious stones. The Indus Valley use of jade, amethyst and agate was enriched with the addition of pearls, rubies, emeralds and diamonds, resulting in splendid creations. Enamelling and filigree were also used in the jewellery which enhanced the courts of the emperors.

With the fall of the Mughals, jewellery and other crafts which had developed under their patronage declined. The era of the British Raj produced much duller workmanship. In this century there was a resurgence of Mughal styles before Independence, and high standards are maintained today. The styles of the old jewellery, distinguished by exquisite taste and craftsmanship, are coming back into fashion, being followed in the principal cities, such as Calcutta and Bombay, chiefly by Bengali jewellers. Lucknow, Delhi and Jaipur were the main Mughal centres and they have striven still to

The gilding and niello work on the Southeast Asian teapot (above) *is similar to styles of technique found in India, Pakistan and Persia.*

deserve their fame. Karimnagar, Murshidabad and many other towns and cities have turned their skills to producing fine, delicate and imaginative pieces in accord with modern demands. The strong Muslim heritage can still be seen in such areas as Orissa State where jewellery designs and workmanship bear a close resemblance to pieces from the Arabian Peninsula.

Brief mention should be made of the Islamic influence in South East Asia, in the thousands of islands between Australasia and southern China. The Indians and Chinese settled there in the first and second centuries AD, and local traditions stem from the folklore of these vast and ancient subcontinents. But Islam too has a strong influence on the way of life, where it has blended with local folklore in curious ways.

Archaeologists have discovered traces of many ancient civilisations in the archipelago of Indonesia. Statues of human and animal figures found in Sumatra, Borneo, the Celebes and Moluccas, dating from the Bronze and Iron Ages, demonstrate that the people imbued their art with monumental and symbolic characteristics. The variety of arts and crafts in South-East Asia is remarkable, and each region has retained an individuality of technique and style.

Nevertheless, one common feature of most Indonesian metalwork is that the form, colour and pattern of a piece are considered to be more important than the intrinsic value of the metal used to create it. Very often gold leaf will cover wood or iron objects. The craftsmen mix their metals for aesthetic purposes, aiming to marry colour and texture and draw their inspiration from nature, so that bird, flower and animal motifs abound in their work.

Arts and crafts developed swiftly in this region around 400 AD, particularly in Java and Sumatra, when traders arrived from the Indian subcontinent. The introduction of Hindu philosophy blended well with the indigenous beliefs of the islanders. Buddhism followed and both were modified by contact with the local culture. Many traders settled and married Indonesian, Malaysian and Philippine girls. Indian culture had a marked effect on the area; the horse and elephant were used, new irrigation methods were developed, learning and literature stimulated. Architectural techniques and ideas promoted the building of cities, in which sculpture and the decorative arts attained new heights.

Links with India remained close. Islam was brought to the islands by merchant traders from Gujarat. The tribes of northern Sumatra were the first to adopt the new faith. Muslim influence was so apparent there that when Marco Polo visited the area in 1292 he called it "the Islamic City." By the end of the fifteenth century, many independent Muslim states existed.

Portuguese traders came in 1511. At the end of the sixteenth century the East India Company vied with them for the spice trade. The Dutch arrived later, were to stay longest and become the dominant European influence. Chinese ideas filtered into Indonesian culture, but were never to gain as strong a hold as either Hinduism or Islam.

Precious metals are refined in Java, Bali, the southern Celebes and parts of Borneo and Sumatra, which were the regions in which Hinduism was most influential and where trading produced prosperity which gave rise to local demand for articles of luxury and to a certain ostentation as a mark of power and wealth. Smithing in gold and silver is not as old a tradition in South-East Asia as work in iron and bronze, but the craftsmen of Bali, Java, Atjeh, Sumatra and the Celebes developed fine techniques in filigree, chasing and engraving. Enamelling was practised in Atjeh, where the method had probably been imported from China.

Fine weaponry has always been produced throughout Indonesia. Geometric ornamentation, with chased foliage and floral motifs, transform hilts, knives and swords into works of art. Particular care and attention is lavished on them because of their important role on ceremonial occasions.

A process of alloying copper and gold, known as *suwasa*, is frequently used for many objects of precious metal and in jewellery. The alloy is combined with silver to make dishes, platters, *sirib* cases and other objects as well as for jewellery. Necklaces, bracelets, leg bands, buckles, belts, rings and ceremonial ornaments are all made by this method.

Another process found in Atjeh and the Batak areas is based on a more ancient method of brass casting. Objects are decorated with silver globules or filigree bands. Many beautiful pieces of gold and silver filigree also emanate from there, especially from Atjeh itself, where large chest ornaments are popular.

On the Padang Plateau, objects such as boxes and imitation fruit are made and small parts, such as the caps of ornamental bamboo receptacles, are decorated with filigree. In the predominantly Muslim areas, like Java, bronze working has almost disappeared; in Hindu areas like Bali, sculpture and bronze casting continue.

South-East Asian craftsmen create unexpected combinations of patterns and exquisite designs. Some pieces contain niello and gilt in a richness of decoration which may cover the entire piece. Much of this silverwork displays Indian features, notably in the abundant use of floral motifs and varying lotus combinations. Many South-East Asian silver pieces are decorated with Arabic calligraphy and some items are signed in Arabic. Jewellery is strikingly worn on festive occasions throughout South-East Asia, the colour of the ornaments complement flamboyant Asian silks, making an impressive spectacle, especially during a dance.

Above: *The dragon motifs, openwork and delicate floral decorations on this bone-handled spoon and fork are typical of South-east Asian silverworks.*

ARAB AND ISLAMIC SILVER

This partly gilded Turkomanian breast decoration (above) *is inlaid with agate and the edges of the ornament are scalloped. The main piece of this ornament* (right) *is inlaid with various glass stones and worn on the forehead and often forms part of the bridal regalia in India and Pakistan. Multiple pendants adorn this Pakistani headdress* (opposite) *which is fixed with three chains and pins.*

CENTRAL AND SOUTH-EAST ASIA

181

ARAB AND ISLAMIC SILVER

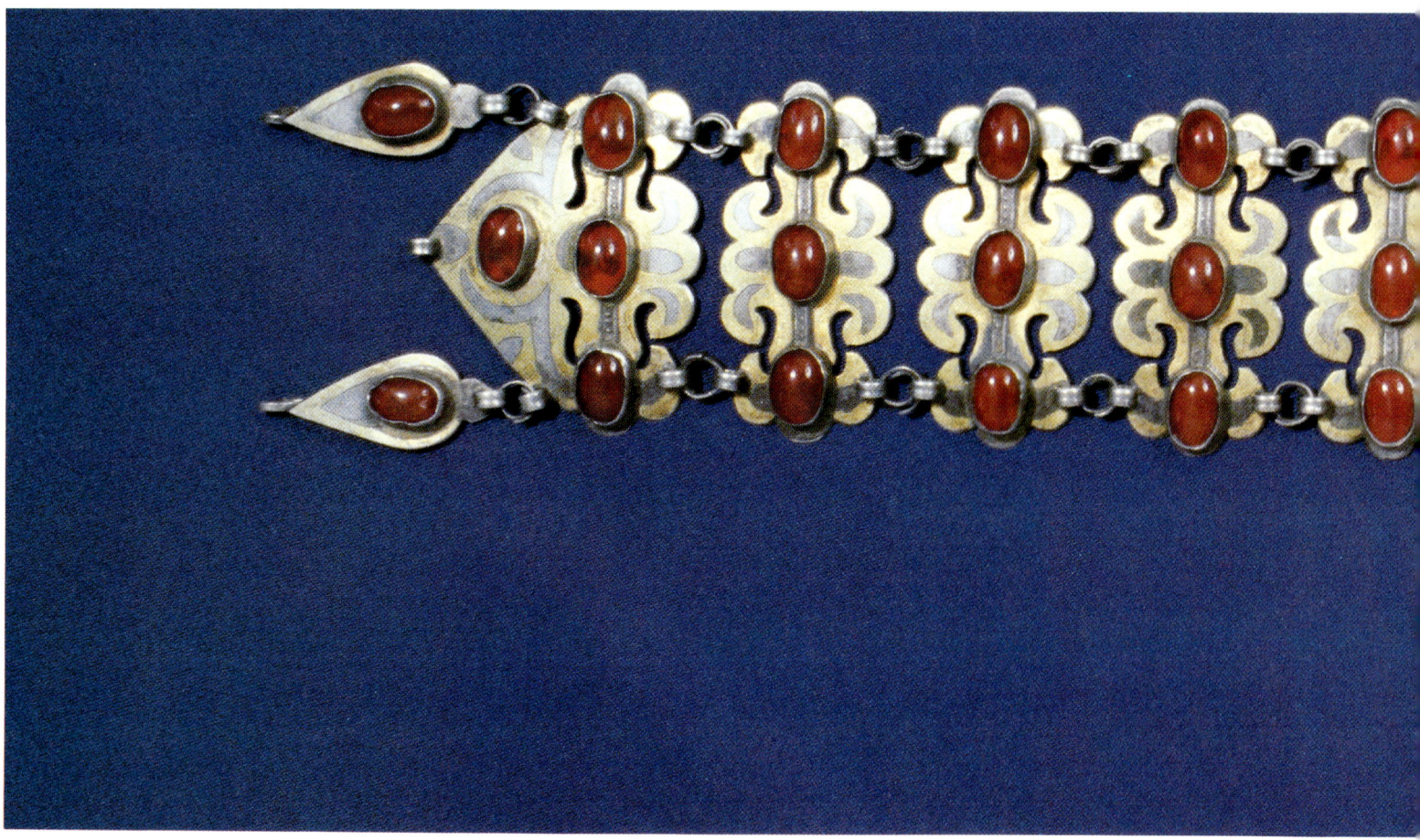

CENTRAL AND SOUTH-EAST ASIA

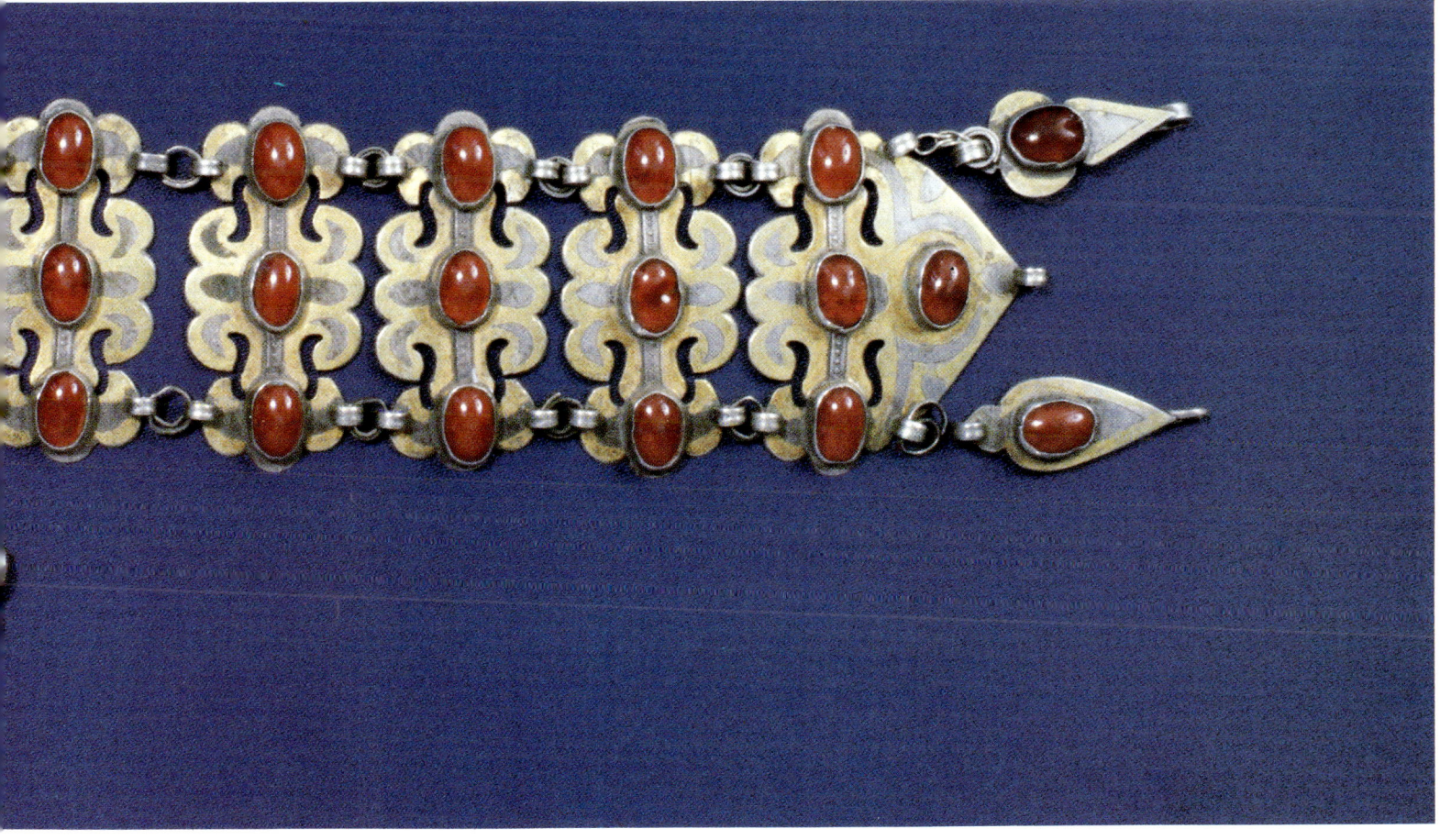

Above and top: *These two different styles of Turkomanian* iklil *are partly gilded and inlaid with stones.*

ARAB AND ISLAMIC SILVER

Above: *A Pakistani set of a hair ornament, a brooch, a ring and two other silver pieces, one of which is a toothpick and the other an ear-cleaner.* Right: *One of a pair of Afghan silver hairdresses which are worn on either side of the head.* Far right: *An Afghani hairdress in which the main ornament is inlaid with a red stone and carries an amuletic box, which is also commonly found in Arabia and Morocco and elsewhere in the Islamic world.*

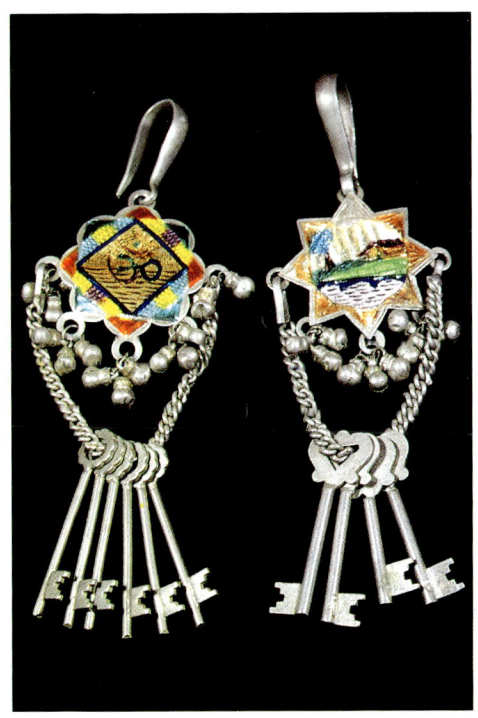

Various types of Pakistani earrings (top) *which are all inlaid with glass. Old Pakistani earrings* (above) *are often big and heavy like these which are also gilded, inlaid with jewels, granulated and have geometrical and floral decoration. Left: Keys and bells are common pendant designs in Pakistani jewellery.*

ARAB AND ISLAMIC SILVER

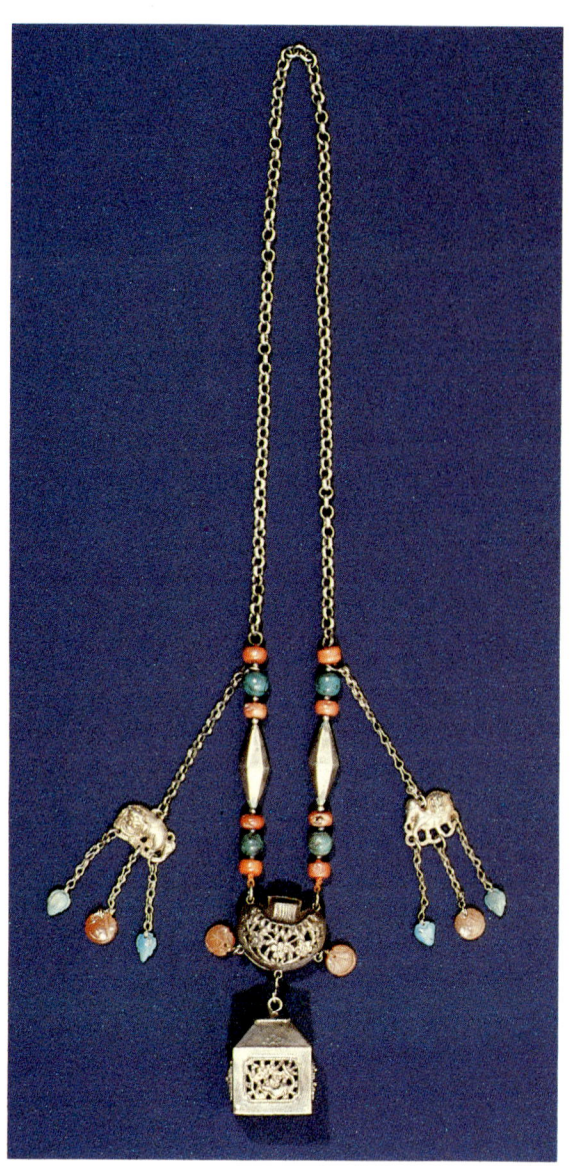

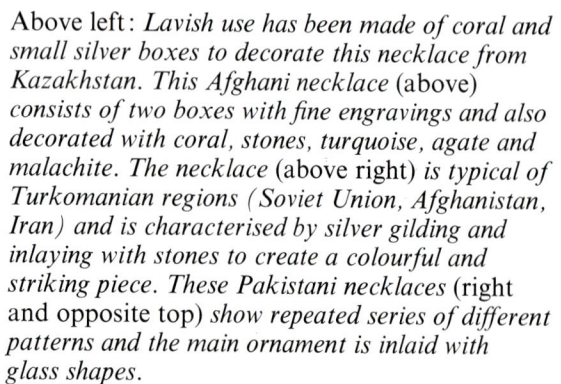

Above left: *Lavish use has been made of coral and small silver boxes to decorate this necklace from Kazakhstan.* This Afghani necklace (above) *consists of two boxes with fine engravings and also decorated with coral, stones, turquoise, agate and malachite.* The necklace (above right) *is typical of Turkomanian regions (Soviet Union, Afghanistan, Iran) and is characterised by silver gilding and inlaying with stones to create a colourful and striking piece.* These Pakistani necklaces (right and opposite top) *show repeated series of different patterns and the main ornament is inlaid with glass shapes.*

CENTRAL AND SOUTH-EAST ASIA

The pendants of this Pakistani necklace (above) *are strung on thick strands of wool and fine floral and bird decorations appear on heavy silver discs. Pendants embellish this heart-shaped Indian ornament* (above right) *which forms part of a necklace.*

187

ARAB AND ISLAMIC SILVER

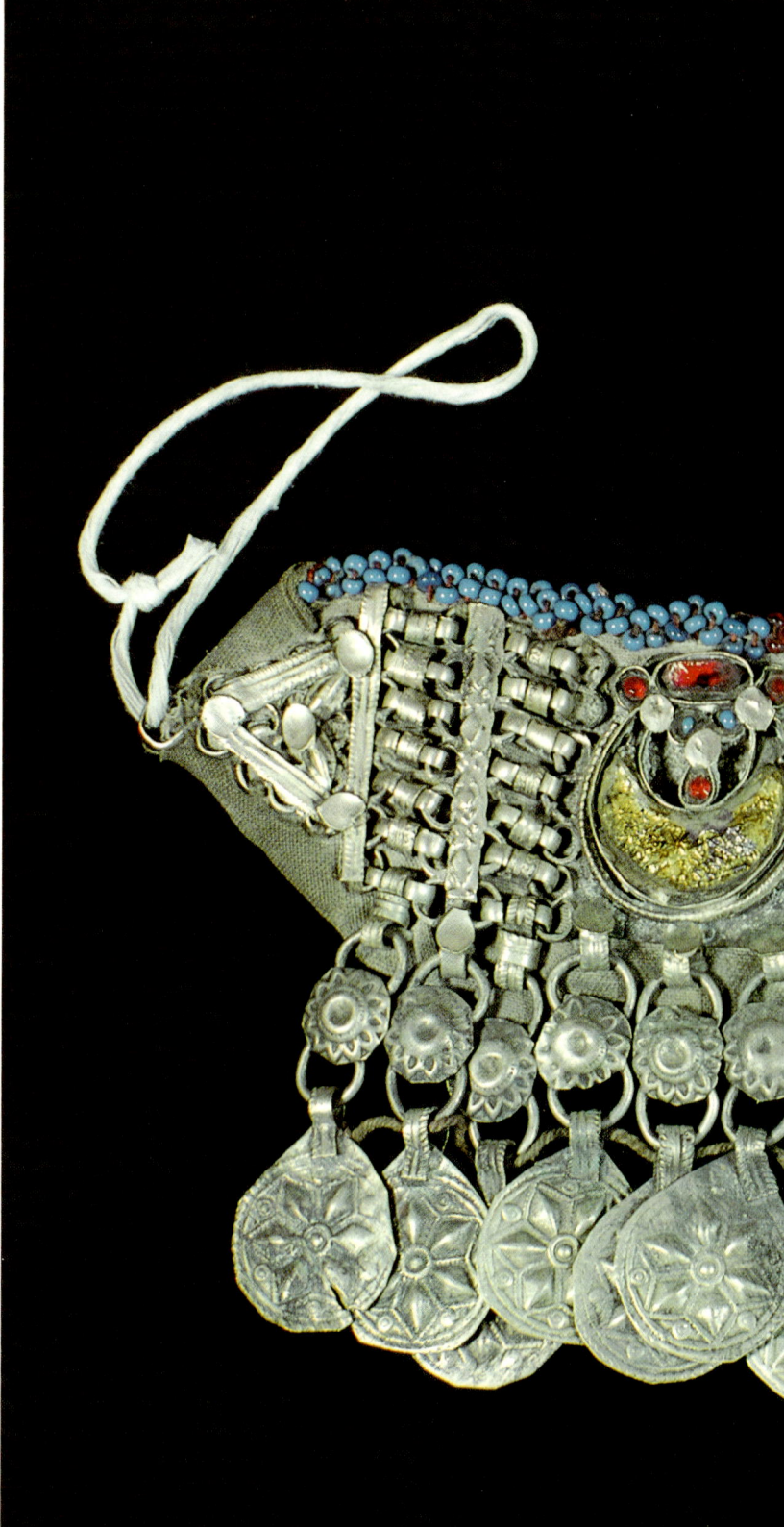

Glass inlaying gives a gilded impression in this Pakistani necklace (top left). Much detailed work is produced in this part of the world which is similar to that done in Yemen. Second from top left: An Afghan necklace inlaid with glass. An attractive Pakistani necklace (above left) consists of repoussé panels with inlaid glass pendants which are balanced by tiny strung blue beads at the top of the ornament.

CENTRAL AND SOUTH-EAST ASIA

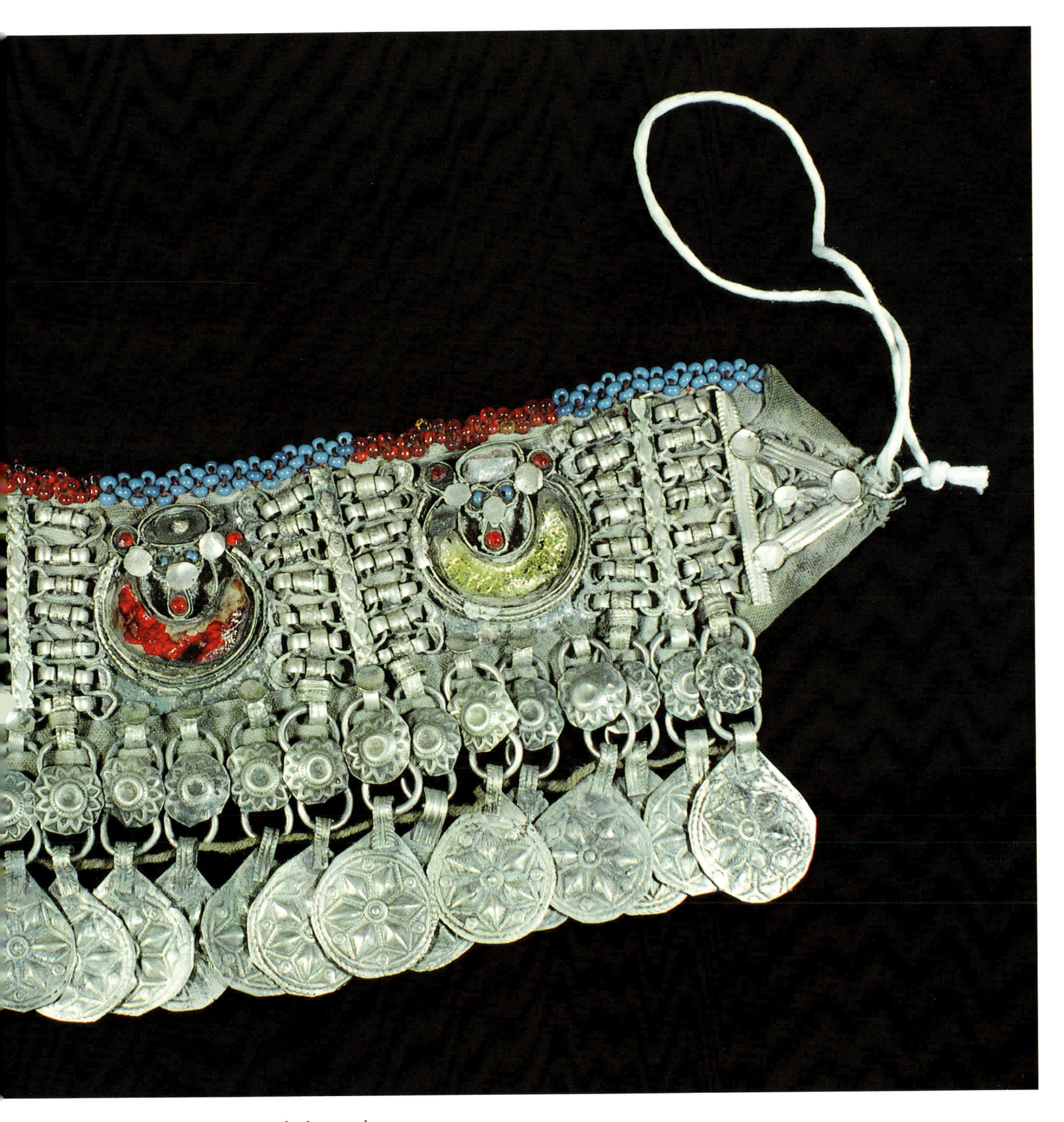

Intricate patterns appear in the low grade silver of this rural Afghan necklace (above). Opposite bottom left: This set, which comprises a necklace, earrings and a ring in turquoise which has been mounted on silver gilt, is a fine example of Indian work.

189

ARAB AND ISLAMIC SILVER

The warm glass colours of this Pakistani necklace (above) give the whole piece an attractive character. The use of small silver balls in another Pakistani necklace (above right) is also typical of Algerian and Omani jewellery.

CENTRAL AND SOUTH-EAST ASIA

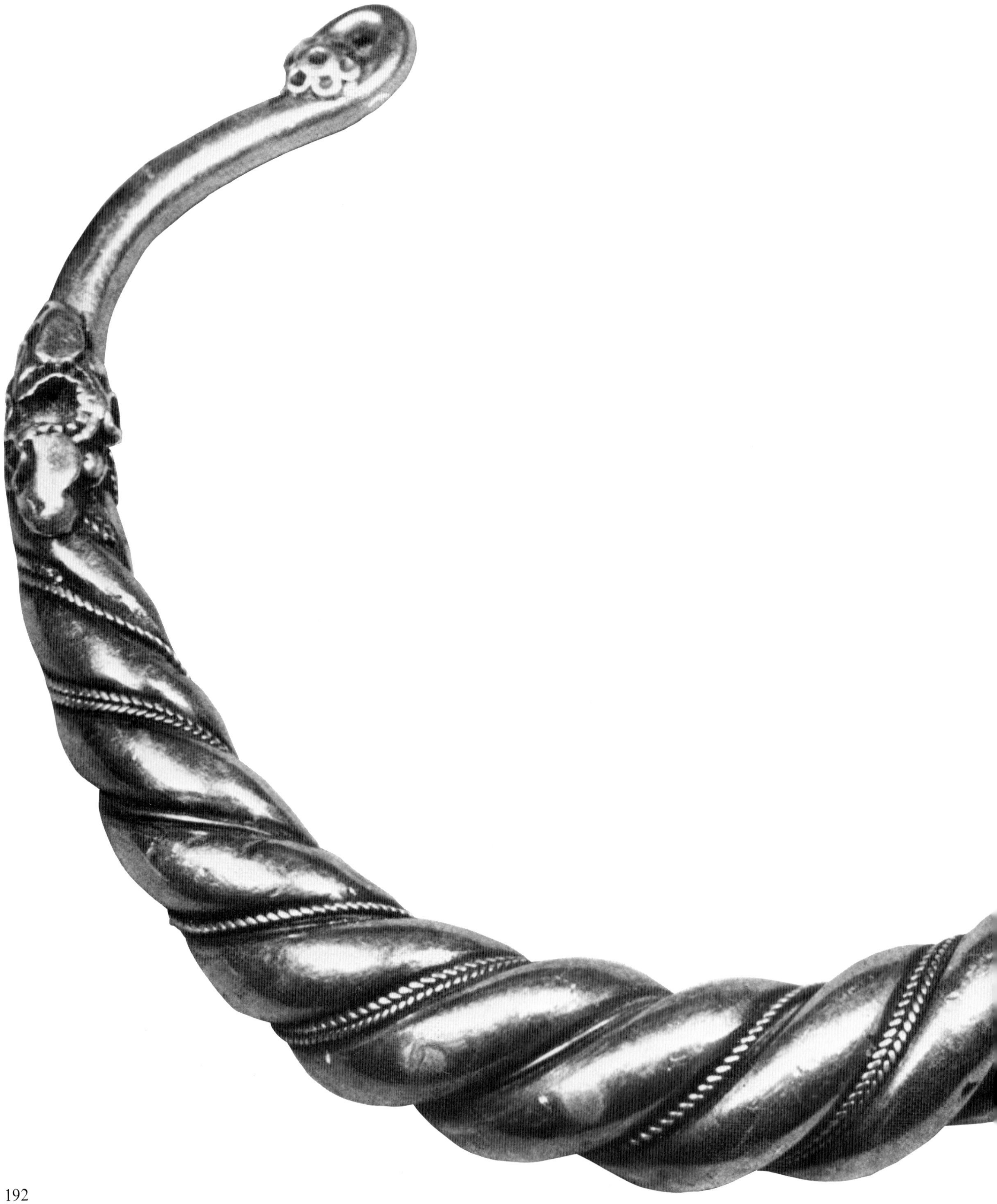

CENTRAL AND SOUTH-EAST ASIA

Top: *Different styles of chain abound in India.* Above: *This heavy Pakistani torque is inlaid with solid silver flowers and silver balls.* Opposite: *Both thick and thin silver wire have been twisted and worked together to create this plain and elegant Pakistani torque.*

193

ARAB AND ISLAMIC SILVER

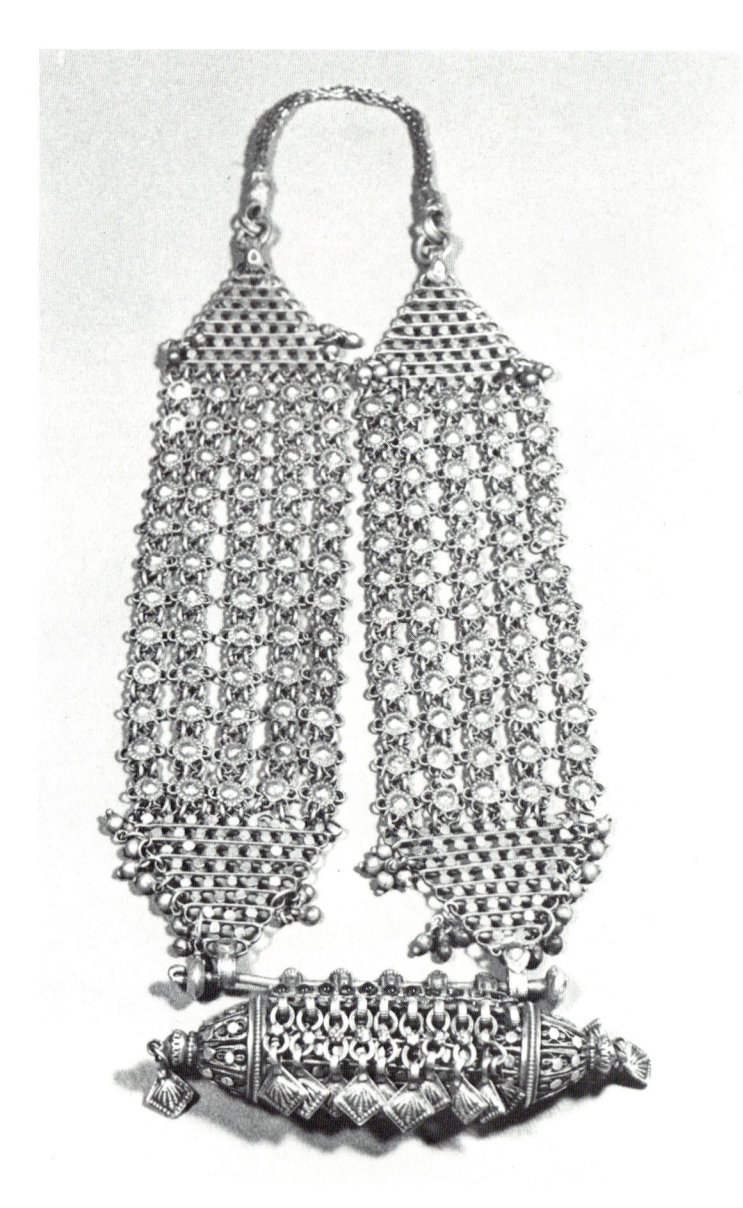

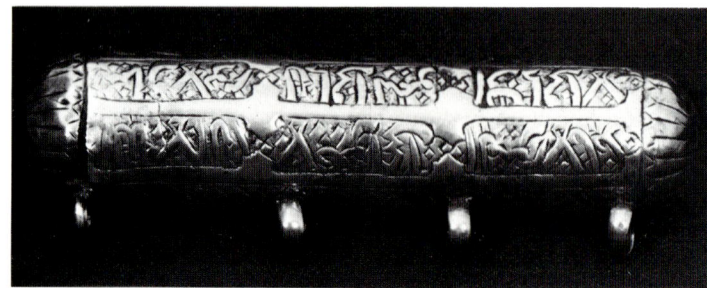

This ornate and heavy Pakistani necklace (top) has four triangular decorated panels joined by five lengths of florally fashioned shapes. The Arabic calligraphy on this cylindrical Afghan amulet (above) reads "the Verse of the Throne". An Afghan perfume container (right) forms part of a necklace in which the main pieces have pendants and inlaid blue stones.

194

CENTRAL AND SOUTH-EAST ASIA

This well composed Afghan breast ornament (left) *is inlaid with stones and decorated with floral patterns. This necklace* (below) *is typical of Turkomanian regions. Bottom: Various Pakistani pendants form part of larger pieces of jewellery that are sometimes worn singly.*

195

ARAB AND ISLAMIC SILVER

A kriss *or dagger* (above) *from Indonesia displays Islamic geometrical and floral designs. An Indian belt* (right) *consists of various hollow panels of floral decoration and chains with an ornate buckle in a stepped pyramid shape.*

CENTRAL AND SOUTH-EAST ASIA

197

ARAB AND ISLAMIC SILVER

The Indian buckle (top right) *displays human, animal and floral openwork decoration. The south-east Asian buckle* (above) *is engraved with floral decoration and nielloed and further embellished with two eight-pointed stars.* Right: *Floral and geometrical decoration are pronounced on this Pakistani bracelet, which is bowl-shaped and hollow.*

CENTRAL AND SOUTH-EAST ASIA

Partly gilded and enamelled, these Pakistani anklets (left) *are old, heavy and big. The Pakistani bracelet* (below left) *is beautifully made and granulated and has twisted silver wire on the inside rim. Below: In this bracelet, anklet and necklaces, various patterns of Indian chainwork are represented.*

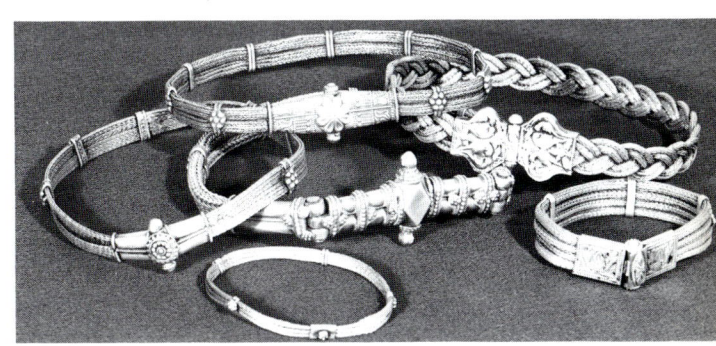

Two patterns of Pakistani bracelet and anklet (above right). *The latter is flexible to enable the wearer to vary its size. These linked Pakistani rings* (above) *are made one for four fingers and one for three.*

199

ARAB AND ISLAMIC SILVER

Above left: *Modern Pakistani coffee pots which imitate old designs are mostly made for export to the Arab world. Characteristic Islamic patterns decorate this Indian tea set* (above) *which comprises a tea-pot, sugar bowl, milk jug and tray. This plain silver Pakistani coffee pot* (below left) *is well proportioned. Repoussé work and floral design adorn this Pakistani tea set* (below). *A Pakistani coffee pot* (opposite) *which is partly decorated with repoussé work and floral designs.*

CENTRAL AND SOUTH-EAST ASIA

ARAB AND ISLAMIC SILVER

A Pakistani filigreed dish (above) *has floral designs and is decorated with solid silver balls. Beautifully proportioned, the heavily gilded Pakistani dish* (opposite top) *has floral decorations. A Pakistani tray* (opposite far right) *displays repoussé floral design. The shell-shaped compartments in this Pakistani tray* (opposite right) *are for spices and also for* paan.

CENTRAL AND SOUTH-EAST ASIA

ARAB AND ISLAMIC SILVER

CENTRAL AND SOUTH-EAST ASIA

A bowl and tumbler (opposite top), *both of which are enamelled and gilded, display fine animal and floral decoration.* Opposite centre: *Various types of sweetmeat dishes. An engraved salt, pepper and mustard set* (opposite bottom) *from Pakistan is further embellished by a camel image.*

An Indian bowl (above) *is heavily engraved and ended with animal and floral decoration. A distinctive Arabesque design covers this Indian tumbler* (above right). *Cake, bread or cheese can be presented on this grand Pakistani openwork container* (below), *used for entertaining guests.*

205

ARAB AND ISLAMIC SILVER

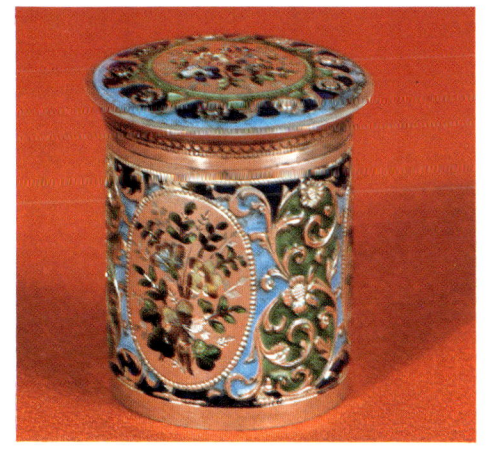

CENTRAL AND SOUTH-EAST ASIA

Reminiscent of a mosque's dome shape this Pakistani box (opposite top) *has a floral design with repoussé and openwork. Four useful types of Indian and Pakistani boxes* (opposite below) *demonstrate various techniques. Various South-east Asian boxes* (top) *represent the different shapes and standards of workmanship which occur in different areas.* Above left and centre: *These Indian enamelled, engraved and partly gilded floral boxes.* Above right: *Typically Islamic flowing patterns are demonstrated on this deeply engraved Pakistani cigarette box.*

207

ARAB AND ISLAMIC SILVER

Realistic flower design enhances this repousséd Pakistani vase (right) *fashioned in a floral shape.* Below: *These small nail-shaped instruments are for serving betel nut or* paan *from this Pakistani box.*

The special holes in this interestingly shaped Pakistani incense burner (above) *are to hold sticks of incense.* Right: *A delicate Pakistani vase.*

CENTRAL AND SOUTH-EAST ASIA

This incense burner (above) *is tree-shaped with filigree openwork repoussé: finished above with a crescent and eight-pointed star, below with small circular shaped pendants.*

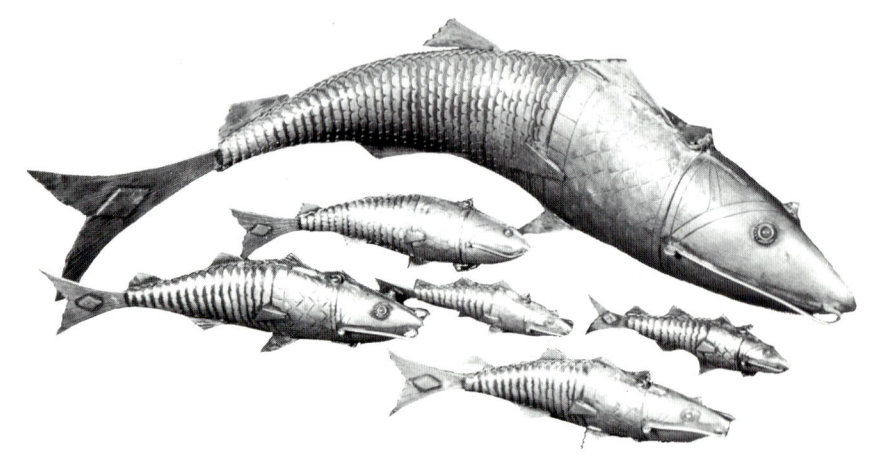

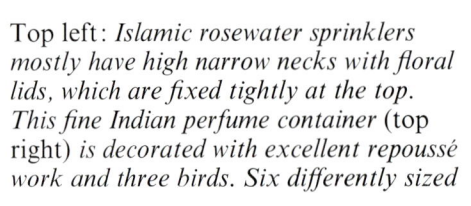

ARAB AND ISLAMIC SILVER

Top left: *Islamic rosewater sprinklers mostly have high narrow necks with floral lids, which are fixed tightly at the top. This fine Indian perfume container (top right) is decorated with excellent repoussé work and three birds. Six differently sized* hollow fishes with overlapping scales (above left), *in which the heads open to make boxes and are sometimes a hiding place for jewellery.* Above: *Various different techniques are demonstrated in these six Pakistani scent bottles.*

CENTRAL AND SOUTH-EAST ASIA

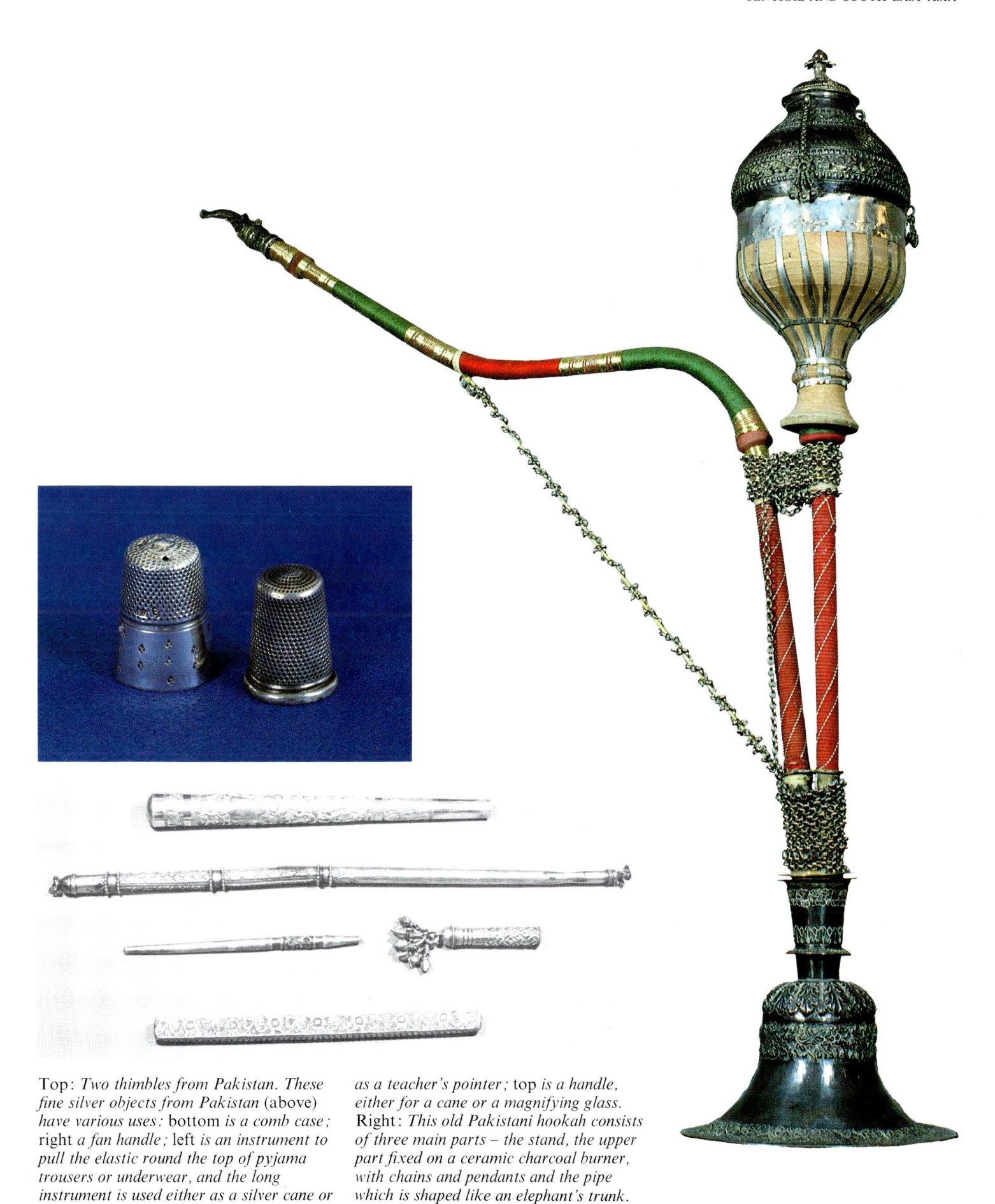

Top: *Two thimbles from Pakistan. These fine silver objects from Pakistan (above) have various uses:* bottom *is a comb case;* right *a fan handle;* left *is an instrument to pull the elastic round the top of pyjama trousers or underwear, and the long instrument is used either as a silver cane or as a teacher's pointer;* top *is a handle, either for a cane or a magnifying glass.*
Right: *This old Pakistani hookah consists of three main parts – the stand, the upper part fixed on a ceramic charcoal burner, with chains and pendants and the pipe which is shaped like an elephant's trunk.*

211

Conclusion

In presenting this book, I have tried to give some idea of my own feeling for the wonderful workmanship of Arab and Islamic silversmiths. I believe my collection to be unique in its historic and artistic quality, its wide geographical scope and in the sheer quantity of superb pieces – locked away, unfortunately, in the strong rooms of banks. As an individual I can do no more. My greatest wish is that the pieces I have collected throughout most of my adult life can somehow be removed from the darkness of bank vaults and brought to life again, that they may be shared and enjoyed by everyone and perhaps even serve, in some small way, to link the modern Islamic world with its past and its inheritance.

My hope now is that this book may stimulate the setting up of a fund or of some organisation which could provide for a permanent exhibition, and that such an initiative might form the nucleus of reference material on Islamic silversmithing, its historical origins, cultural influence and techniques. This would be of great value to modern silversmiths and archaeologists and historians, but an exhibition would surely also delight many non-specialists by the sheer excellence of the work of the ancient craftsmen.

BIBLIOGRAPHY

African History, Longmans, London

Al-Ali, Zaki Omar, *Women's Adornment and Jewellery in the Abbasid Period*, Ministry of Information, Baghdad, 1976 (Arabic)

Allam, Nimat Ismail, *Middle East Arts in the Islamic Periods*, Dar al Maarif, Cairo (Arabic)

Arts and Crafts in Indonesia, Djakarta, 1958

Barrett, Douglas, *Islamic Metalworks in the British Museum*, British Museum Publications, London 1949

Ben-Wanish, Faridah, *Jewellery in Algeria*, Algiers, 1976 (Arabic)

Beresneva, L., *The Decorative and Applied Art of Turkomenia*, Aurora Art, Leningrad (Russian)

Colyer Ross, Heather, *Bedouin Jewellery in Saudi Arabia*, Stacey International, London 1979

Engel, Josef, *Grosser Historischer Weltatlas*, Bayerischer, Schulbuch Verlag, Munich 1958 (German)

ed. Ettinghausen, Richard, *Islamic Art in the Metropolitan Museum of Art*, Kevorkian Foundation, New York, 1972

Fehervari, Geza, *Islamic Metalwork*, Faber and Faber, London, 1976

Gerard, Bernard, *Yemen*, Editions Delroisse, Paris (English, French and Arabic)

Harris, George L., *Jordan*, Hraf Press

Hawley, Ruth, *Omani Silver*, T. A. Constable Ltd., London and New York, 1978

Himeur, Agnes Francesci, *"Costumes et Bijoux Arts et Traditions Populaires"*, article in *L'Oeil*, Revue d'Art, no. 294–295

Jewellery Through 7000 Years, British Museum Publications, London 1976

Jordan, Ministry of Information, Jordan, 1978 (Arabic)

Kasha, Suheil, "Jewellery in Mesopotamia", article in *Alturath Al Shabi*, No. 3, 1978

Kuhnel, Ernst, *Encyclopaedia of World Art*, article in Vol. VIII, McGraw Hill Inc. 1963

Marshak, B. E., *Sogdiiskoye Serebro* (Sogdian Silver), Glarnaya Redaktsia, Vastochnai Literaturi, Moscow, 1971 (Russian)

Morneo, Manuel Jometh, *Islamic Art in Spain*, translated by Lufti Abdel Badi and Mahmoud Abdul Aziz Salem, General Egyptian Association of Books, 1977

Munro, John, "Islam in Russia", article in *Aramco World Magazine*, Jan/Feb 1976

Norton, Mary, "Islam in Al Andalus", article in *Aramco World Magazine*, Sept/Oct 1976

Norton, Mary, "The Bright Thread", article in *Aramco World Magazine*, Sept/Oct 1977

Obojiski, Robert, "Coins of History", article in *Aramco World Magazine*, August 1978

Pakistan Past and Present, Stacey International, London 1977

Roth, H. Ling, *Oriental Silverwork*, Malay and Chinese, Truslove and Hanson, London 1910

Smirnov, Y. I., *Vostochnoye Serebro* (Eastern Silver), Imperial Archaeological Commission, Petersburg 1909 (Russian)

Sovietsky Khudozhnik, (Dhagestan Decorative Art), Moscow 1971 (Russian)

Swarup, Shanti, *5000 Years of Arts and Crafts in India and Pakistan*, Russi Jal Taraporevala for D. B. Taraporevala Ltd., Bombay, 1967

Wealth of the Roman World, British Museum Publications, London 1977

Weekes, Richard V., *Muslim Peoples*, Greenwood Press Inc. Connecticut, 1978

Wilber, Donald N., *Iran Past and Present*, University Press, Princeton, New Jersey, 1963

Zaki, Abdul Rahman, *Jewellery in History and Art* (Arabic)

Zein-al-Abadin, Ali, *Folk Jewellery in Egypt*, Cairo, 1974 (Arabic)

MUSEUMS
The following list of international museums containing Arab and Islamic works in precious metals is not exhaustive but has been complied from my personal knowledge. There is not a large collection in any one of them and most only display items from one region or country.

AL AIN MUSEUM, AL AIN, ABU DHABI.
NATURHISTORISCHES MUSEUM, VIENNA, AUSTRIA.
OSTERREICHISCHER MUSEUM FUR KUNST UND INDUSTRIE, VIENNA, AUSTRIA.
MORAVIAN APPLIED ART MUSEUM, BRNO, CZECHOSLOVAKIA.
MORAVIAN COMMERCE MUSEUM, BRNO, CZECHOSLOVAKIA.
DAVID COLLECTION, COPENHAGEN, DENMARK.
STATE MUSEUM, EAST BERLIN, EAST GERMANY.
MUSEUM FUR VOLKERKUNDE, LEIPZIG, EAST GERMANY.
MUSEUM OF ISLAMIC ART, CAIRO, EGYPT.
EGYPTIAN MUSEUM, CAIRO, EGYPT.
MUSEE DES ARTS DECORATIFS, PARIS, FRANCE.
BIBLIOTHEQUE NATIONALE, PARIS, FRANCE.
MUSEE DE L'HOMME, PARIS, FRANCE.
MUSEE DU LOUVRES, PARIS, FRANCE.
MUSEE NATIONALE DES ARTS AFRICAINES ET OCEANIAS, PARIS, FRANCE.
SAN ISIDRO MUSEUM, LYON, FRANCE.
BENAKI MUSEUM, ATHENS, GREECE.
RIJKSMUSEUM, AMSTERDAM, HOLLAND.
TROPENMUSEUM, AMSTERDAM, HOLLAND.
HOPP MUSEUM, BUDAPEST, HUNGARY.
ETHNOGRAPHIC MUSEUM, BUDAPEST, HUNGARY.
NATIONAL MUSEUM, BUDAPEST, HUNGARY.
MUSEO CIVICO, BOLOGNA, ITALY.
MUSEO DI CAPODIMONTE, NAPLES, ITALY.
NATIONAL MUSEUM OF ORIENTAL ART, ROME, ITALY.
BUSTAN MUSEUM, TEHERAN, IRAN.
IRAQI MUSEUM, BAGHDAD, IRAQ.
TRIPOLI MUSEUM, TRIPOLI, LIBYA.
AL BATHA MUSEUM, FEZ, MOROCCO.
DAR JAMAI MUSEUM, MEKNES, MOROCCO.
DAR SI SAID MUSEUM, MARRAKESH, MOROCCO.
MUSEE DES ARTS TRADITIONELLES, RABAT, MOROCCO.
OUDAIA MUSEUM, RABAT, MOROCCO.
CORDOBA MUSEUM, CORDOBA, SPAIN.
GRANADA MUSEUM, GRANADA, SPAIN.
MADRID MUSEUM, MADRID, SPAIN.
NATIONAL MUSEUM, STOCKHOLM, SWEDEN.
NATIONAL MUSEUM, DAMASCUS, SYRIA.
MUSEE DE BARDO, TUNIS, TUNISIA.
TOPKAPI SARAY MUSEUM, ISTANBUL, TURKEY.
BRITISH MUSEUM, LONDON, U.K.
ORIENTAL GALLERY, TOWER HILL, LONDON, U.K.
VICTORIA AND ALBERT MUSEUM, LONDON, U.K.
MUSEUM OF FINE ARTS, BOSTON, U.S.A.
MUSEUM OF ART, CLEVELAND, U.S.A.
INSTITUTE OF ARTS, DETROIT, U.S.A.
FREER GALLERY OF ART, WASHINGTON, U.S.A.
METROPOLITAN MUSEUM OF ART, NEW YORK, U.S.A.
HERMITAGE MUSEUM, LENINGRAD, U.S.S.R.
BAYERISCHE NATIONAL MUSEUM, MUNICH, WEST GERMANY.
KUNST GENERALE MUSEUM, DRESDEN, WEST GERMANY.
STATE MUSEUM, BERLIN, WEST GERMANY.
SANA'A MUSEUM, SANA'A, YEMEN.

Index

Abbasid Dynasty, 10, 13, 14, *19*, 31, 40, 41, 42, 130, 134, 176
Abyssinia (*see* Ethiopia)
Afghanistan and Afghan centres of silverwork, 8, *22*, 34, 173, 174, 175, *184*, *186*, *188*, *189*, *194*, *195*
   Ghazni, 174
   Herat, 175
   Kabul, 174, 175
   Kandahar, 175
Al-Bu Said Dynasty, 90
Alexander the Great, 19, 92, *99*, 128, 132, 134, 173
Algeria and Algerian centres of silverwork, 8, *16*, 20, 24, 29, 30, 36, 37, *37*, 40, 43, *47*, *52*, *53*, *57*, *58*, *60*, *61*, *64*, *65*, 68, *69*, *73*, 75
   Aet Al-Arba'a, 43
   Beni Yeni, *1*, 43, *64*
   Biskra, 25, 43
   Constantine, 43
   Ghardaia, 43
   Insalah, *61*
   Kabyllie, *1*, 23, *36*, 40, 43, *46*, *62*, *63*, *72*
   Oran, *69*
   Ouargla, *61*
   Tamanrasset, 43, *61*
   Tizi Ouzou, *1*, 43
Amber, 32, 34, 89, *105*, *108*
Amr ibn Al-As, 42, 89
Amulets and amulet boxes (*hirz*, *du'a* and *bas bend*), *2*, *3*, 16, 17, *17*, 23, 27, 34, 45, *62*, *64*, 78, *106*, *108*, *116*, *135*, 143, *172*, 175, *184*, 194
Andalusia, (*see also* Spain), 10, 40, 42, 43
Anklets (*Al-Khalkhal*), 16, *16*, *18*, 25 (*full list*), *25*, 44, *74*, *124*, *150*, *151*, 175, 179, 199
Ayyubid Dynasty, 13, 31, 42

Bahrain, 92, 93
Balls, *22*, *52*, *72*, *106*, *110*, *111*, *142*, *190*, *193*, 202
Bangladesh, 176
Beads, 16, *22*, 34, *44*, *50*, *52*, *53*, *58*, *63*, *65*, *72*, *73*, *102*, *105*, *106*, *116*, *120*, *138*, *188*
Bedouin, 8, 35, 91, *101*, 128
Bells, 21, 24, 25, *111*, *147*, *148*, *150*, *185*
Belts (*Al-Hizam*), *2*, *3*, *14*, 16, 19, 24 (*full list*), *68*, *69*, *71*, *110*, *135*, *177*, 179, *196*
Berbers, 40, 45
Body ornaments, *50*, *58*
Boxes, *165*, *207*
   for toilet (*see also* Silverwork), 19, 27, *32*
   for cigarettes, 19, 27, *45*, *77*, 133, *133*, *164*, *165*, 207
   as decorations, *22*, *26*, *164*, *186*
   for pen and ink, 27, *161*, *176*
   for jewellery, 41, *77*, *210*
   for seals, *208*
Bracelets (*Al-Siwar*), 16, *16*, 25 (*full list*), 44, *72*, *73*, *74*, *75*, *95*, *120*, *123*, *145*, *150*, *172*, 173, 179, *198*, *199*
Brass, 23, 26, 177
Breast decoration, *52*, *110*, *172*, *180*, *195*
British influence, 93, 175
Bronze, 19, 26, 28, 41, *42*
Brooches and pins, *1*, 23 (*full list*), *23*, 24, *43*, *52*, *53*, *56*, *57*, *58*, *128*, *140*, *141*, 175, *180*, *184*
Buckles, clasps and locks, *21*, 23, 24, 25, 35, 130, *131*, *135*, *148*, *151*, 179, *196*, *198*
Buddhism, 173, 174, 175
Buttons, *21*, 29
Buyid Dynasty, 14, 132, 175
Byzantine influence, 11, 12, 13, 28, 29, 134

Canaanites, 128, 129
Candlesticks, 26, 41, *169*
Caucasus and Caucasian silverwork, 13, 34, 131, *135*, *147*, *149*
Ceramics, 41, 130, 132, *211*
Chains (*Al-Silsilah*), 16, 21, *22*, *22*, 23, 25, 26 (*full list*), 35, 45, *52*, *95*, *100*, *106*, *110*, *136*, *142*, *150*, *161*, *172*, 180, *193*, *196*, *199*, *211*
Children's jewellery, *17*, *17*, *24*, *24*, 25, *150*

Chinese influence, 12, 26, 133, *169*, 173, 175, 179
Christian influence, 13, 28, 31, 40, 41, 42, 128, 129, *142*, 175
Copper, *22*, 26, 41, 42, *99*, *106*, *121*, *131*, 177
Copts, 13, 40
Coral, *16*, *22*, *22*, 23, 24, 25, 28, 32, 34, *46*, *50*, *53*, *62*, *63*, *68*, *89*, *95*, *98*, *105*, *106*, *116*, *142*, *186*

Daggers (*khanjar*, *kinjal* and *kriss*), 16, 19, 24, 28, 43, *71*, *90*, *91*, *113*, *116*, *117*, *118*, 132, *148*, *149*, 177, *196*
Damascene (*koftgari* or *bidri*), 27, 28, 31, 129, 176, 177
Dancing, 16, *22*, 179
Dhagestan and Dhagestani centres of silverwork, 135
   Amouzgui, 135
   Kharbuk, 135
   Kubachi, 135
   Kumukh, 135
Djibouti, 16

Earrings, 21 (*full list*), *22*, *22*, 41, 45, *60*, *95*, *172*, *185*, *189*
Egypt and Egyptian centres of silverwork, 10, 14, 19, 30, 33, 36, 40, 42, 43, *66*, *74*, *78*, *82*, *83*, *84*, *85*, *89*, 129
   Alexandria, 12
   Cairo (Al-Qahira) 13, 28, 42, 130
   Kairouan, 40, 42
   Sidi Bou Said, 40
Ethiopia, 11, 12, 13, 28, 40
Etruscan influence, 14, *99*

Farouk, King of Egypt, *66*, *77*
Fatimid Dynasty, 10, 41, 42
French influence, 11

German influence, 12, 13
Ghaznavid Dynasty, 10, 174, 176
Ghenghis Khan, 13, 130, 134, 173, 174
Glass, 20, 21, 24, 25, 32, *41*, 42, *50*, *74*, 175, *175*, *185*, *188*, *190*
Gold, 16, 18, 19, 23, 24, 25, 28, 31, *33*, 43, 44, 91, *123*, *164*, *172*, 177, 179
Greek silverwork and influence, 12, 14, 30, 33, 129, 132, 134, *172*, 175
Gunpowder flasks (*talahiq*), *119*

Hallmarks, 20, *22*, 45
Headdresses, 20 (*full list*), 23, 24, *31*, 45, *46*, *47*, *94*, *95*, *136*, *138*, *139*, *140*, *172*, 173, *180*, *183*, *184*
Hindu influence, 33, 175, 176
Hookahs, (*nergileh*), 25, 135, *161*, 175, *211*

Illumination of manuscripts, 42, 43, 129, 130, 173
India and Indian centres of silverwork, 22, 24, 25, 30, *35*, 36, 44, 173, *175*, *176*, 177, *187*, *189*, *193*, *196*, *198*, *199*, *200*, *205*, *207*, *210*
   Ahmadabad, 176
   Alwar, 177
   Bidar, 177
   Delhi, 8, 176
   Gujarat, 176, 178, 179
   Jaipur, 177, 178
   Kashmir, 177, 178
   Lucknow, 177, 178
   Rampur, 177, 178
   Vijayanagar, 176
Indus valley and civilisation, 89, 175, 176
Iran (Persia) and Iranian centres of silverwork, 8, 11, 13, 19, 25, 26, *26*, 28, *31*, 35, 36, 128, 129, 131, 132, 133, *133*, *148*, *149*, *152*, *153*, *154*, *155*, *156*, *161*, *164*, *165*, *166*, *169*, 175
   Isfahan, 13, 132, 134
   Kermanshah, 134
   Qazvin, 132, 133
   Sultaniya, 132
   Tabriz, 132, 133, 134
   Tehran, 134
   Yezd, 132
Iraq and Iraqi centres of silverwork, *5*, *17*, 19, 23, 25, 29, 31, *33*, 35, 42, 130, *136*, *139*, *141*, *143*, *145*, *147*, *148*, *149*, *150*, *151*, *156*, *158*, *161*, *164*, *165*, *168*, *169*
   Baghdad, 8, 13, 14, 16, 40, 42, 130, 132
   Mosul, 13, 14, 42, 43, 129, *142*

Samara'a, 130
Wasit, *19*
Islamic poets and historians
   Al-Biruni, 174
   Firdausi, 174
   Ibn Hawqal, 42
   Ibn Khaldoon, 15
   Makrizi, 15, 42
   Nasir Khusro, 42, 176
Islamic Society, 8, 31, 36, 45, 91, 135, 178
Italian influence, 31, 43, 131
Ivory, 20, 28, 41, 42, 43, 175

Jewellery *see* Amulets, Anklets, Beads, Bells, Bracelets, Brooches, Buckles, Buttons, Chains, Children's Earrings, Headdresses, Necklaces, Nose-rings, Pectorals, Pendants, Rings, Weddings
Jordan and Jordanian centres of silverwork, 22, 36, 128
   Amman, 128
   Petra, 128

Karmathians, 31
Kurdish silverwork, 35, 130, 131, *138*, *140*, *147*
Kuwait, 16, 88, 93

Leather, 20, 42, *66*, *111*
Lebanese silverwork, 16, 29, 42, *66*, *111*
Libya and Libyan centres of silverwork, 8, *18*, 20, *22*, *24*, 34, *44*, *45*, *47*, *50*, *53*, *55*, *56*, *58*, *60*, *62*, *63*, *65*, *68*, *72*, *73*, *74*
   Benghazi, 68
   Misurata, 68
   Tripoli, 68

Macedonia *see* Greek silverwork
Mameluke Dynasty, 13, 43
Melting down silver, 16, 35
Mesopotamia, 11, 14, 19, 22, 24, 89, 91, 92, 128, 132, 175
Miniature painting, 134, 177
Mahmoud of Ghazni, 174
Mongols, 43, 131, 173
Morocco and Moroccan centres of silverwork, 8, 13, 19, *23*, 25, 31, 34, 40, *41*, *52*, *57*, *71*, *74*, *78*
   Agadir, 43
   Fez, 43
   Meknes, 43
   Rif, 43
   Tangier, 43
   Terudent, 43
   Tetouan, 41, *41*
   Tiznit, 43, *56*
Mosques, 23, 26, 40, 42, 129, 130, 132, 134, 173, 174, 177
Mother of pearl, 128, *128*
Mughals, 10, 13, 175, 176, 177, 178
Museums, 214 (*full list*)

Necklaces (*Al-Qiladah*), 21, 22 (*full list*), 23, *23*, *36*, 45, *61*, *62*, *63*, *64*, *65*, *66*, *96*, *98*, *99*, *100*, *101*, *102*, *105*, *108*, *141*, *142*, *143*, *145*, *172*, *172*, *173*, 179, *186*, *188*, *189*, *190*, *193*, *194*, *195*, *199*
Niger, *73*
Nigerian silverwork, *80*, *82*
Nile, river and civilisation, 11, 22, 40
Noserings (*Al-Khazzamah*), 16, 19, 22 (*full list*)
Nubia, 12, 13, 40

Oman and Omani centres of silverwork, 8, 19, 20, *21*, *22*, *24*, 29, *32*, 34, 88, 89, 90, 91, 93, *94*, *95*, *99*, *100*, *106*, *107*, *111*, *113*, *116*, *119*, *120*, *121*, *123*, *124*
   Bahla, 91
   Dhofar, 89
   Ibri, 91
   Masirah, 89
   Matrah, 91
   Muscat, 8, 89, 90, 91
   Nizwa, 8, 90
   Qalhat, 90
   Quryat, 90
   Rostaq, 91
   Sohar, 89, 90
Ottomans, 29, 43, 130, 131, 134, *142*, *159*

ARAB AND ISLAMIC SILVER

Pakistan and Pakistani centres of silverwork, *7, 16, 21*, 22, *175, 175, 180, 184, 185, 186, 187, 188, 190, 193, 194, 195, 198, 199, 200, 202, 205, 207, 208, 210, 211*
   Baluchistan, 176
   Hyderabad, 175
   Karachi, 8, 32, 175
   Lahore, 176
   Multan, 174, 176
   North-West Frontier, 176
   Peshawar, 176
   Punjab, 175, 176
   Sialkot, 176
   Sind, 175
Palestine and Palestinian centres of silverwork, 36, 128
   Akka, 128
   Bethlehem, 128
   Bir Al-Saba'a, 128
   Gaza, 128
   Al-Khalil, 128
   Nabuls, 128
   Al-Nassira, 128
   Al-Ramla, 128
   Ya'afa, 128
Parthia *see* Iran
Pearls, 22, 42, 45, 92
Pectorals, *10, 31*
Pendants, *1*, 21, *21, 22,* 29, 43, *50, 53, 55, 56, 57, 60, 62, 63,* 89, *90, 96, 101, 106, 141,* 173, *180, 185, 187, 195, 209, 211*
Persia *see* Iran
Phoenician silverwork, 14, 40, 29
Pictures and picture frames, *9,* 19, *165*
Plastic, 16, 25
Portuguese influence, 89, 90, 175, 179
Pre-Islamic silverwork, 11, 28
Prophet Mohammed, 12, 24, 91, 93, 129
   hadith of, 18, 33

Qatar, 88, 93
Quran, verses (*surah*) and inscriptions, *9,* 11, 16, *17, 18,* 19, *23,* 26, 27, 29, 43, *44, 78,* 88, *88,* 91, *135, 140, 194*

Rings (*Al-Khatem*) 19, 21, 24, *24,* 25 (*full list*), 72, *121, 172,* 179, *184, 189, 199*
Roman silverwork, 12, 14, 19, 24, 28, 30, 33, 40, 88, 128, 129, 134, 135
Rope, 22, *22,* 105
Russia *see* U.S.S.R.

Saba'a, Queen of, 88, 89
Safavid Dynasty, 10, 132, 133, *141*
Saharan silverwork, 8, 25, 34, 43, *60, 61*
Salah El-Din (Saladin), *131*
Sassanian silverwork, 12, 29, 91, 129, 131, 132
Saudi Arabia and Saudi centres of silverwork, 16, 88, 91
   Al-Hasa, 92
   Hijaz, 91
   Mecca, 11, 31, 91
   Medina, 11, 31, 91
   Riyadh, 16
   Taif, 11, 91
Seals, 22, 24, 77
Seljuk Dynasty, 10, 13, *14, 19,* 130, 131, 134, 174
Silver currency, 11, 19, *19,* 28, 29, 34, 45, *46, 53, 65, 66, 107, 123, 140, 141, 142, 143, 145,* 161
Silversmiths, 17, 30–35
Silverwork, ancient hoards of, 12
Silverwork, animal ornamentation in, 19, 45, *168*
Silverwork, comparison of rural and urban, 16, 18, 20, 43, 45, 173, 175, *189*
Silverwork, domestic objects in
   Baskets, *156*
   Bowls, 22, 42; *80, 83,* 91, *135,* 174, 175, 177, *205*
   Coffee and tea pots, 15, 19, 26, *34,* 41, 45, 91, 128, *130,* 133, 134, *158,* 175, *178,* 200
   Cups, *159,*
   Cup and glass holders, *158, 159*
   Ewers, 42, 135, 174
   Glasses, 133, 134
   Incense burners, *5, 15,* 19, 27, *28,* 41, 42, 91, 174, *208, 209*
   Kettles, 26
   Mirrors, 19, 175

Plates and dishes, 19, 42, *83,* 91, 134, *152, 153, 154, 155,* 168, *202, 205*
Rosewater sprinklers, 19, 27, 42, 91, 174, 177, *210*
Salt, pepper and mustard pots, 19, *161, 203*
Samovars, 19, 26, 45
Sugar bowls, 26, *133, 200*
Tea caddy, *169*
Teaspoons, 161, *179*
Tongs, *26, 161*
Trays, 26, 27, *82*
Tumblers, *205*
Urns, 26
Vases, *6,* 26, 27, 128, 134, *166,* 174, 175, 177, *208*
Silverwork, shapes and motifs in,
   Animal, 14, 25, 26, 27, 33, *56, 164, 166, 198, 205*
   Arabesque, 26, 28, 42, 128, 134, *172,* 176, *205*
   Arch, 42
   Bird, *18,* 27, *28, 161,* 174, *187, 210*
   Calligraphic, 14, 33, 34, *42, 45, 53, 83, 84, 85, 106, 116,* 128, *161, 166,* 174, 176
   Circular, 21, 23, 24, 33, *164*
   Conical, 21, 22
   Crescent, 21, *23, 45, 209*
   Dome, 24
   Fish, 77
   Floral, 14, *16, 18, 22, 23, 24,* 26, 33, *42, 45, 56, 64, 65, 68, 73, 77, 83, 84, 90, 111, 147, 149, 156, 161, 164, 166,* 174, *176, 185, 187, 195, 196, 198, 200, 202, 205, 207, 298, 210*
   Foliage, *138*
   Geometric, 14, 18, 22, 32, 33, *47, 63, 66, 68, 73, 77, 90,* 176, *185, 198*
   Hand, 22
   Heart, 25, *172, 187*
   Hexagonal, *164*
   Horse-shoe, 23, 42
   Human, 14, 26, 33, *132, 156, 161, 198*
   Lozenge, *172*
   Mythical, 25, 33, *179*
   Octagonal, *169*
   Pentagonal, 33
   Plaiting, *82, 84, 147*
   Pyramidical, 24
   Semi-circular, 22
   Shell, *77, 202*
   Snake, 25, *64, 75, 150*
   Square, 24, 33, *164*
   Star, 43, *50, 83, 84, 148, 164, 198, 209*
   Triangular, 21, 23, 33
   Zodiacal, 26
Silverwork, toilet articles in
   Combcases, *211*
   Earpicks, 19, *184*
   Handles, *211*
   Kohl boxes, *124*
   Meel, 19, 32
   Perfume boxes and bottles, 41, 177, *194, 210*
   Powder box, *164*
   Shaving equipment, 19
   Thimbles, *211*
   Toothbrushes, 19
   Toothpicks, 19, *184*
Silverwork, value of 19, 20, 29, 35, 175
Somalia, 28, 40
South-East Asia and South-East Asian centres of silverwork, 11, 25, *178,* 179, *198, 207*
   Atjeh, 179
   Bali, 179
   Batak, 179
   Borneo, 179
   Celebes, 179
   Indonesia, 8, *196*
   Java, 179
   Moluccas, 179
   Philippines, 179
   Sumatra, 179
Spain and Spanish centres of silverwork, 13, 28
   Almeria, 28
   Cordoba, 13, 40, 41, 42
   Granada, 28, 40, 41
   Seville, 28, 40
   Toledo, 28, 41
   Valencia, 41
Stones, precious, 16, 19, 42, 175, 176, 178
   Diamonds, 32
   Ruby, 25
Stones, semi-precious, 25, 135, *136,* 175, 178

Agate, 23, 24, 25, *26,* 32, *95, 105, 116,* 120, 121, *138, 141, 150, 165, 172,* 180, 186
Cornelian, 11, 89, *172*
Malachite, *186*
Tiger-eye, *138*
Turquoise, 22, 24, 25, 32, 43, *89, 138, 142, 143, 147, 165,* 186, *189*
Sudanese silverwork, 45, *45,* 78
Sulaiman bin Daoud (Solomon), 88, 89
Sumerian culture, 92, 129
Superstitions, 16, 23, 43, (*see also* Amulets)
Symbols in silverwork, 18, *60, 63,* 90, *90,* 128, 176
Syria and Syrian centres of silverwork, 12, 14, 22, 23, 31, 42, 129, *143*
   Aleppo, 13, 16, 129, 130
   Damascus, 13, 28, 41, 129, 130, 132
   Homs, 16

Techniques in silverwork, 30–35
   Casting, 26, 32, 175
   Chasing, *58, 65,* 71, *72, 74,* 106, 148
   Cutting or incising, 32, 175
   Embossing, 32, 42, *62, 63,* 75, *82, 83, 84, 85,* 108, 120, *155, 161,* 174, 175
   Enamelling, (*meenakari*), *23,* 24, 25, 28, 41, 43, 44, *56, 63, 64,* 71, *72, 74,* 77, *83,* 116, 128, *133, 133,* 135, *155, 161, 175, 175,* 177, *177, 178,* 199, 205, 207
   Engraving, 32, 34, *47, 58, 62,* 64, 77, *135,* 148, *149, 156, 161,* 174, 175, *198, 205, 207*
   Filigree, *23,* 26, *34, 60, 73,* 128, 130, 135, *145, 147, 161,* 175, *179, 202, 209*
   Granulation, 28, 32, *60, 89, 95, 101, 108, 116, 123,* 130, *135,* 148, *150,* 175, *185,* 199
   Hammering, 32, 68, 73
   Inlaying, 28, 43, *46, 72, 73, 74,* 106, *108,* 128, *150,* 174, 175, *183, 185, 186, 195*
   Moulding, 32
   Niello, 28, 31, 34, 43, 130, *130, 131,* 135, *145, 147, 149, 151, 158, 159, 161, 165,* 168, *169, 178,* 179, *198*
   Repoussé, 22, *73, 74,* 120, 121, *148, 156,* 175, *200, 207, 209, 210*
Touareg Silverwork, 16, 19, 24, 30, 34, 43, *63, 66, 73*
Tunisian silverwork, 8, 20, 36, 40, 43, 44
Turkish silverwork, *9, 15,* 23, *28, 34,* 131, 132, 134, 135, *140, 142, 149, 159, 161,* 166
Turkomania and Turkomanian centres of silverwork, 12, *172, 172,* 180, *183, 186, 195*
   Bukhara, 173
   Khiva, 173
   Samarkand, 13, 132, 173, 174
Tutenkhamen, *11,* 44

Ummayad Dynasty, 10, 13, *19,* 29, 40, 41, 128, 129
United Arab Emirates (UAE.) and centres of silverwork, 16, 34, 88, 92, *124*
   Abu Dhabi, 8, 35, 92
   Al-Ain, 92, 93
   Buraimi, 92
   Hili, 92
   Ras Al-Khaima (Julfar), 92, 93
   Umm Al-Qawwain, 92
U.S.S.R., 12, *15, 172, 172*

Weaponry, (*see also* Daggers), 19, 28, 45, *143,* 173
Weaving, 42, 43, 92
Weddings, 172
   Dowry, 16, 92
   Jewellery, 16, 22, 25, 31, 45, *47,* 92, 135, *140, 172,* 177, *180*
   Traditions, 16, 45, *47,* 135, *172,* 177
Wire, 25, 26, *52, 62, 63, 72, 95, 102, 110, 121, 193, 199*
Wood and carving, 41, 42, 43

Yemen (Y.A.R. and P.D.R.Y.) and Yemeni centres of silverworks, *2, 3,* 11, 19, *23,* 28, 29, 31, 34, 88, *89,* 92, 94, *95, 96, 98, 100, 101, 102, 105, 106, 107, 108, 110, 111, 116, 117, 118, 119, 120, 121, 123, 124*
   Aden, 8
   Mukalla, 89
   Sana'a, 8, 31

Zoroastrianism, 172

216